IMAGES
of America

HOLLAND

On the Cover: This is the original Elsworth and Son General Store. Established by Isaac Elsworth and his son Frank, the store was open for business from 1875 to 1910. It was on the south side of Mill Street (now Capitol Heights), second lot from the corner of Main Street. In 1910, after the great fire had destroyed sections of the town's business area, Elsworth built a modern brick building and relocated the store to Main Street. (Courtesy of Holland Historical Society.)

IMAGES
of America

HOLLAND

Karen L. Kline and Sandra B. Smith
for the Town of Holland

ARCADIA
PUBLISHING

ISBN 978-1-4671-2747-9

Published by Arcadia Publishing
Charleston, South Carolina

Printed in the United States of America

Library of Congress Control Number: 2017952575

For all general information, please contact Arcadia Publishing:
Telephone 843-853-2070
Fax 843-853-0044
E-mail sales@arcadiapublishing.com
For customer service and orders:
Toll-Free 1-888-313-2665

Visit us on the Internet at www.arcadiapublishing.com

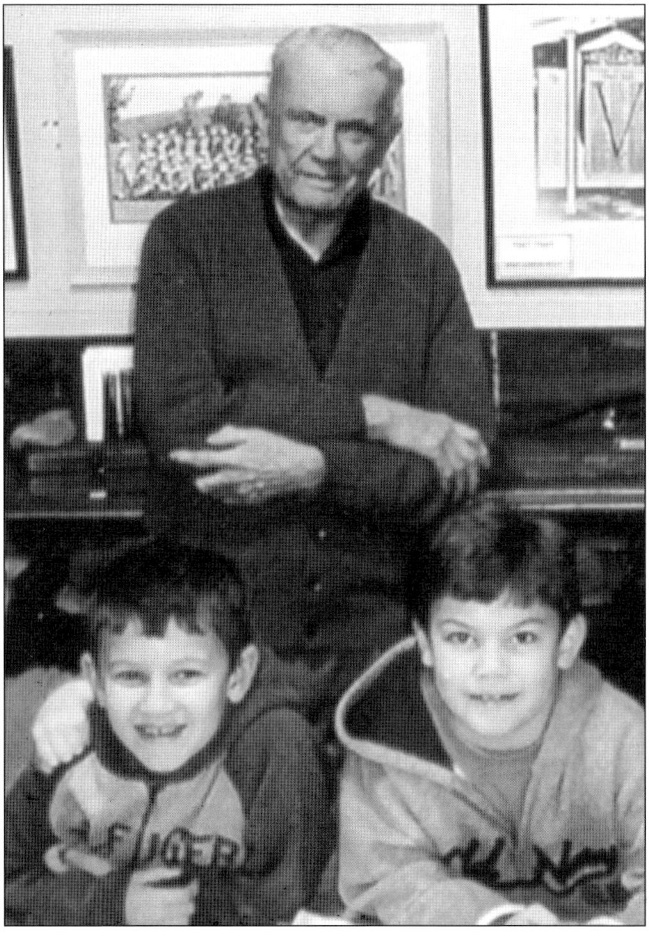

This book is dedicated to Kenneth K. Tanner (September 24, 1924–April 13, 2008). Without his photographic talents, there would be no documentation of Holland's history. (Courtesy of Holland Historical Society.)

Contents

FOREWORD

Think about what it must have been like to be in Holland, New York, in 1818. We, as a nation, had just a generation earlier fought for and won our independence. Just a few years earlier, our new nation fought the War of 1812, and our own Fort Humphrey was built to protect our early settlers. Holland was the western frontier!

There were few open fields. Forest covered most of our 36 square miles. Roads were just paths through the woods. Farms, homes, businesses, and schools were just in their infancy. Churches, mills, hotels, and manufacturing would come later.

We have endured as a community for 200 years and now look forward. Our community DNA has been forged by our history and our vision of the future.

As you enjoy this book's look back, I encourage you to envision yourself as one of those pioneers who created Holland literally out of the wilderness. I also hope you can share a vision for future generations who live and work in Holland.

Sincerely,
Michael C. Kasprzyk
Supervisor, Town of Holland

Acknowledgments

We would like to begin by thanking those who provided images and related stories to us during the process of creating this book. A special thank-you goes to the Holland Historical Society for providing resources from its collection. Unless otherwise noted, all images are from the society's archives. We also want to thank the Town of Holland and the Bicentennial Committee for their unwavering support. This book was fondly created to coincide with the town's bicentennial in 2018.

Secondly, thanks to Brian Koss—your talents as a photographer and all-around media guru turned this possibility into a reality. The hours you spent scanning and resizing photographs and taking extra pictures were incredible. Thank you, and Peg, for giving up your valuable time to work on this special project.

Former town historian Norma Fischer provided valuable recollections and photographs, and Joy Bucknam, president of the Holland Historical Society, contributed extra help with editing and proofreading. We thank you both.

And lastly, thanks to our families, who instilled in us the love of history and taught us to embrace our heritage and value our town.

It is our hope that this book sparks happy memories of the past and serves as a resource for those in the future.

Introduction

In 1807, Holland's three founders traveled from Vermont by oxen and settled in a beautiful valley that was once an Indian trail. Perhaps the founders thought the valley resembled Vermont and so they chose to settle here and look no further. Perhaps it was the fertile soil, trickling creeks, and lush vegetation. Whatever the reason, Arthur Humphrey, Abner Currier, and Jared Scott decided to stay and make their home in this valley.

Arthur Humphrey was the first to set his claim. Accompanied by his wife, Alethea, and their small children, he made the long trip in a covered wagon over hill and dale. All three men went to work to build a log cabin for the Humphreys, most likely because they came with a young family. This was made easier by the thick woods that lined the valley on both sides.

Abner Currier and Jared Scott persuaded their families to stay in Vermont on the original trip and promised to return home for them once they found suitable sites. Currier settled just south of Humphrey's land on property with a clear creek running through it. Jared Scott's claim must have been nearby, but little is known about his exact location. It is known that Currier and Scott returned to Vermont for their families the next year.

News that Humphrey, Currier, and Scott found a fertile valley where there was plenty of room for others soon reached other adventurous families in the east. In 1808 and 1809, the Colbys arrived; Ezekiel and Jonathan Colby settled in the same valley, while Nathan Colby located on the hillside later named Vermont Hill.

Joseph Cooper and his son, Joseph, lived near the border of Vermont and New Hampshire. The father had been a cook in George Washington's army during the Revolutionary War. They started for the western hills of New York and arrived around 1811. This was a 500-mile trip. Later generations of the Cooper family ran a successful sawmill business in Holland.

As families arrived, the need for a school was soon realized. The first school in the valley (known as the Humphrey settlement) was built on a site near Abner Currier's property just before the War of 1812, and lessons were taught by Abner Currier during the winter months.

News of the burning of Buffalo, New York, and the capture of Fort Niagara during the War of 1812 soon reached Holland. In 1812, Fort Humphrey was built by the settlers on Arthur Humphrey's property in anticipation of another attack. The stockade fort was built large enough to house their livestock, food and water, and other supplies. A moat was also dug around the fort, which fortunately never saw action. Eventually, the fort was dismantled and the logs used to build area homes and barns. This is the reason that Arthur Humphrey's homestead is referred to as the "Fort Farm."

By 1816, it was reported that 40 families had come to this area, arriving in covered wagons from the east. Settlers made their homesteads on land south of the original valley as well as properties on the East and West Hills.

A village began to take shape when a gristmill was built on the Cazenovia Creek by Gen. William Warren and Ephraim Woodruff. Soon, sawmills and other gristmills followed. These mills were owned by families named Orr, Wurst, and Griggs.

Caleb Cutler was another pioneer who arrived with his family from Vermont. In 1816, he settled on the West Hill, near Holland Glenwood and Burlingham Roads. Family history notes that Cutler's son, William Cheney, drove six cows the entire distance from Vermont. Generations of Cutlers farmed his homestead for many years.

The year 1816 was notable for the "cold summer"—there were frosts every month of the year. This caused severe hardship, as food was scarce until grain could be harvested the following year.

Holland continued to grow and prosper: Joshua Barron opened the first tavern in 1816, Leander Cook opened the first store in 1817, and the first village school opened on Continental Avenue.

Up until this time, Holland was a part of the Town of Willink and belonged to Niagara County. On April 15, 1818, by an act of the New York state legislature, Willink was divided into three towns, Aurora, Holland, and Wales, and the Town of Willink was dissolved. Holland was likely named for the Holland Land Company, a group of Americans who held land in trust for several wealthy men from the Netherlands (who could not own the land as they were not American citizens). The Holland Land Company purchased the land from Robert Morris, the celebrated financier of the American Revolution.

There was now a need for local government. The first town meeting took place in the spring of 1819, and Arthur Humphrey was elected supervisor. The first town clerk was Samuel Corliss; assessors were Richard Buffum, Caleb Cutler, and Elisha Newhall; the commissioners of highways were Richard Buffum Jr., Amazrah Morey, and Chapen Wheelock. Also elected were two constables, John Abbott and Samuel Corliss; the poormaster was Charles Crook; the commissioners of schools were Rudolphus Burr, Elon Clark, and Ira Johnson; and the inspectors of schools were Elon Clark, Ira Johnson, and Abner Nutting. When Erie County was organized in 1821, Holland was considered one of the most flourishing towns in the county. In 1822, Lyman Clark became the first postmaster. There were now 17 road districts, which indicate a considerable number of settlers at that time.

In 1827, a tract of land was separated from Holland forming the Township of Colden.

One-room schoolhouses were built in the 1820s and 1830s for families located outside the Village School in the hamlet. Eight district schools were in use during this time, and they were named for their vicinity or the families they served. A sampling of the districts included Vermont Hill, Hunters Creek, Sleeper, and Colby.

Various support industries for farming continued to develop in the hamlet. Blacksmith shops, cheese factories, cooper shops, wagon and carriage works, and icehouses were viable businesses. A stagecoach line out of Buffalo made Holland a halfway stop for trips farther south to Franklinville, New York. Because of this, hotels started to appear in Holland.

By 1840, a large number of Germans had settled in the Hunters Creek area. Hunters Creek Road is named in honor of Capt. John French, known for his success as an expert hunter. Frederick River was one of the first to settle in this area. Many were Baptists who worshipped in a small house on Philip Fischer's land. Sidney Sleeper donated land for a church building in 1865.

A. Rumsey and Company built a large tannery at the north end of the village. Owners of one of the largest tanneries in Buffalo, Aaron Rumsey and sons Bronson and Dexter expanded to Holland in 1850. The tannery profited from the hemlock forests in the area; the hemlock trees were used for lumber, and the hemlock bark was used in the tanning process. Rumsey Road was built from the tannery to the railroad track.

During the Civil War, 28 young men enrolled from Holland. Their graves can be found in local cemeteries, including Holland Cemetery and Hunters Creek Cemetery. After the war, Holland resident Charles A. Orr was awarded the Congressional Medal of Honor for his action on October 27, 1864, at Hatcher's Run, Virginia. Orr's brother, Sgt. Robert Orr, was killed in action at Fredericksburg, Virginia, in 1862. Holland formed a Grand Army of the Republic post in 1885 and named it Robert Orr Post No. 553 in his honor.

In 1871, the Buffalo, New York & Philadelphia Railroad was extended through Holland on the east side of the Cazenovia valley. It later became the Pennsylvania Railroad, then Penn-Central, and lastly Conrail. This greatly facilitated economic growth in this rural town.

With the coming of the railroad, the dairy industry flourished, as farmers could now ship whole milk to the growing nearby city of Buffalo. Icehouses were built and ice was harvested in the winter, stored, and used to keep milk cool in the summer.

Horace Selleck built a planing mill in 1876. The wagon and blacksmith shop of M. Keller was established in 1871. Frank Dillon also had a blacksmith shop, and Henry Bangert was a woodworker who made sleighs, spokes for wagons, and the like.

A fire department materialized in 1893 and was officially chartered in 1894 with 10 members. The organization was named Holland Fire Department. Eighteen new members joined the department at the following meeting. The company's first equipment consisted of a hand-drawn hose cart, and its first motor-driven firetruck was purchased in 1931.

The Bank of Holland was organized in 1893. Its first president was William B. Jackson. Located on Main Street in the Whitney Block, the bank, along with most of the business district, was wiped out by the great fire of 1910. Businesses wasted no time and rebuilt the following year; Holland's people definitely came from hardy stock.

Beginning in 1928, Holland's school superintendent, William Bensley, and Principal Harold Brumsted campaigned to combine the district's rural schoolhouses into one centralized school to be located in the hamlet. A vote was finally taken in 1931 in which residents wholeheartedly supported the move. Holland Central School became the first school in Western New York to centralize.

What follows is the story of the Town of Holland and its people, presented through photographs and captions. Many of today's residents are descendants of pioneers who, along with the newer population, continue to treasure its rural life, rolling hills, and picturesque change of seasons.

One

SETTLING HOLLAND

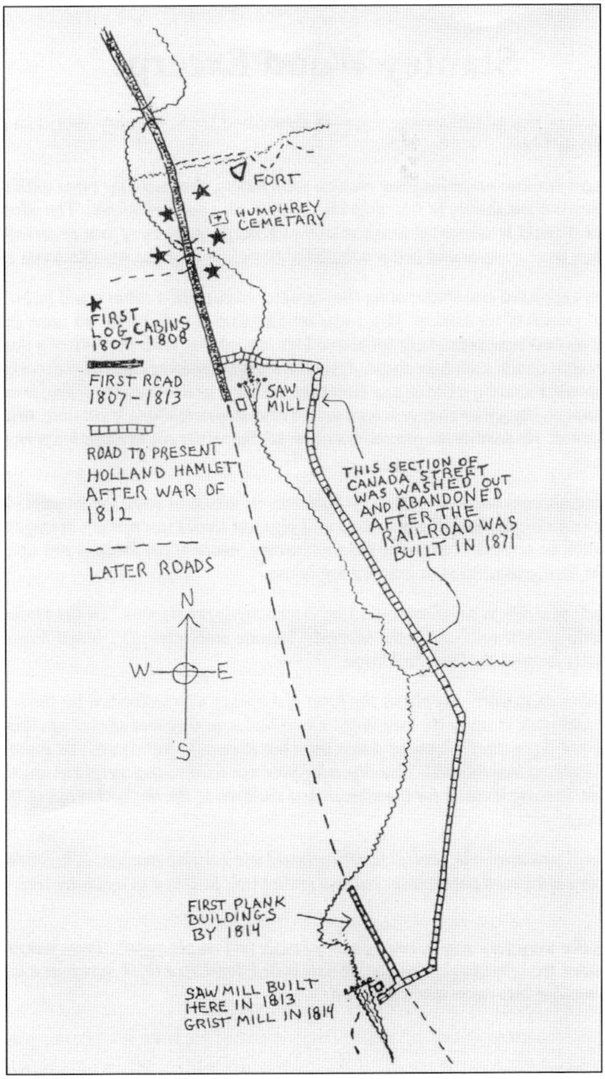

The first area of Holland to be settled was the Humphrey valley, in the northern part of Holland along what is now Route 16 or Olean Road. The original settlers were Arthur Humphrey, Abner Currier, and Jared Scott. Their 1807 journey from Vermont eventually led them along an old Indian trail flanked by the foothills of the Allegheny Mountains. This map depicts the beginning of what was to become Holland.

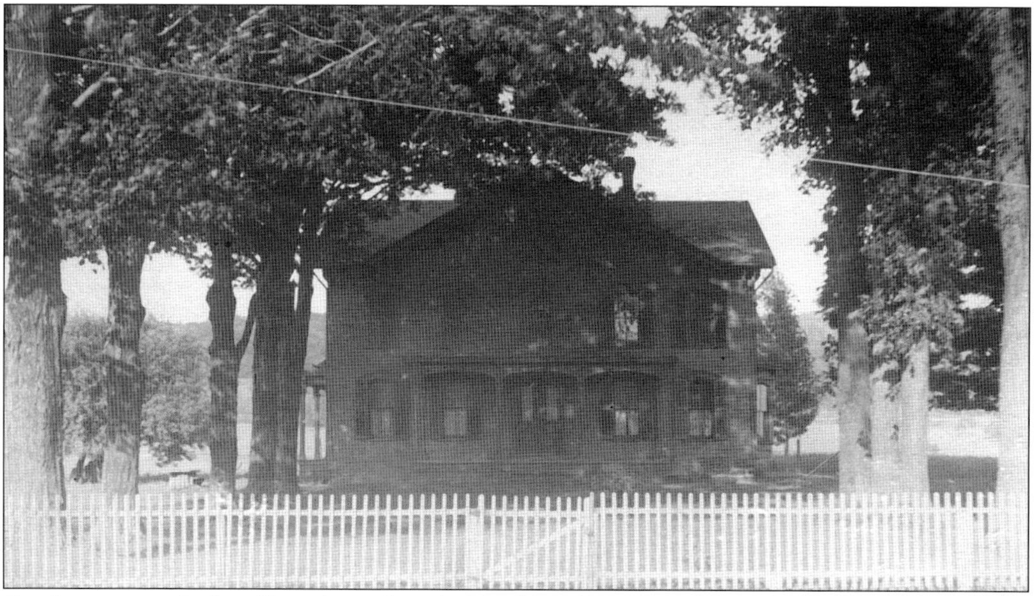

By all accounts, Arthur Humphrey chose his land site first. Humphrey, Currier, and Scott worked together to build the first log cabin on Humphrey's land. This picture shows the homestead that was built some 50 years after Humphrey first settled here. The house was built around 1860 by either John Riley or Jonas Selleck, subsequent owners of the Humphrey farm. It shows the home as it was in the late 1890s or early 1900s. (Courtesy of John Rickettson.)

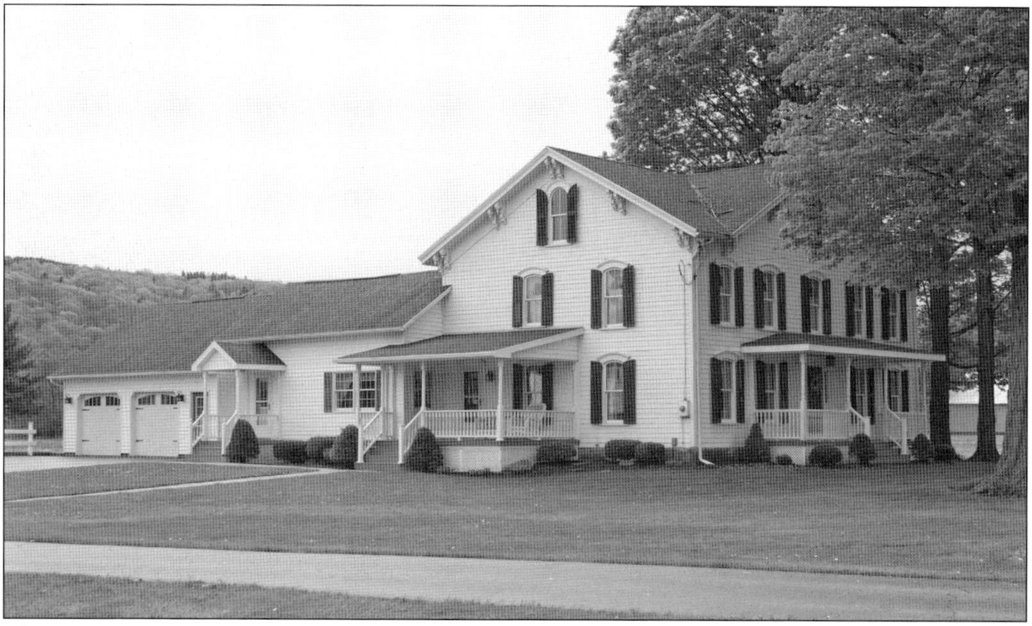

This is a more recent photograph of the 1860s home, nicknamed the "Fort Farm" as a fort was built on this property during the War of 1812. After previous owners Humphrey, Riley, and Selleck, the property was sold to Edward Rickettson, and it is now owned by Rickettson's grandson William McArthur and his wife, Judith Davies McArthur. The black walnut staircase and trim on the exterior of the house are said to have been imported from England.

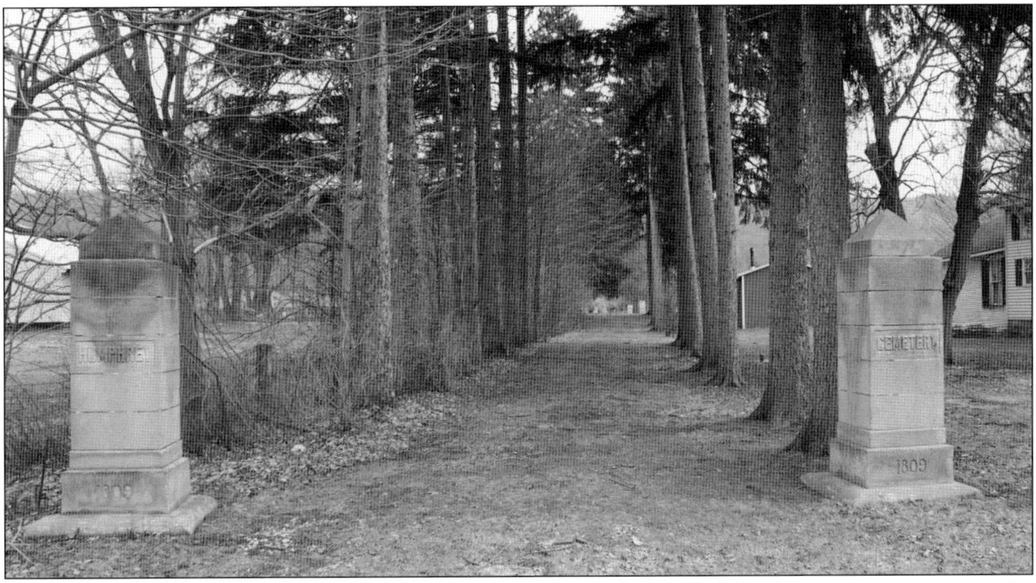

The stones flanking the entrance to Humphrey Cemetery, Holland's oldest cemetery, bear the date 1809. The cemetery was named after Arthur Humphrey, one of Holland's first settlers and its first supervisor. The cemetery is on the east side of Route 16 north of the hamlet on the land that was settled by the Humphrey family. Most of Holland's Revolutionary War and War of 1812 soldiers are buried here.

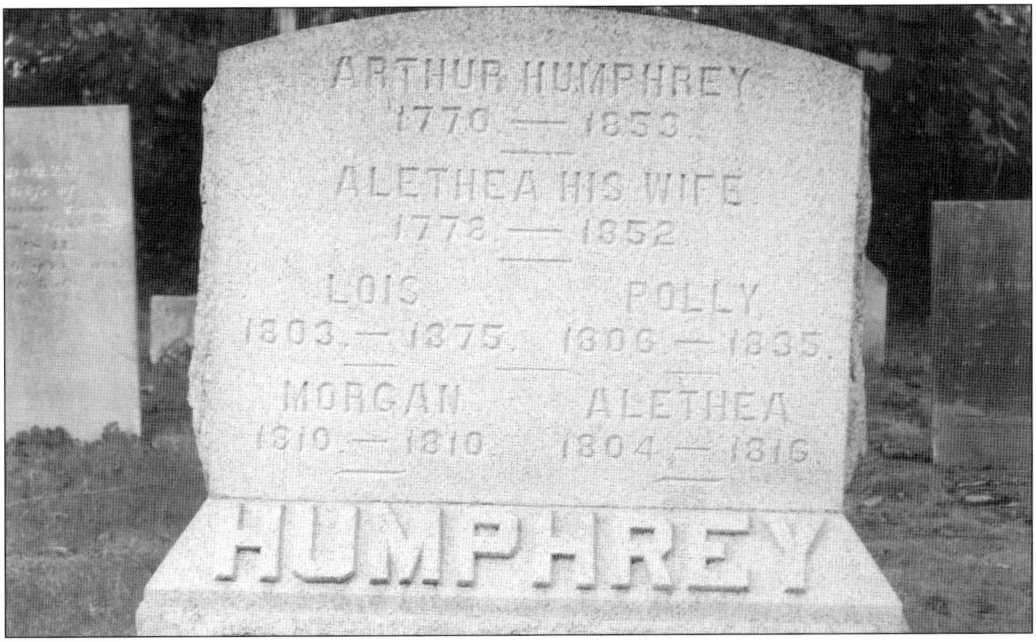

Two of Holland's three founding settlers are buried in Humphrey Cemetery. This is the headstone for Arthur Humphrey, his wife, Alethea, and four of their eight children. Humphrey became Holland's first supervisor in 1818. His son James was a leading lawyer in Buffalo and a member of Congress. Alethea was the only wife of the three original founders who made the initial trip from Vermont with her husband. Founders Abner Currier and Jared Scott returned to Vermont and brought their wives and families to Holland the following season.

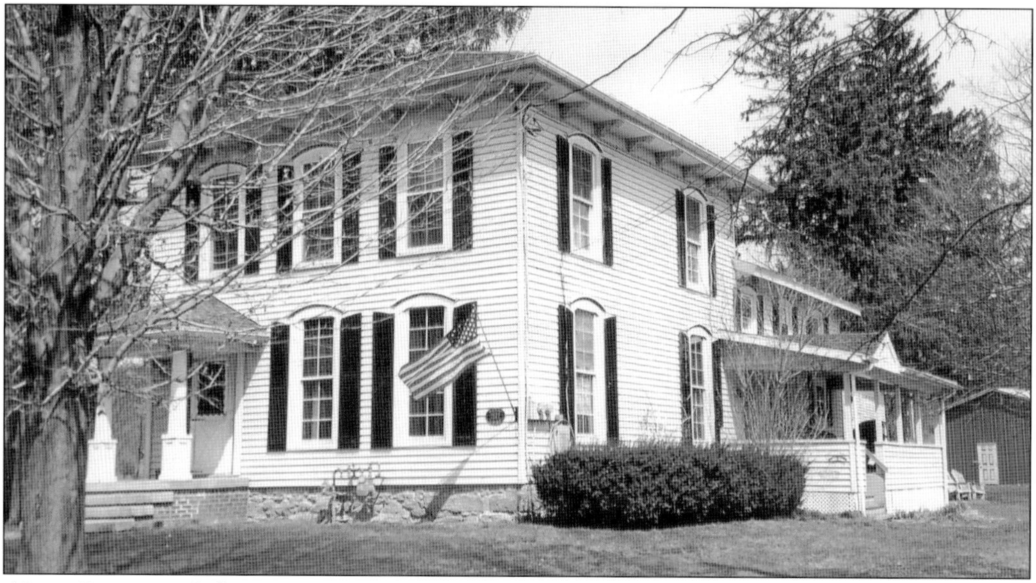

Abner Currier settled on property just south of Arthur Humphrey's in 1807. His old frame house was said to have been a chicken house, now long gone from this site. The pictured homestead, built in 1873 by Abner Currier's son Chauncey Currier, sits near a branch of the Cazenovia Creek. It features a 23-step staircase with a rosewood bannister. The first school in the settlement was located here just before the War of 1812 and was taught by Abner Currier during the winter months. Other owners included Charles "Will" Gerstung when the property was named Brookside Farm, Plinn Geiger, Oscar Heitman, Kenneth Major, and currently Timothy Rickettson of Rickettson Farms.

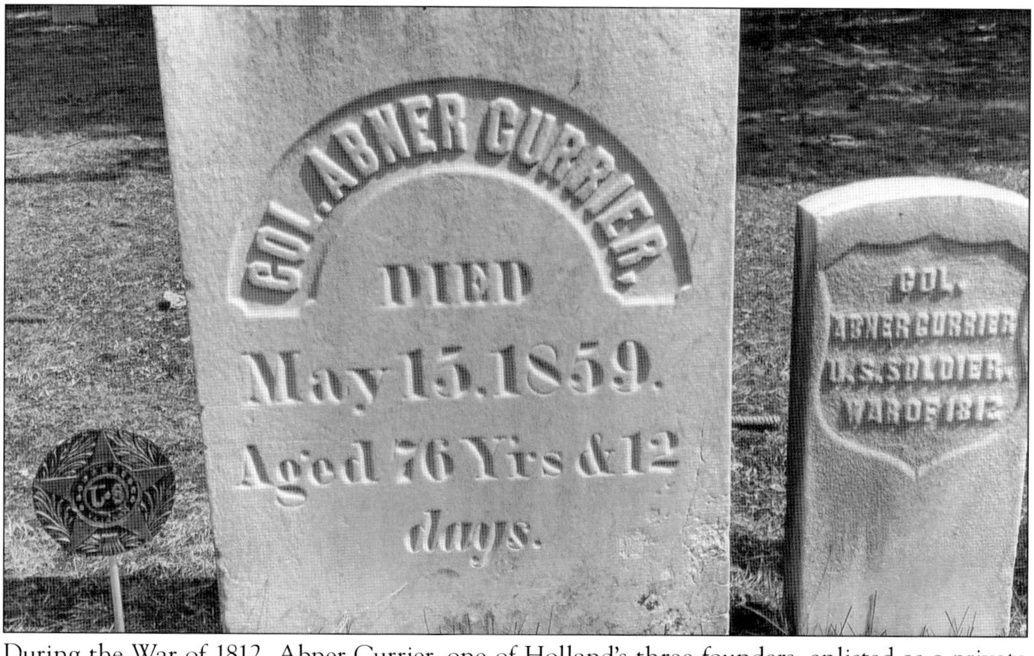

During the War of 1812, Abner Currier, one of Holland's three founders, enlisted as a private and served along the Niagara frontier. Currier became a prominent citizen and was appointed a colonel of the state militia around 1820. He and his wife, Susannah, are buried in Humphrey Cemetery on Olean Road in Holland.

During the War of 1812, the settlers became concerned about British and Indian invasions. In the summer of 1813, they unified and built a stockade on Arthur Humphrey's farm, enclosing about an acre of land. The fort was built of 600 to 700 logs cut into 15-foot lengths, hewn to fit closely together and set upright, side by side, about three feet in the ground. Moats and ditches were dug around the triangular fort, with water supplied by the hill creek. Loop holes were cut in the standing logs for muskets and rifles. This defense was called Fort Humphrey, and the Humphrey farm was thereafter known as the Fort Farm. Fortunately, the fort never had to be used. It was later dismantled, and the logs were used in the construction of area barns. This model of Fort Humphrey was constructed using information from Holland's early history records.

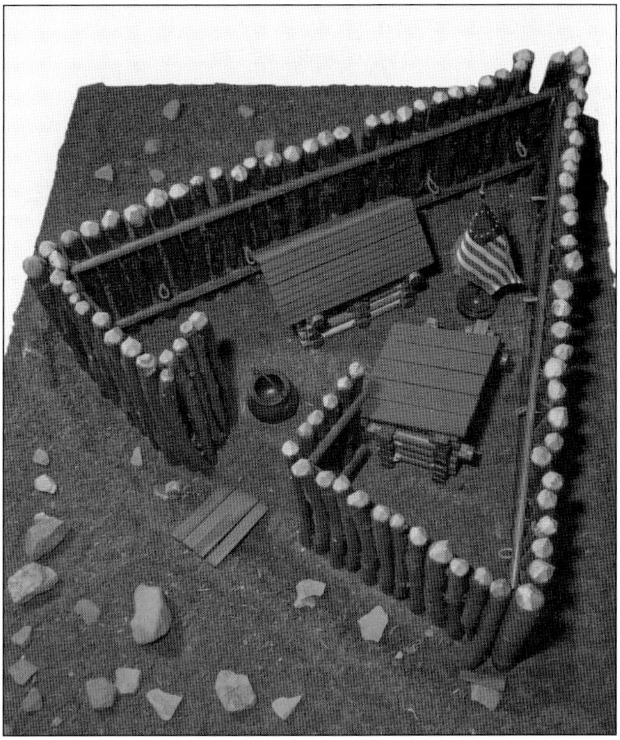

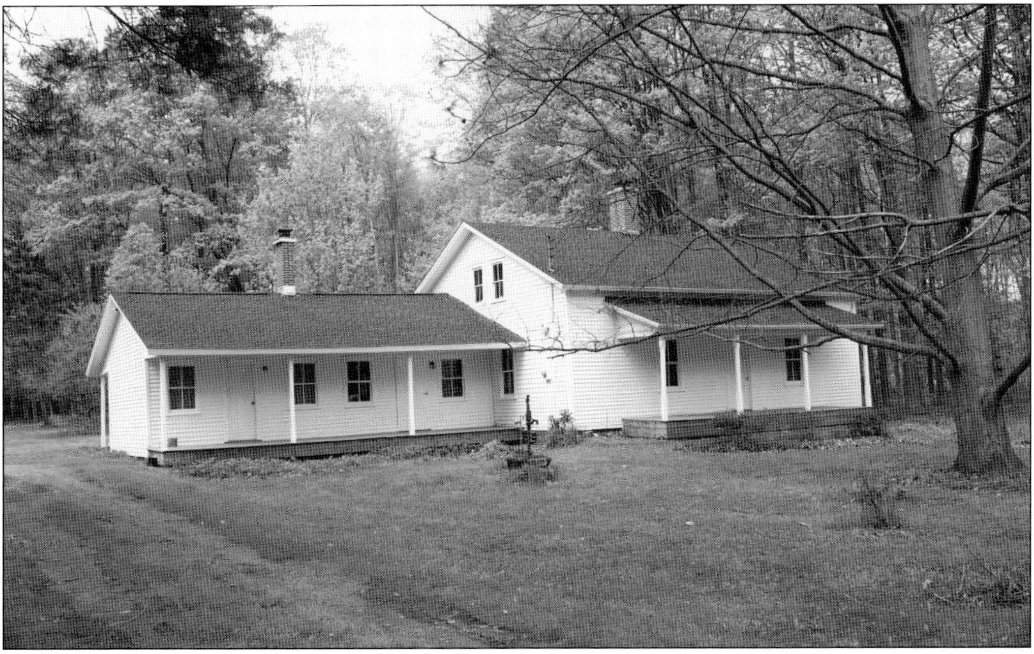

Built in 1818 by Ezekiel Colby, this is most likely the oldest house on a homestead lot in Holland. Colby was a Revolutionary War veteran who came to this area from Corinth, Vermont, in 1808. The house features original wainscoting with a feather-painted surface and original doors, latches, corner beams, and windows. At 7898 Olean Road, the house has been in the Colby family for eight generations.

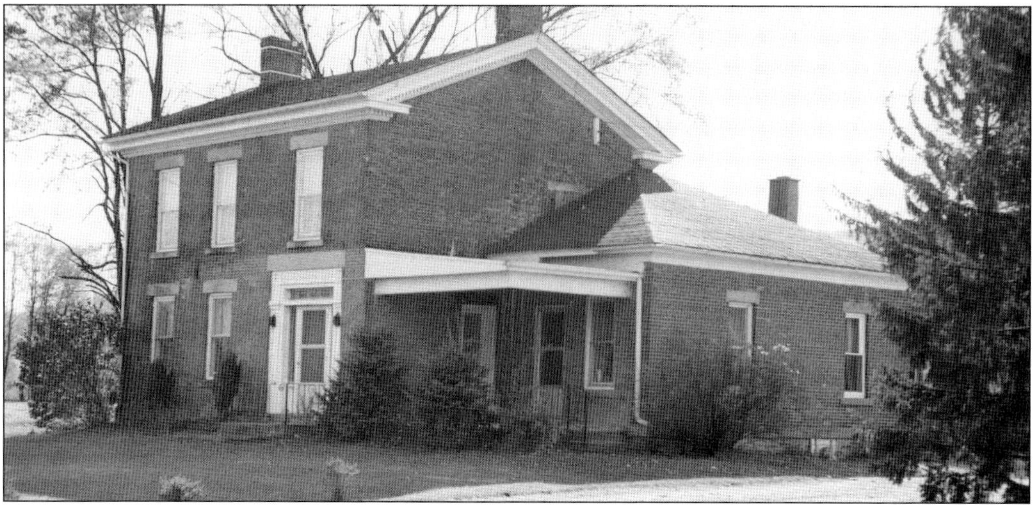

This house is referred to as the Dickerman-Wanamaker home. The property was bought from the Holland Land Company by Daniel McKean from Corinth, Vermont, in 1817. Ownership passed to Joseph Currier, Albert Tracy, and then Isaac Dickerman, who built the brick house in 1829. Dickerman had the marble for the fireplace floor and the stone slabs for the window lintels and front doorway sent from Vermont via the Erie Canal. It was drawn by oxcart from the canal to its location on Olean Road. Dickerman later sold the homestead to Addison Ryder, who eventually sold to the Wanamaker family.

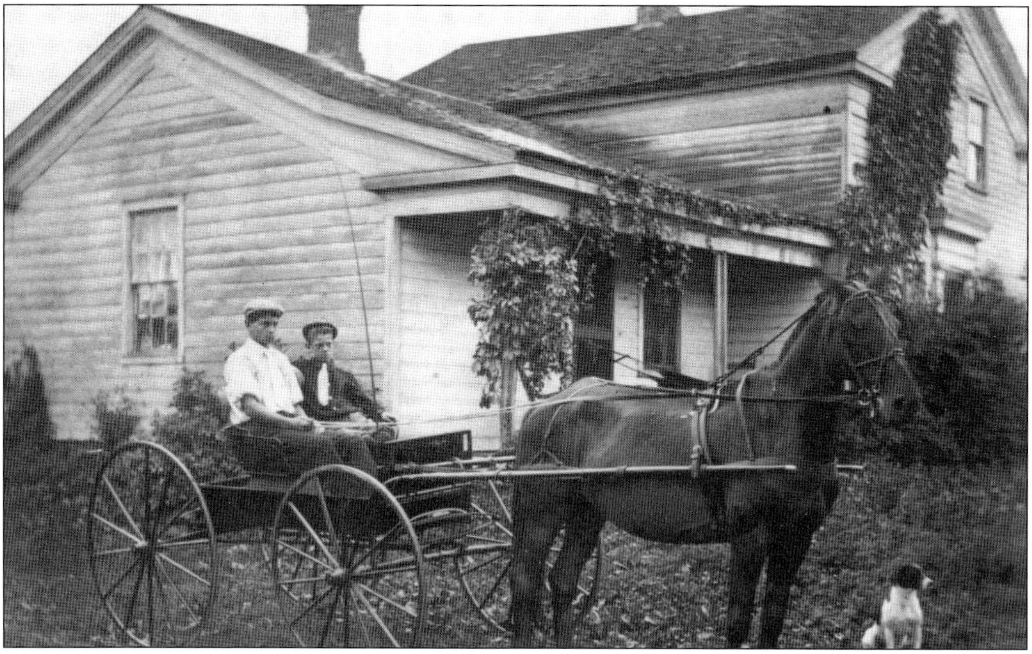

William Barron's two sons are shown with the family's horse and buggy on South Protection Road. The house was built around 1837, and this picture is dated 1900, before the second story was added. Descendants of the Barron family have lived here for eight generations. The Barrons were early settlers and trace their roots to 1816, when Joshua Barron opened the first tavern in a house built by Col. William Warren. The tavern was located in the hamlet near Mill Street, which was renamed Capitol Heights.

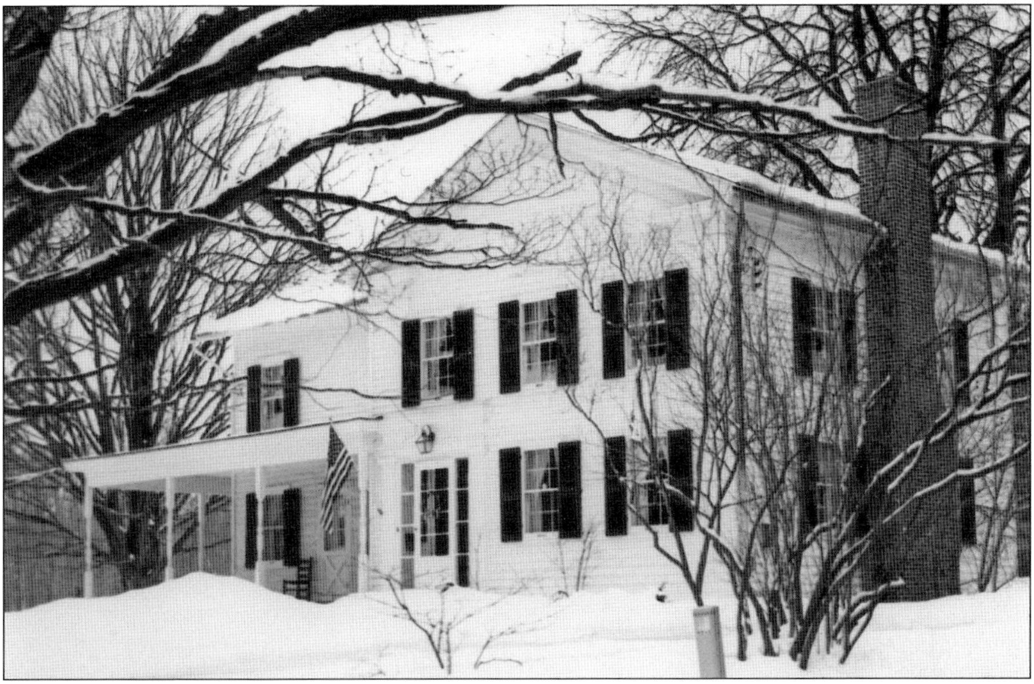

Pictured is the Jonathan Kent House, or Goodman home, which was built in 1836. Jonathan and his wife, Polly, came from Vermont in 1811 and owned a large tract of land on Vermont Hill Road. Kent built this home on Olean Road in the area known as the Colby settlement. He hired local men and Indians to help with the labor. Part of the house was first used as a trading store where exchanges were made with the Indians and neighbors. Barrel marks can still be seen on the plank dining room floor.

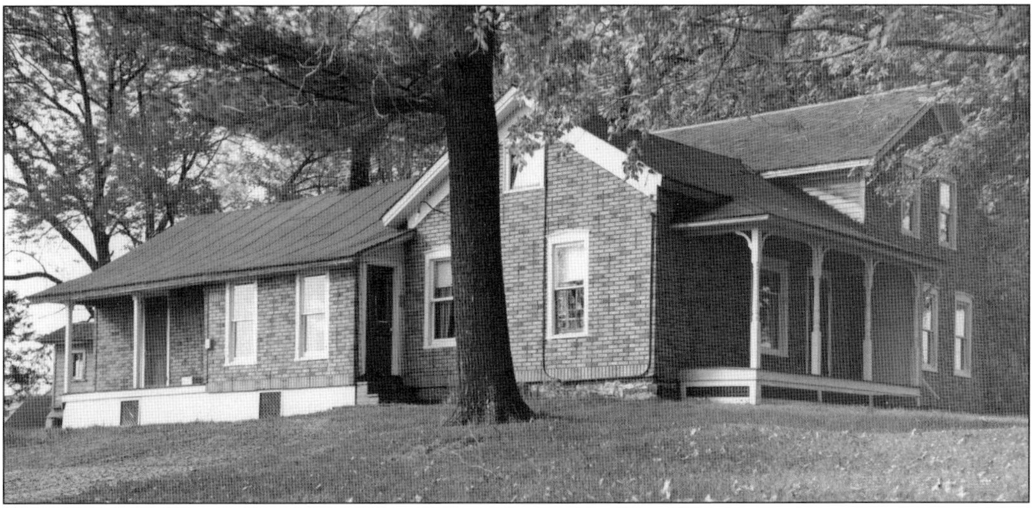

In 1816, Caleb Cutler came from Wardsboro, Vermont, and settled on the farm now located at 11555 Holland Glenwood Road. He was 45 years old at the time and brought his wife and large family of eight children by horse and wagon; the older boys walked and drove six cows the entire distance, which took 22 days. The pictured homestead was built in 1865. Cutler, a veteran of the Revolutionary War, and his descendants owned and farmed this land for over 150 years. Many residents can trace their roots to the Cutler-McArthur family.

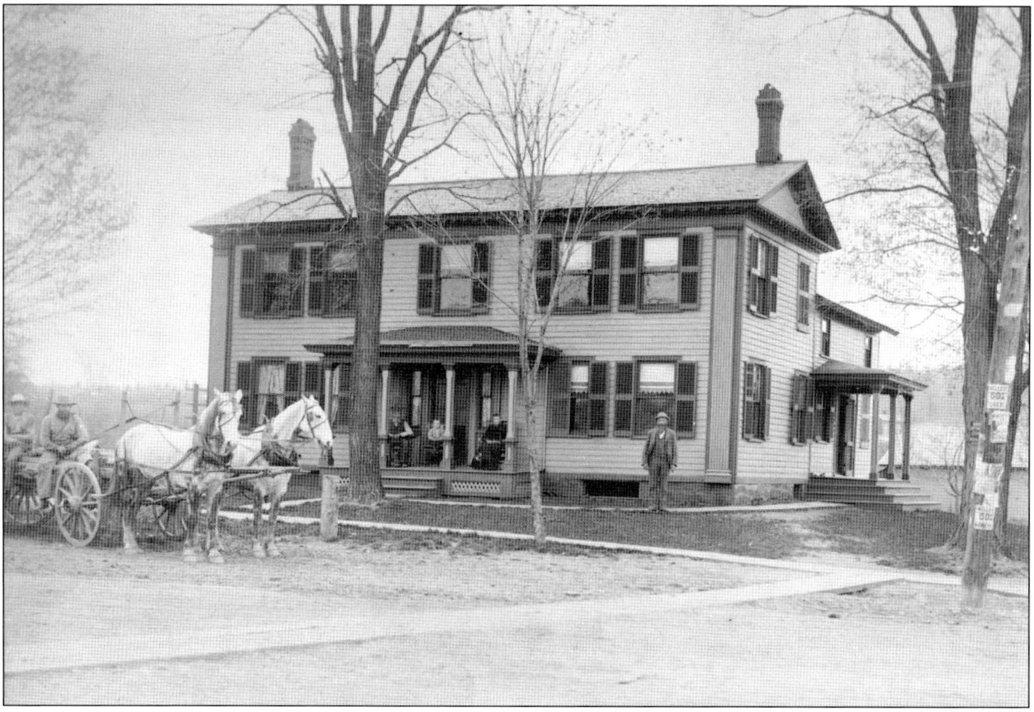

Alvin Orr built this home at 7 South Main Street in the 1840s, and it still stands today. The Orrs owned a saw- and gristmill nearby. When owned by the Orr family, it was a stop on the Underground Railroad to Canada; the Orrs were known abolitionists.

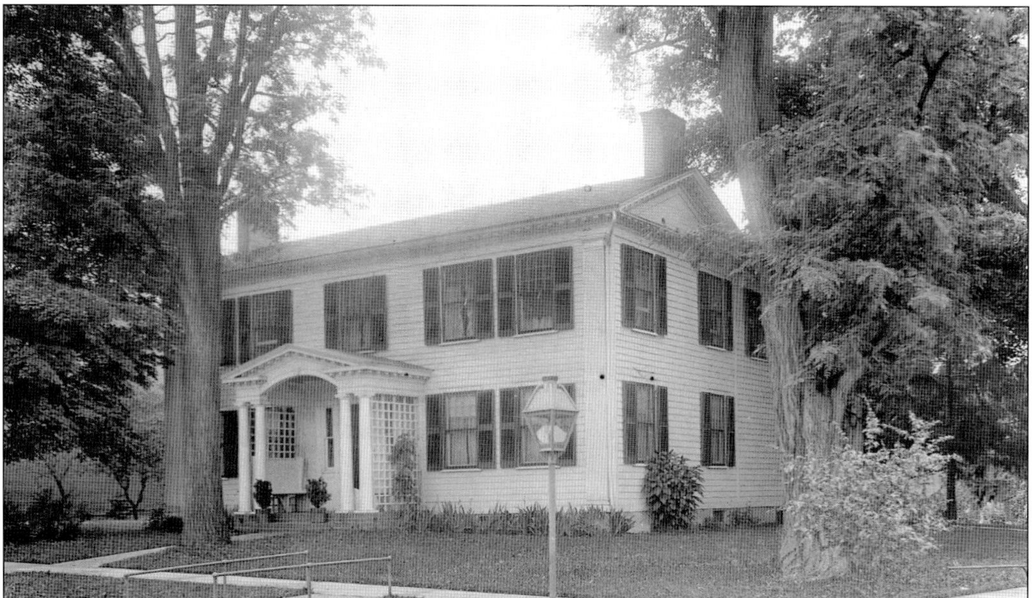

The Orr house was purchased by Paul J. Wurst just before 1900. At that time, the Wurst family also owned the Orr mills. In the 1950s, the home was sold and used as a nursing home; in the 1960s, it was remodeled and became Bucknam Funeral Home. Today, it is an apartment building and looks very much like it did in this photograph.

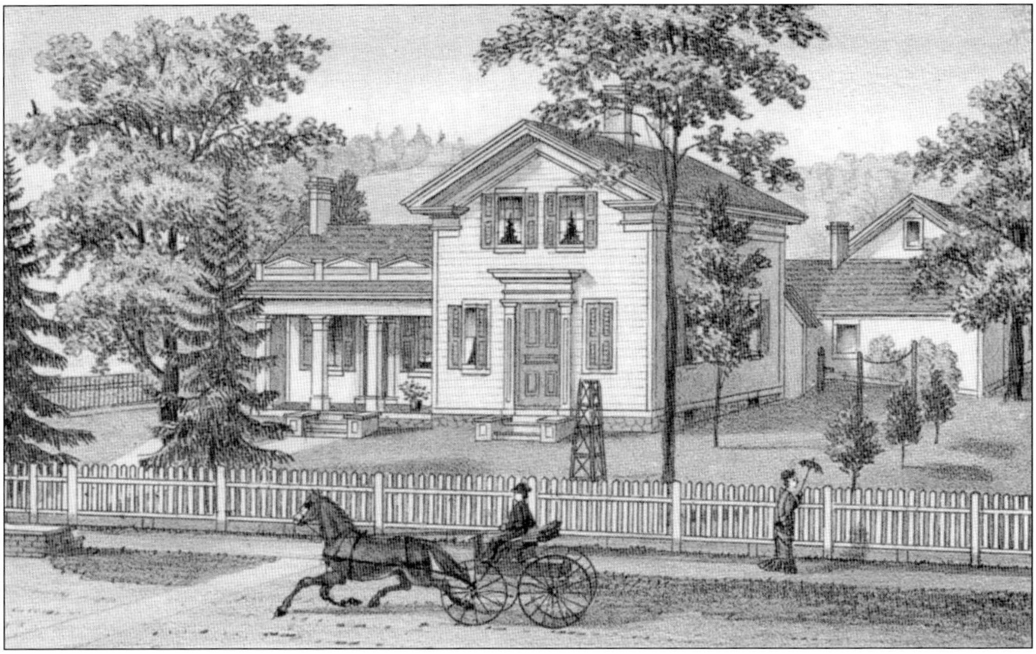

Dr. A.C. Osborn came to Holland around 1868 and settled in a home built in the late 1840s at 100 North Main Street. The property was originally purchased by Abner Currier from the Holland Land Company in 1829. At one time, it was owned by Clarence Bush, and today, it is a hair salon.

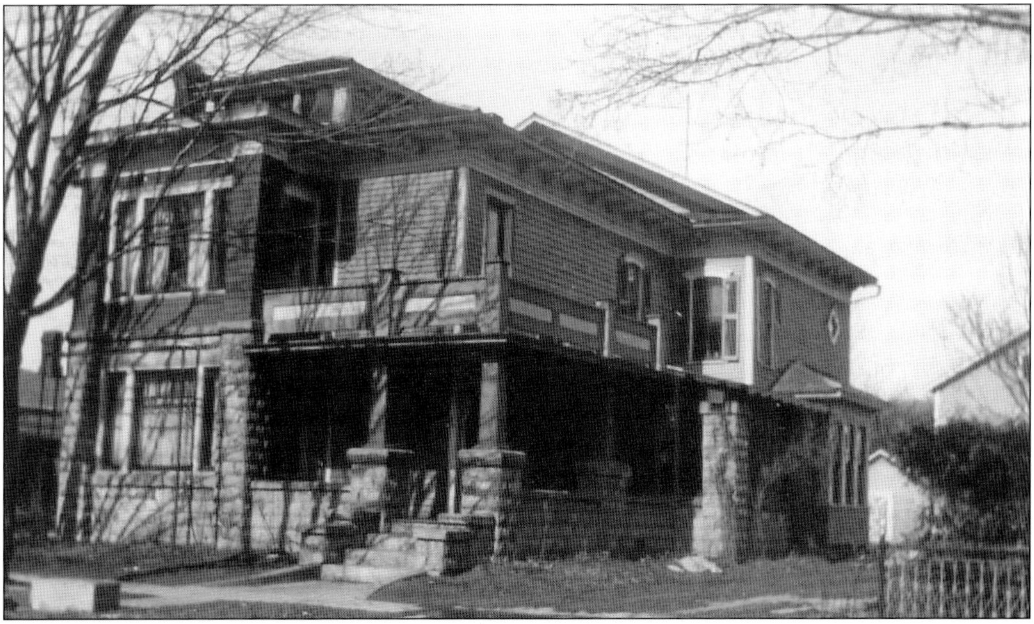

This stately home sits on land purchased from Wilhelm Willink of the Holland Land Company by Abner Currier in 1829. The residence at 81 North Main Street has been home to many recognizable Holland families, including the Rileys, Burlinghams, Stickneys, and Tanners. At one time, Dr. Castilego had his office here. The Lingenfelters have made this their home since the late 1940s.

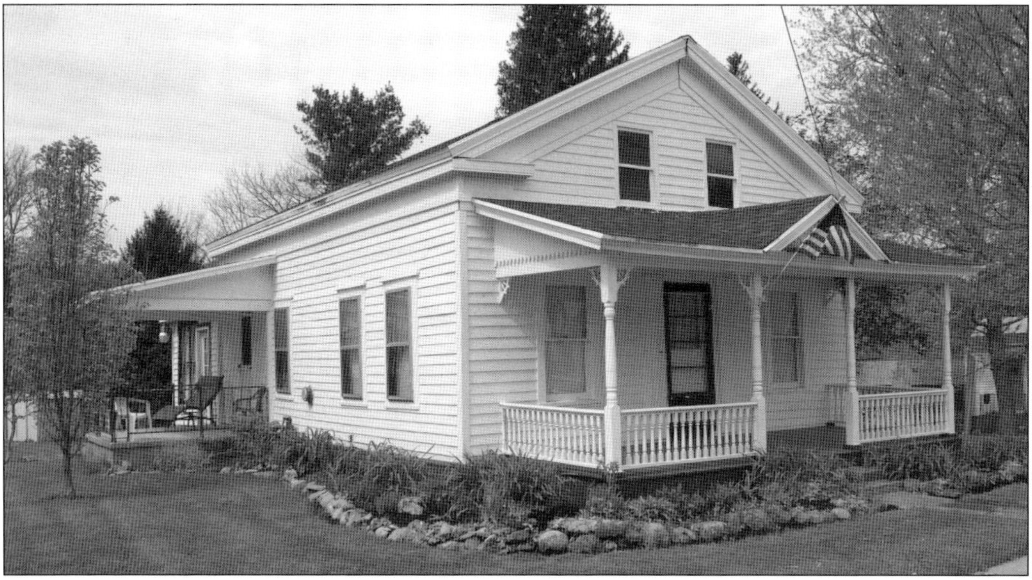

Built in the 1850s, this home was owned by the Wellman Bucknam family for a number of years. While the first owner is unknown, Dr. Clayton Button lived here in the 1890s. His office was in the wing to the right. Dr. Button was also a grocer and a pharmacist in Holland. His family came to Holland in 1815 and settled on the West Hill near the Kramer farm. The house, at 120 North Main Street, is still owned by a relative of the Bucknam-Schott family.

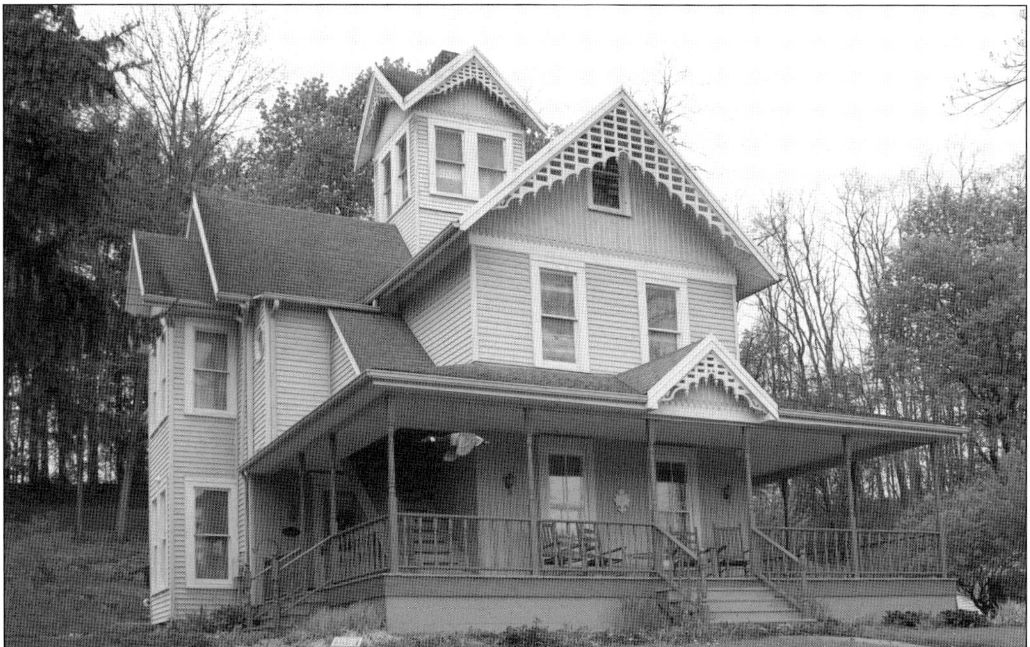

This was the home of Horace Selleck, a prominent and successful businessman who came to Holland in 1868. He purchased property containing a planing and lumber mill, built a house, and sold farm implements. This home, with its intricate trim work, stood across the street from his mills. Selleck was active in town affairs; he served as postmaster in 1897 and was twice elected town assessor.

Two

Historic Homes

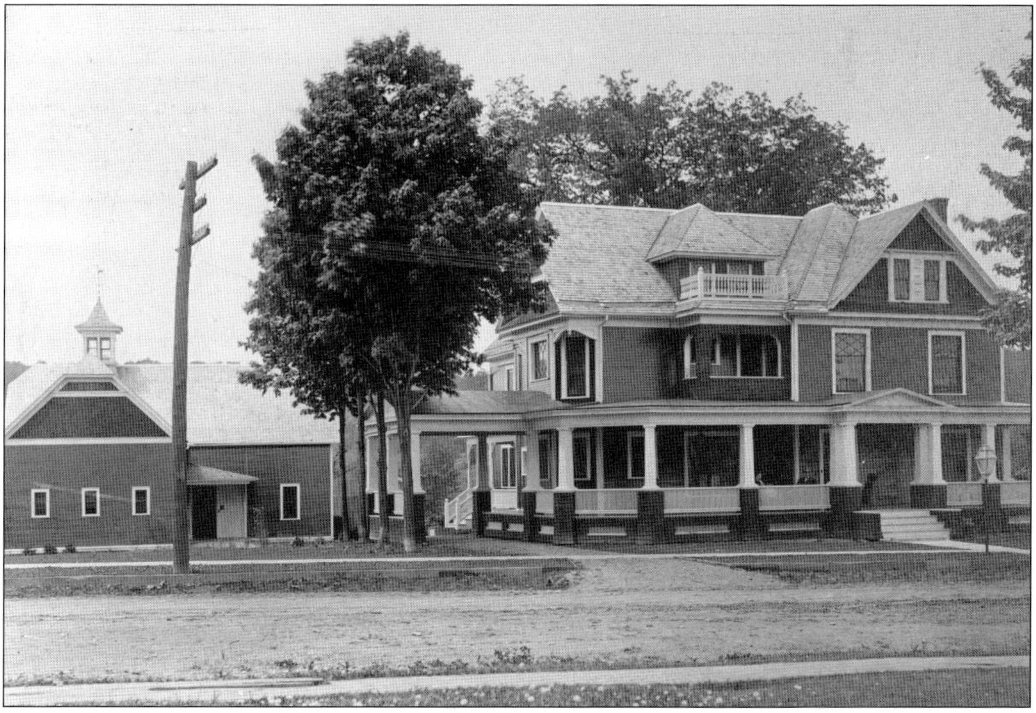

One of the most recognizable homes in Holland is the Riley House, on Main Street in the heart of the business district. Philip D. Riley came to Holland in 1832, opened a general store, and prospered in farming, livestock, and real estate. An affluent man, Riley was also community-minded and served four separate terms as town supervisor, his first in 1848. The Riley House was eventually passed down to his grandson Philip M. Riley, who took over the family business. The home was later purchased by the Moore family, who moved to East Aurora. They traded houses with the Beardsells, who lived here from 1929 to 1983. It was then sold to Robert and Carol Gilbert, who operated a well-known antique shop on the premises. The house was sold to its current owners, Kevin and Laurel Swartz, in 1996.

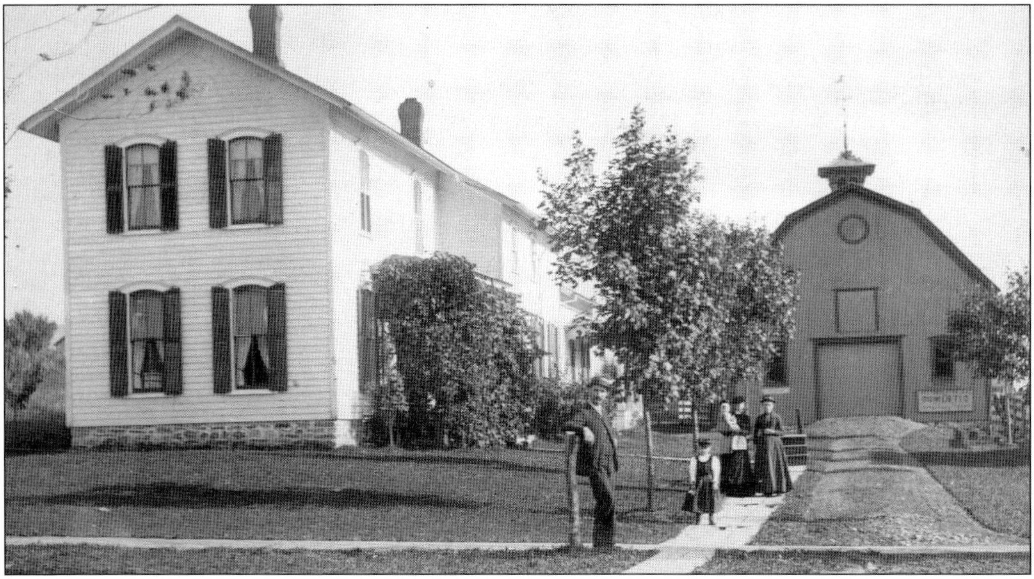

William B. Jackson built this house at 67 Pearl Street in 1888. The handsome horse barn that featured a cupola and weather vane was added in 1891; the cupola is still on the barn. Jackson, a prosperous businessman and very active in town activities, is shown with his family. He was the first president of the Bank of Holland, serving from 1893 to 1906. He was also town supervisor (1894–1904), town highway commissioner, superintendent of town water works, and postmaster (1889). Jackson ran a general store in the late 1800s. (Courtesy of Edwin Stevenson.)

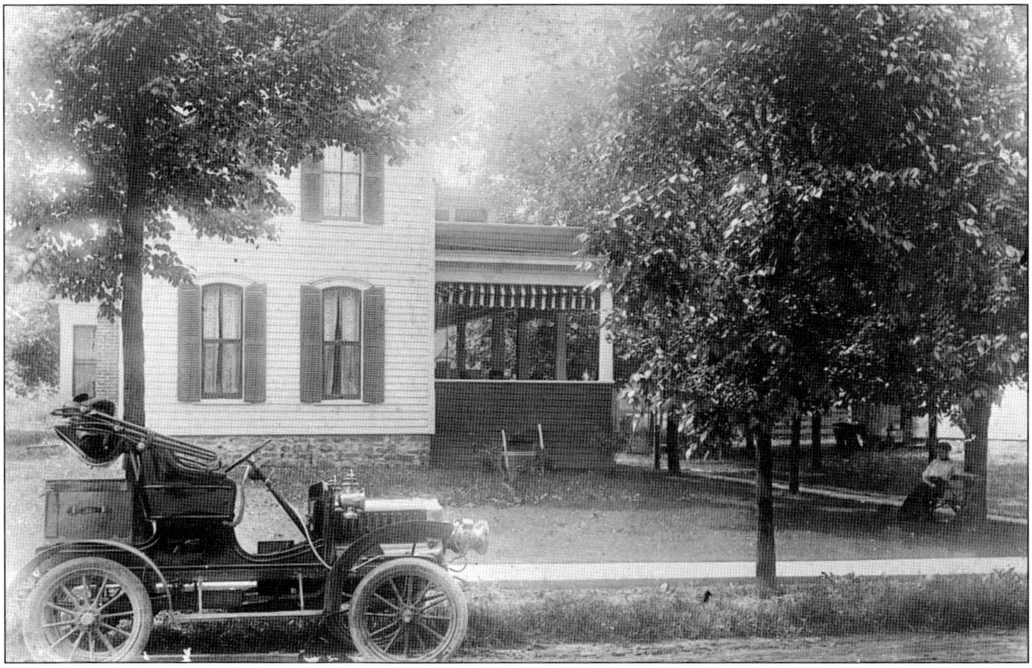

This later photograph shows the home with its unique two-story porches. This stately home is presently an apartment house owned by Edwin and Laureen Stevenson. This picture illustrates one of the many changes that came to the community: Jackson's new car is in the front yard, and his horses are in the stable.

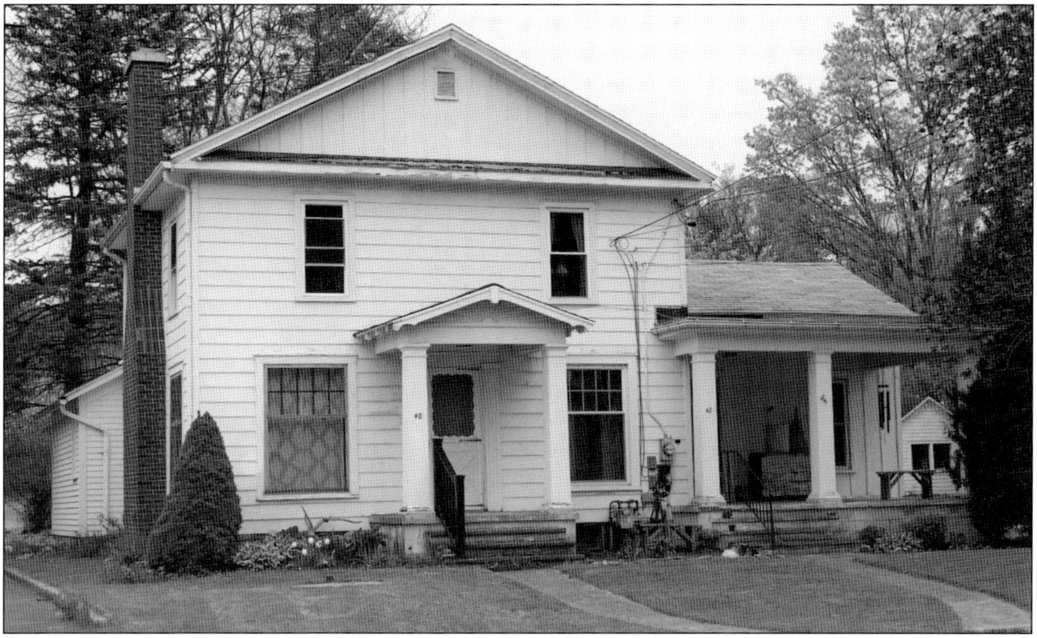

Abner Orr built this home at 42 South Main Street around 1848 and lived here until 1864. Orr was town supervisor in 1852 and 1854 and was related to the Orr family that ran the mill in town. He also owned a hotel and feed store a few doors away. The home passed through several owners and eventually came to Seymour Rogers and his wife, Minnie. In the 1920s, Minnie operated a millinery shop in the left part of the house. In 1929, the house was divided to make a rental apartment. Later, the home was owned by the Kirkby family, who lived there for many years.

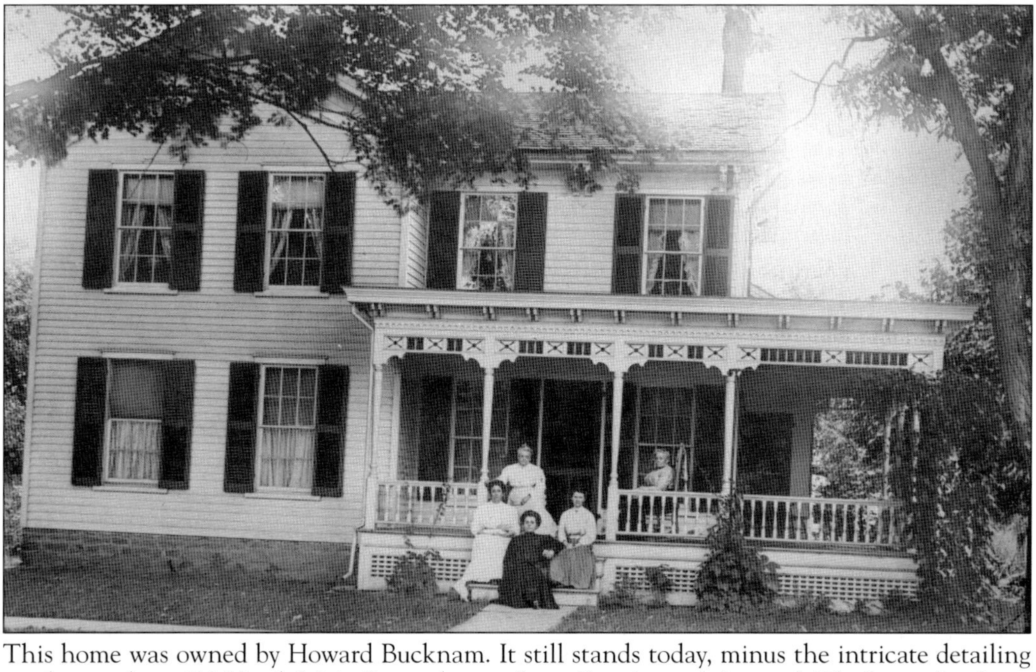

This home was owned by Howard Bucknam. It still stands today, minus the intricate detailing on the porch, at 111 North Main Street (across from Continental Avenue). The house has been converted into apartments.

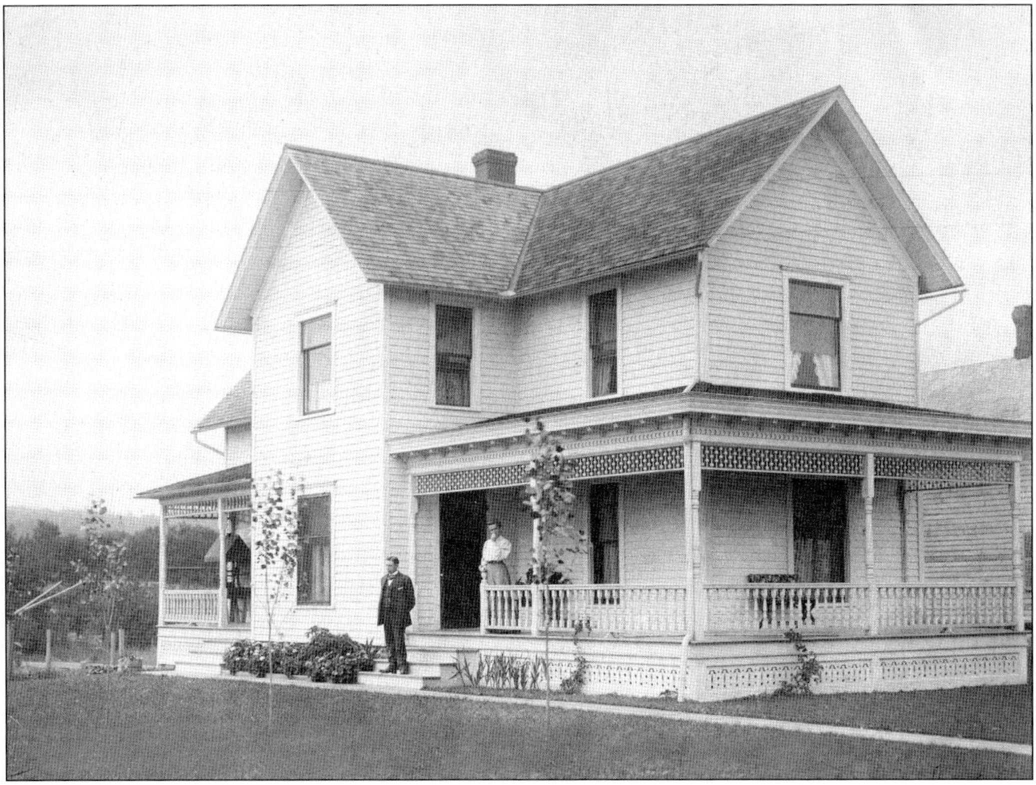

The home of Frank and Stella Selleck can still be seen today at 18 Canada Street. Selleck edited the local newspaper, *Holland Review*. This house has since been renovated into apartments.

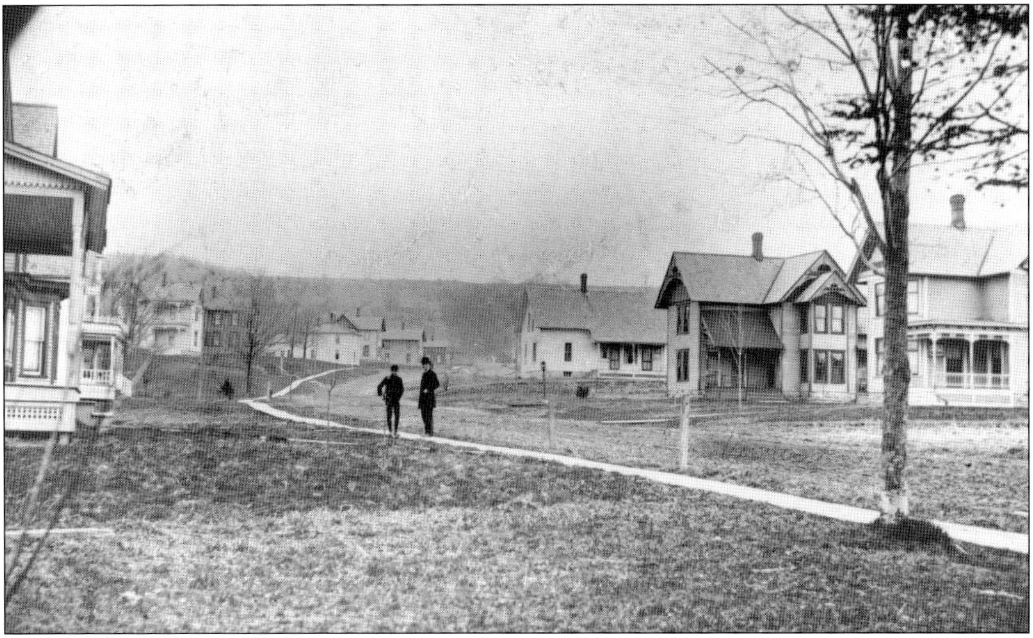

Here is a 1907 view of the homes along Vermont Street, looking toward the railroad tracks. Note the plank sidewalk and dirt road.

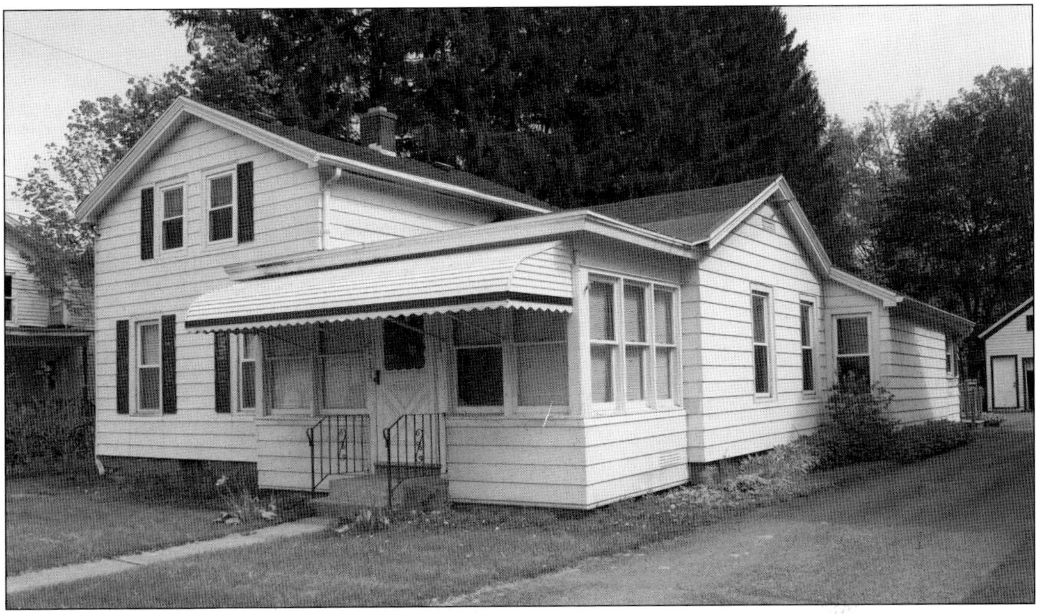

The home of John O. Riley was built in the late 1850s in a Greek Revival style. He was a brother of Philip D. Riley; they were a prosperous, distinguished family who also built homes like this in nearby East Aurora, New York. This house has the distinction of having Susan B. Anthony for an overnight guest in 1880 when she spoke at the Baptist church in Holland. The house passed from the Riley and Wurst families to the Bixbys, Van Names, Kimballs, and Moores, and is presently owned by the Joyce family.

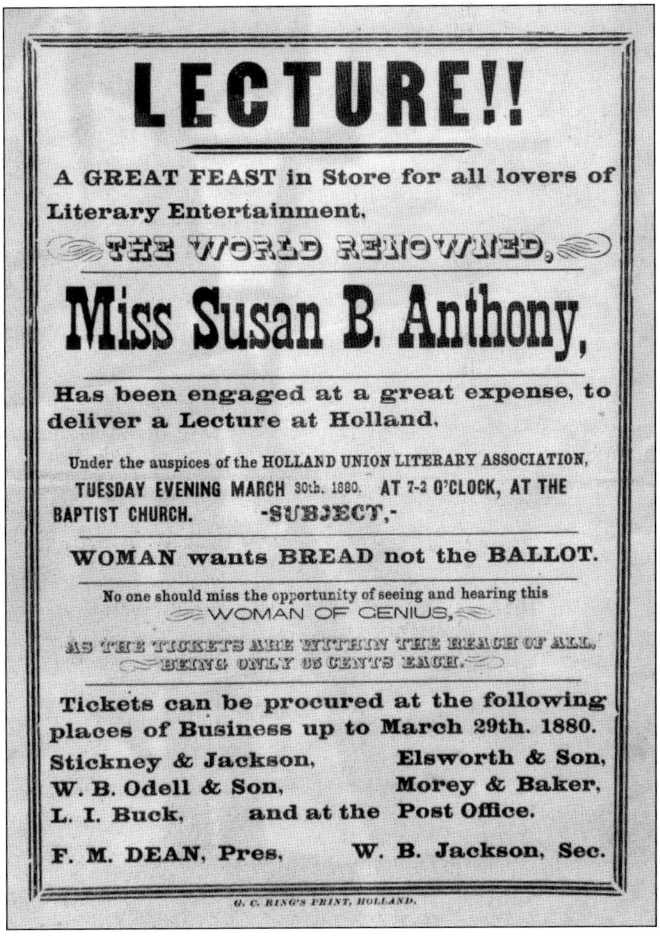

LECTURE!!

A GREAT FEAST in Store for all lovers of Literary Entertainment,

THE WORLD RENOWNED,

Miss Susan B. Anthony,

Has been engaged at a great expense, to deliver a Lecture at Holland,

Under the auspices of the HOLLAND UNION LITERARY ASSOCIATION, TUESDAY EVENING MARCH 30th. 1880. AT 7-2 O'CLOCK, AT THE BAPTIST CHURCH. -SUBJECT,-

WOMAN wants BREAD not the BALLOT.

No one should miss the opportunity of seeing and hearing this

WOMAN OF GENIUS,

AS THE TICKETS ARE WITHIN THE REACH OF ALL, BEING ONLY 35 CENTS EACH.

Tickets can be procured at the following places of Business up to March 29th. 1880.

Stickney & Jackson, Elsworth & Son,
W. B. Odell & Son, Morey & Baker,
L. I. Buck, and at the Post Office.

F. M. DEAN, Pres, W. B. Jackson, Sec.

G. C. KING'S PRINT, HOLLAND.

This is the poster advertising Susan B. Anthony's speaking engagement in Holland on March 30, 1880. Sponsored by the Holland Union Literary Association, the lecture was held at Holland's Baptist church on Main Street.

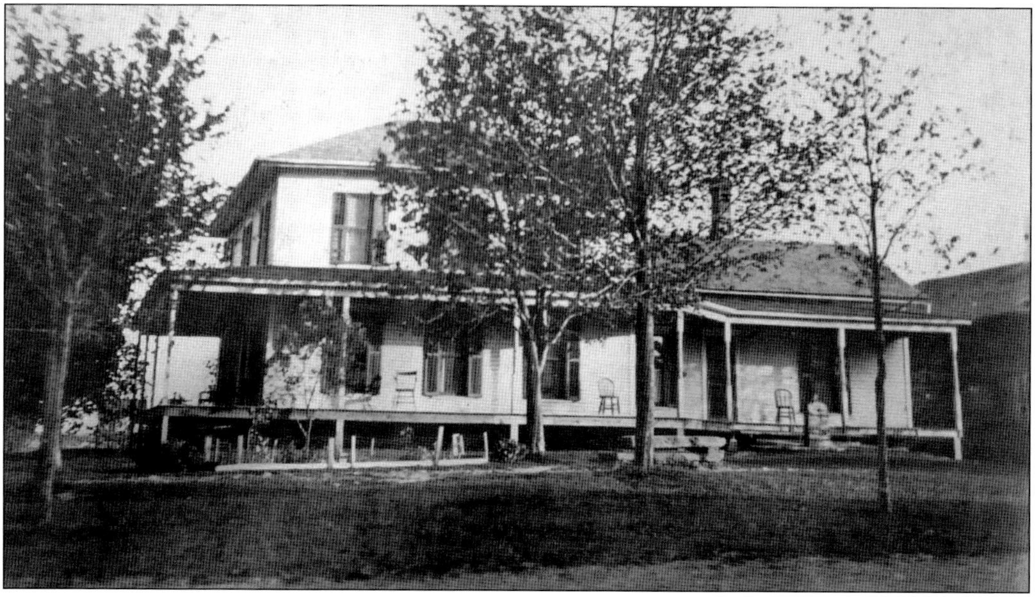

In 1809, the Colbys traveled to Holland from Corinth, Vermont. Their 540 acres were most likely part of the original purchase from the Holland Land Company by Peter Colby in 1835. This home was passed to Jonas Colby and eventually to family member Donald Fischer, its current owner. A log cabin and frame house were torn down and this large square house built around 1884. A group of homestead buildings surrounded the house. An old frame house stood behind it, along with pig pens, a smokehouse, a horse barn, chicken houses, and even a house used to make wooden shingles. All of these outbuildings were in need of repair and were taken down during the 1950s and 1960s.

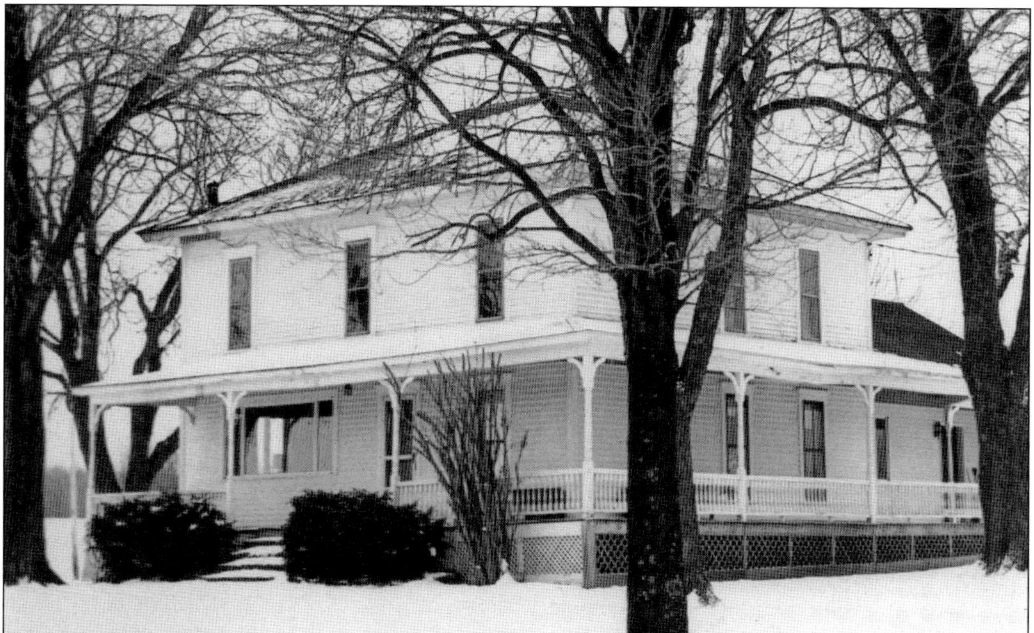

Here is a current picture of the Colby Homestead/Fischer Farm, still owned and lived in by 95-year-old Norma Fischer. At least 10 generations of Colbys have lived here.

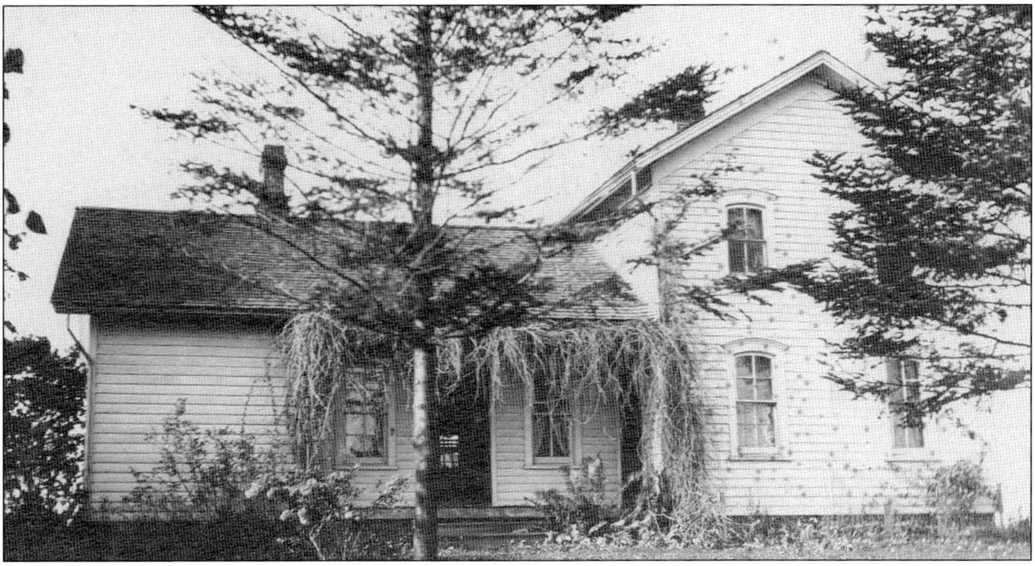

This house was the home of Jefferson Colby on Vermont Hill Road. Given land by his father, Jonas Colby, when he married Philena Hawks, Jefferson built the entire home around 1873. The home was inherited by son Clare and then in the 1960s by Donald Fischer, a Colby relative. Fischer's son Brian has owned the home since 1981. Jefferson Colby was a teacher and a farmer and held several town offices through the years. Next door to this house was a blacksmith shop owned by Jefferson's grandfather Peter Colby.

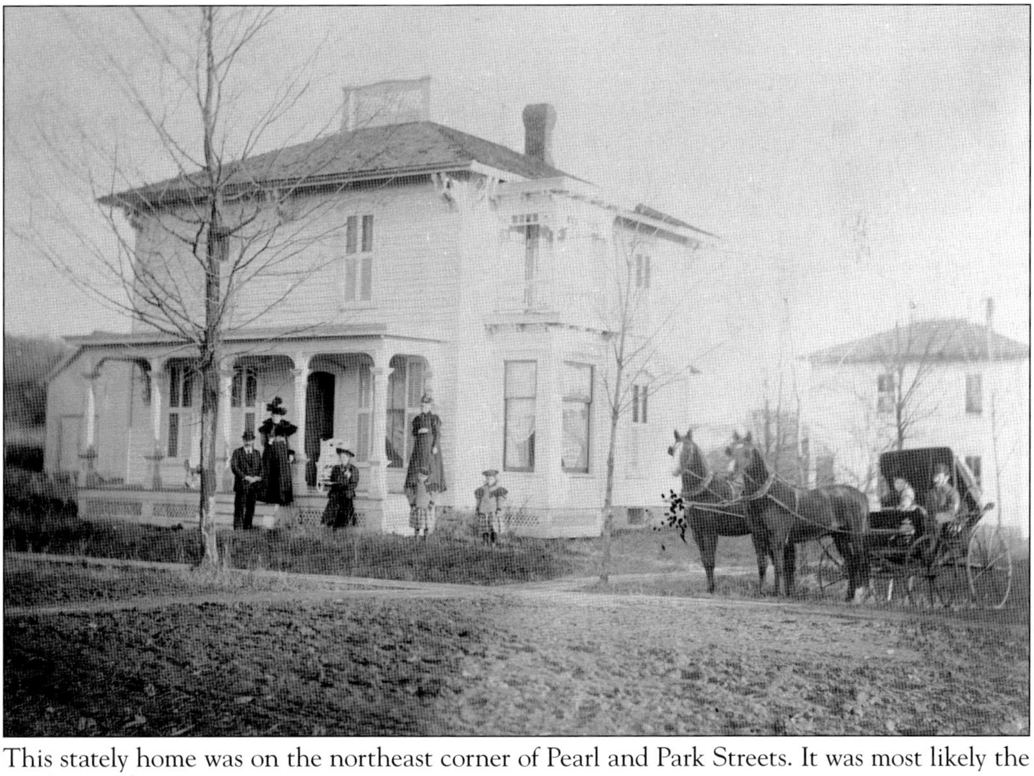

This stately home was on the northeast corner of Pearl and Park Streets. It was most likely the Merlau residence.

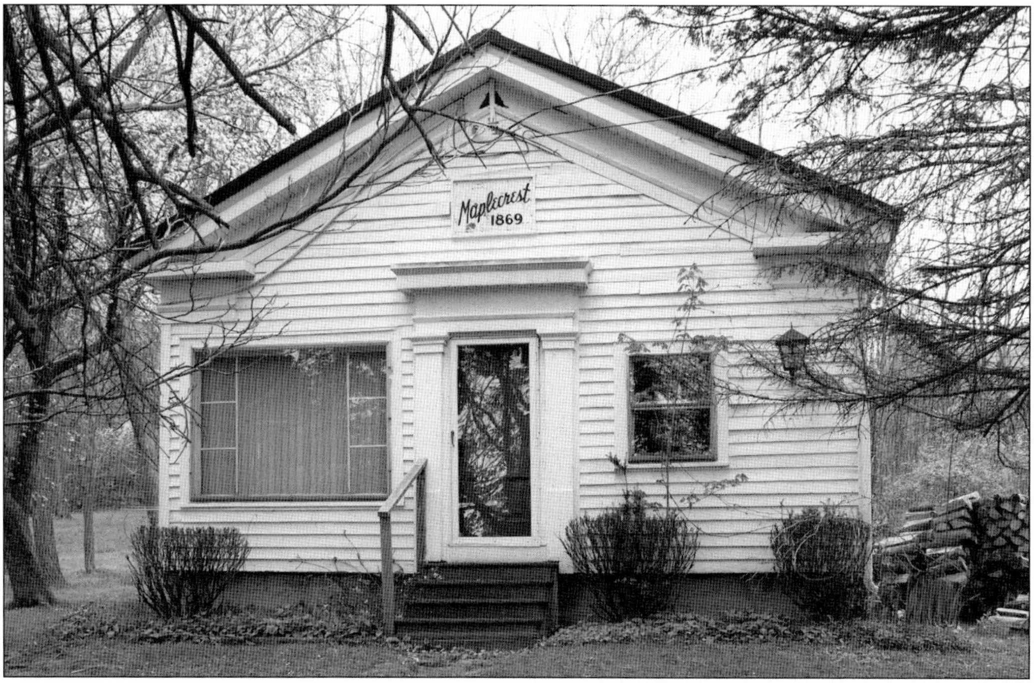

This old schoolhouse, District 1 (formerly District 11), is on Hunters Creek Road and was remodeled into a residence. The schoolhouse was constructed around 1855. The school also served the Hunters Creek community as a church and meeting place until Holland's schools were centralized in the 1930s. The many trees around the building were planted by pupils over the years for Arbor Day celebrations. A tavern and store once owned by Oliver Davis stood to the left of the school, which is near Vermont Street and Hunters Creek Road. The Dobersteins are the present owners.

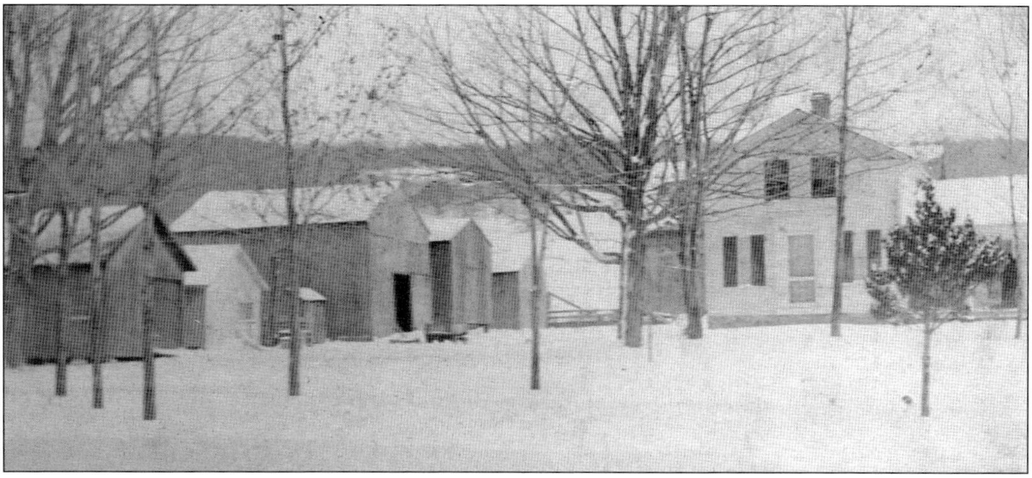

James D. Kimball lived in this homestead at 305 Canada Street. He served as Holland's justice of the peace from 1924 to 1933. Kimball sold his property to Albert Koerner, and in 1944, Koerner started raising turkeys in a very small way. Through the years, he gradually built up a retail turkey trade directed toward the quality-conscious consumer. He raised and marketed some 1,200 turkeys annually, with many of them being sold as gifts. Koerner started a construction business in 1948 and retired around 2010. His business was sold to Edwin Stevenson, who presently carries on the construction business and owns the property. (Courtesy of Edwin Stevenson.)

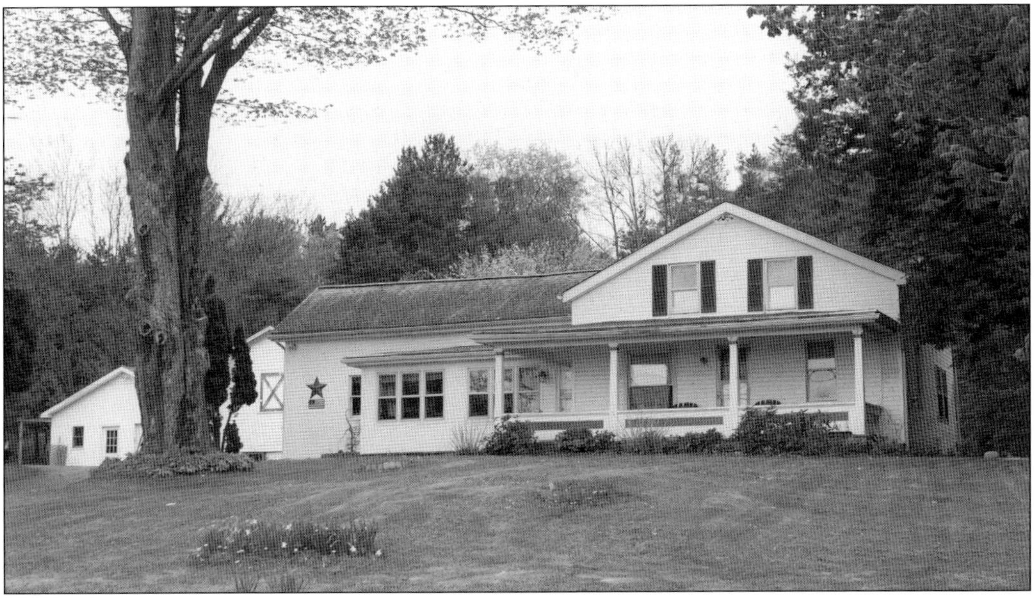

This home is in the area where the Davis family settled; they made the trip to Holland from Corinth, Vermont. William Davis was deeded the property in 1829 from the Holland Land Company, and the house was built in the 1830s. Oliver Davis was the next owner, followed by Wattus Brown and his grandson Robert Brown. The property is on Hunters Creek Road.

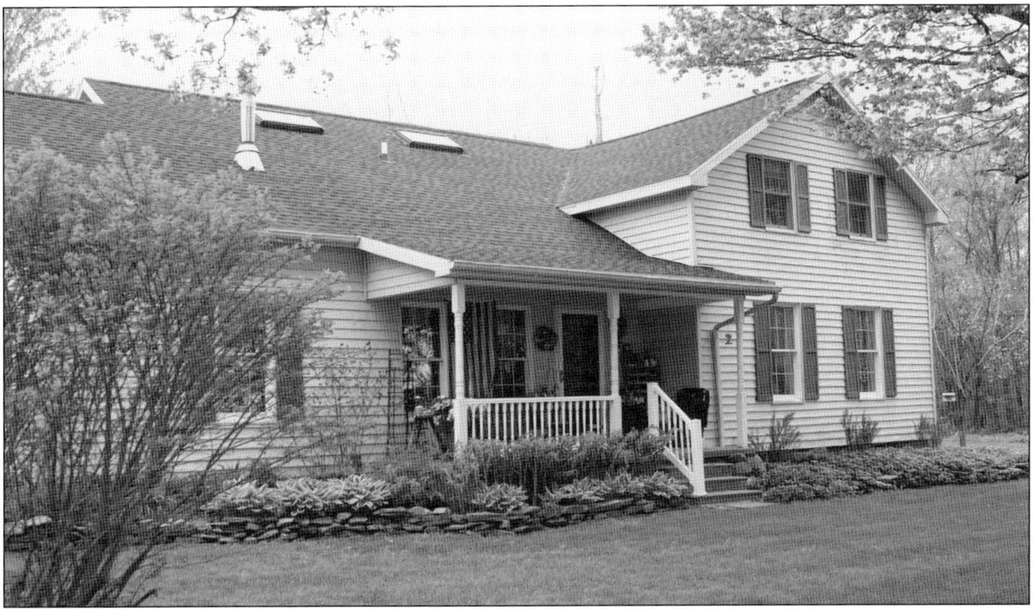

Another Hunters Creek Road property, this early homestead belonged to John Hiller, who came from Germany and eventually settled in Holland. Other owners include Chester Limburg, Henry Seadeek, and presently, Keith Johnson. The home was most likely built in the 1840s by a member of the Jackson family, listed on an 1855 map as living in this area. From the 1940s to 1970s, the house stood empty; however, both the interior and exterior were remodeled extensively in later years.

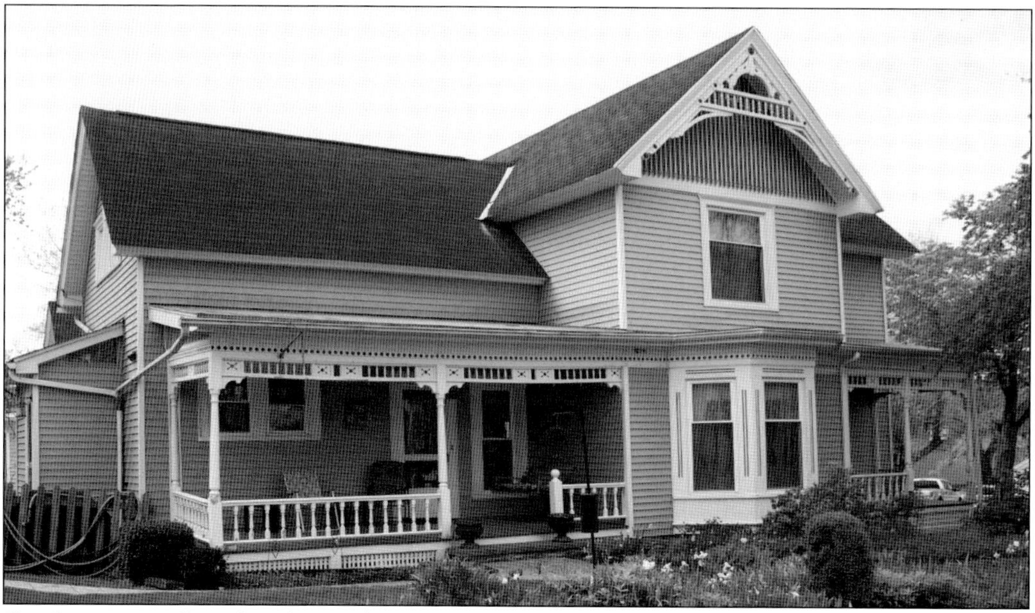

On the corner of Pearl and Canada Streets, this was once the home of Nora C. Kanner, a well-respected teacher, poet, and community member. This grand home was built around 1870 and has only had three owners: Kanner, the Rose family, and Bruce and Barbara Reinagel, who purchased it in 1989. The property once had a carriage barn, which was deteriorating and had to be taken down in the early 1990s.

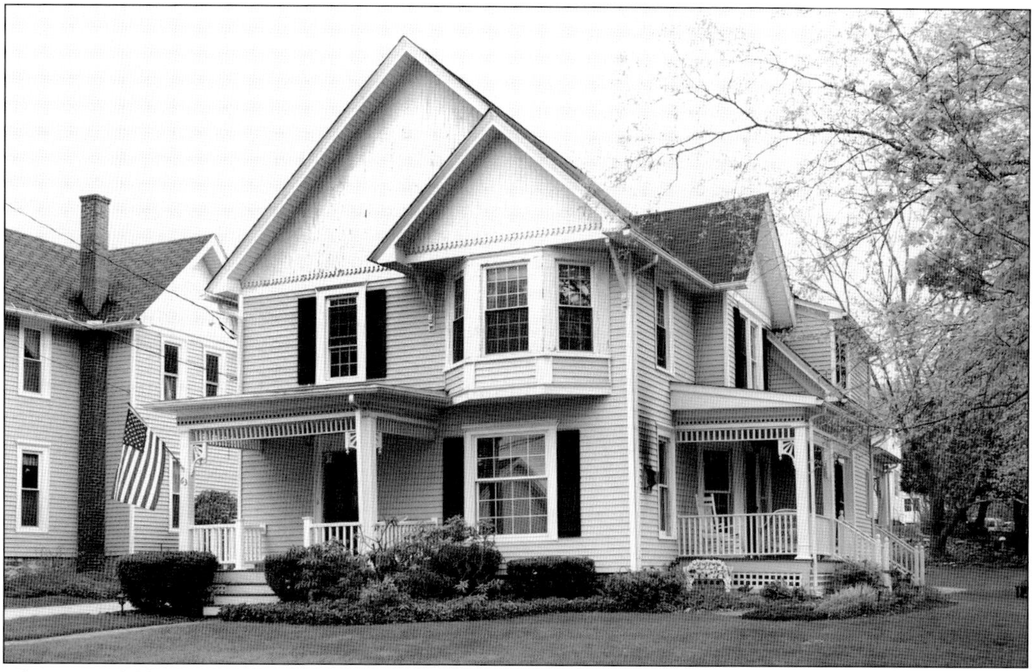

This graceful home at 63 Canada Street was built around the beginning of the 20th century. The stairs, bannister, and hemlock floors are original to the home. It is currently owned by the Fraunfelder family; earlier owners include Currier, Hoit, Hill, Cutler, Baker, Bucknam, Underwood, and Shull. The original land was deeded in 1829 to Wilhelm Willink of the Holland Land Company.

Three

Mills, Dams, and Agriculture

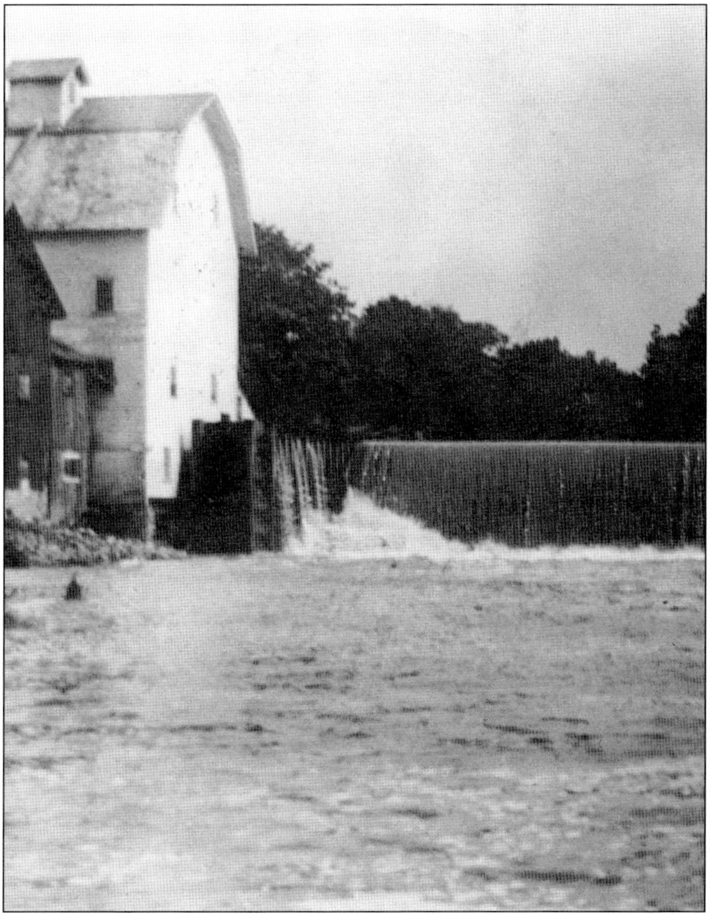

The gristmill and sawmill were built by Gen. William Warren and Ephraim Woodruff on Mill Street, which is now Capitol Heights. This was the beginning of the village of Holland, even though the locality did not then bear that name. In the autumn of 1813, Robert Orr bought the mill properties. He eventually sold the mills to his son Alvin, who operated them until his death in 1877. For the next few years, the mills were run by Orr family members, including Alvin's son Charles and daughters Jennie (Mrs. Gilbert Dodds) and Grace (Mrs. Frank Elsworth). In 1881, the mills were purchased by Jacob Wurst, and they were passed down to his son Paul J. Wurst, who rebuilt and enlarged both. This picture shows the Wurst Mill and Dam.

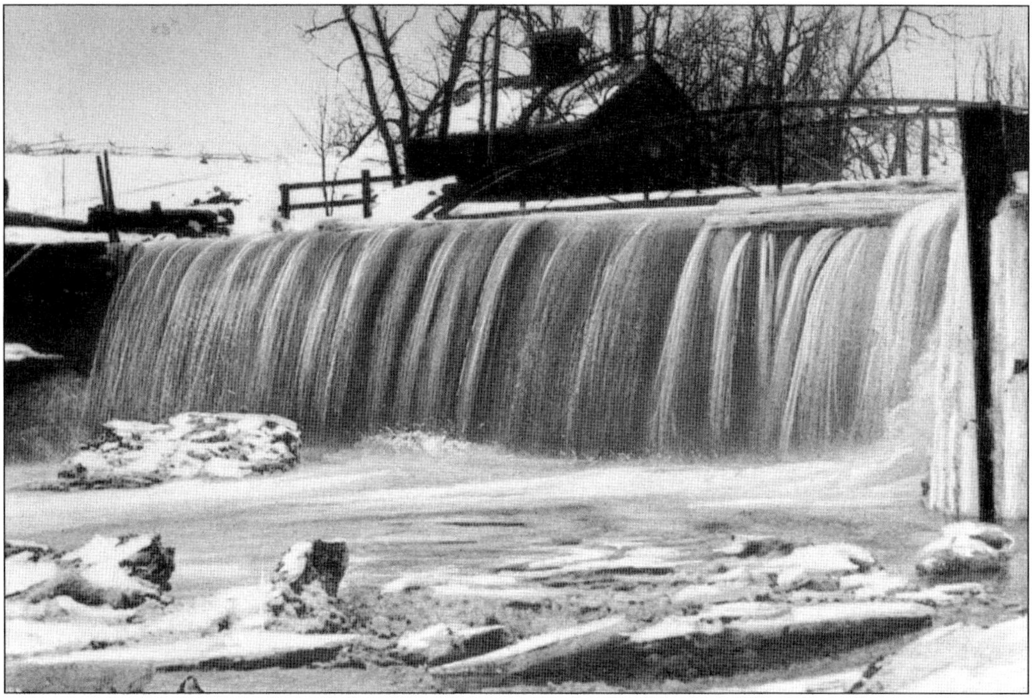

The Wurst Dam furnished power for the gristmill. A steel bridge stood in place of the concrete bridge of today. The prominent Wurst family also owned a sawmill, along with several other businesses in town. Jacob Wurst served Holland as town supervisor from 1888 to 1889. His son Paul J. Wurst built the Wurst Block on Main Street that housed a hardware store, general store, and agricultural implement store. The dam is pictured below with the water drawn off.

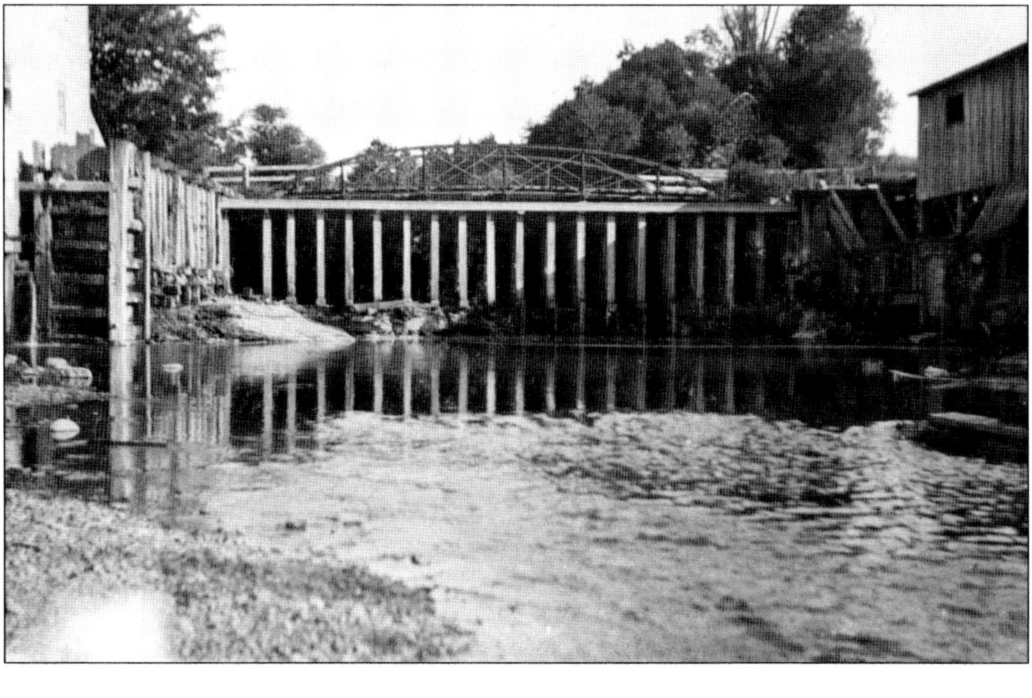

This photograph shows the Wurst Mill and its water run, which carried the swift current and drove the mill wheel. Painters can be seen on the high scaffold giving the building a new coat of paint. The mill was used until 1930.

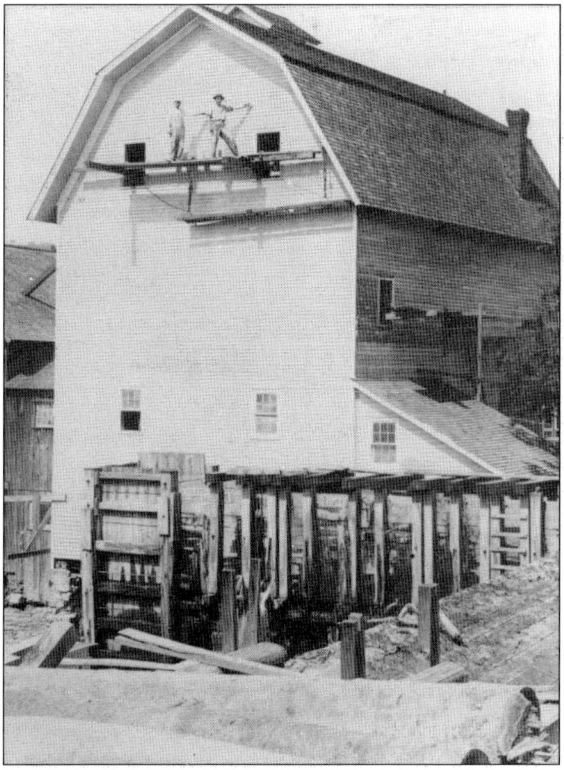

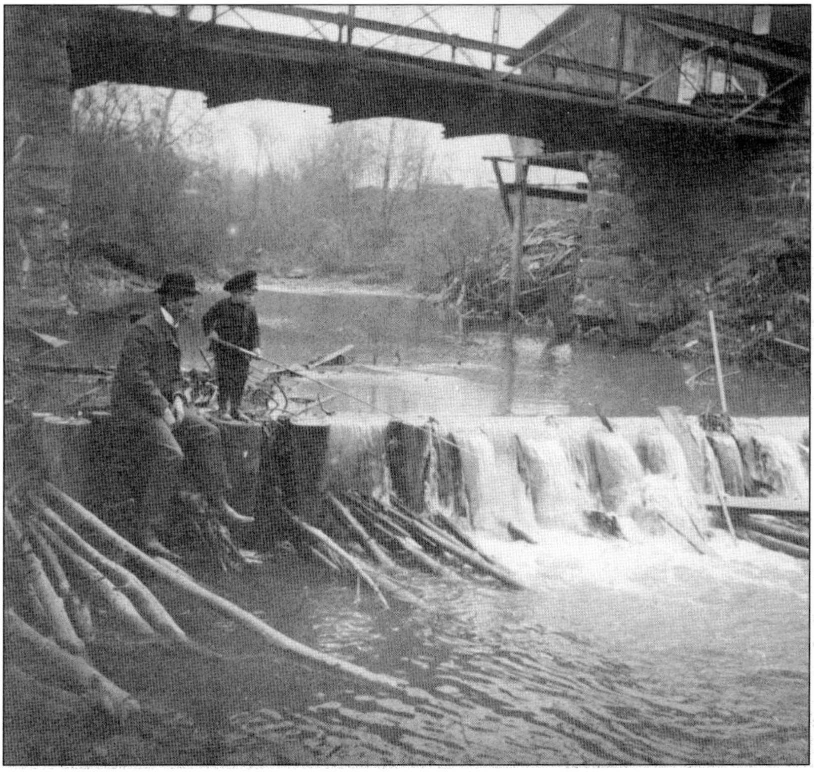

A father and son fish under the bridge near the Griggs Mill complex on Cazenovia Creek.

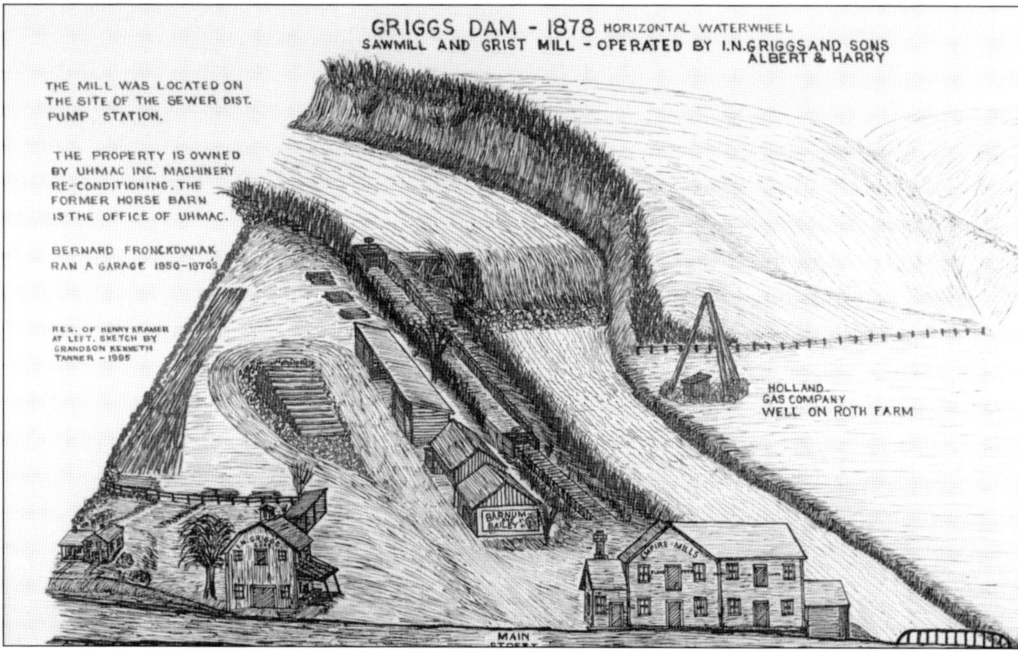

In 1878, Ichabod Griggs built a three-story flour and feed mill near the bridge on North Main Street that crosses the Cazenovia Creek (across from Garfield Street). The Griggs family were early settlers from Hamburg, New York. Today, the property is owned by Uhmac Industries. The former horse barn, which once served as Barney Fronckowiak's garage, has been converted to Uhmac's office. This sketch by Kenneth Tanner shows the Griggs Dam, sawmill, and gristmill complex as it looked in 1878.

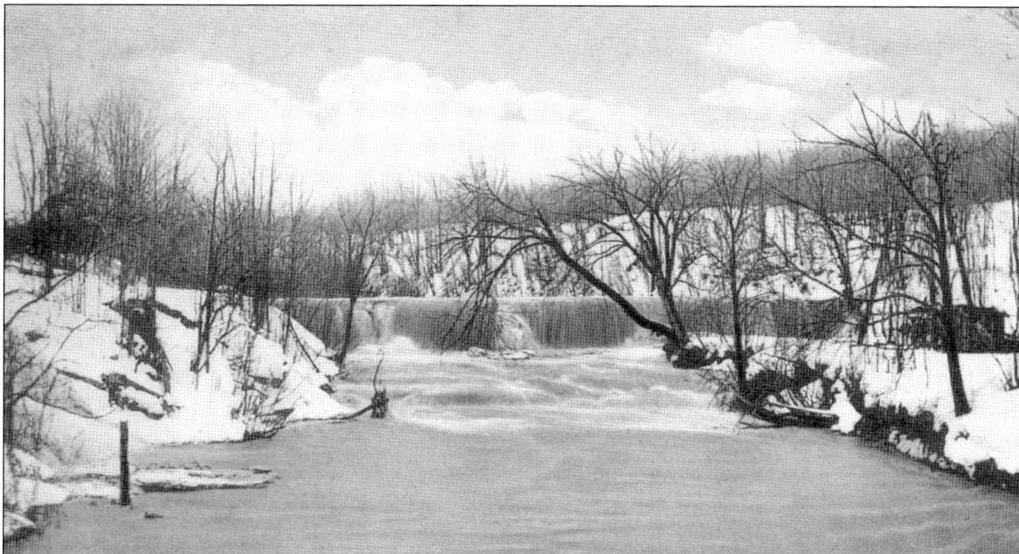

This is a winter scene of Griggs Dam and the Cazenovia Creek, which furnished power for the grist- and sawmills. The location is North Main Street across from Garfield Street. Remains of the dam can still be seen today.

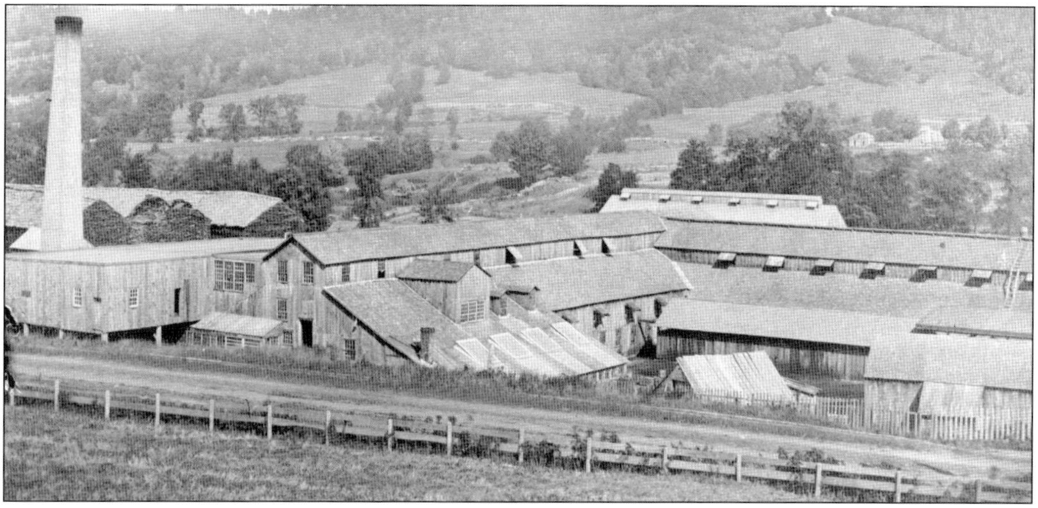

In 1850, a large tannery was built at the north end of the village by A. Rumsey and Company of Buffalo (Aaron Rumsey and sons Bronson and Dexter). The tannery had 600 vats and worked mostly on dry hides. Hemlock bark, used in the tanning process, was purchased from many in the surrounding countryside. It is said that at times there were loads of bark a mile long waiting to be delivered.

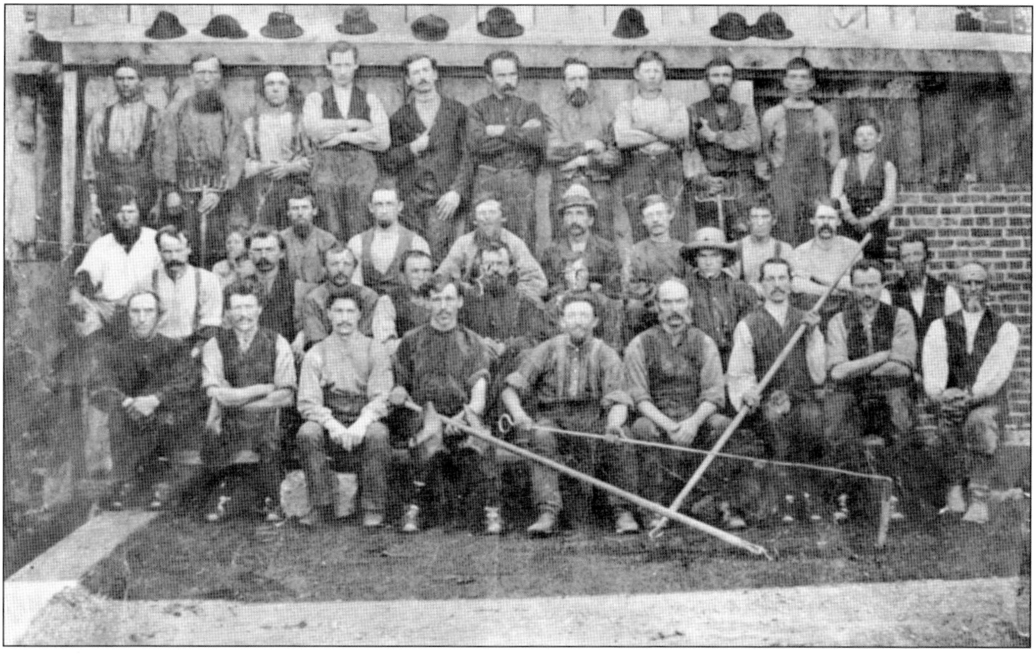

A large group of Rumsey Tannery employees is pictured with their tools of the trade. At its height, the tannery employed 60 men and could produce 60,000 to 70,000 sides of sole leather a year. In the late 1800s, it became one of the largest tanneries in New York State, covering about 10 acres of land.

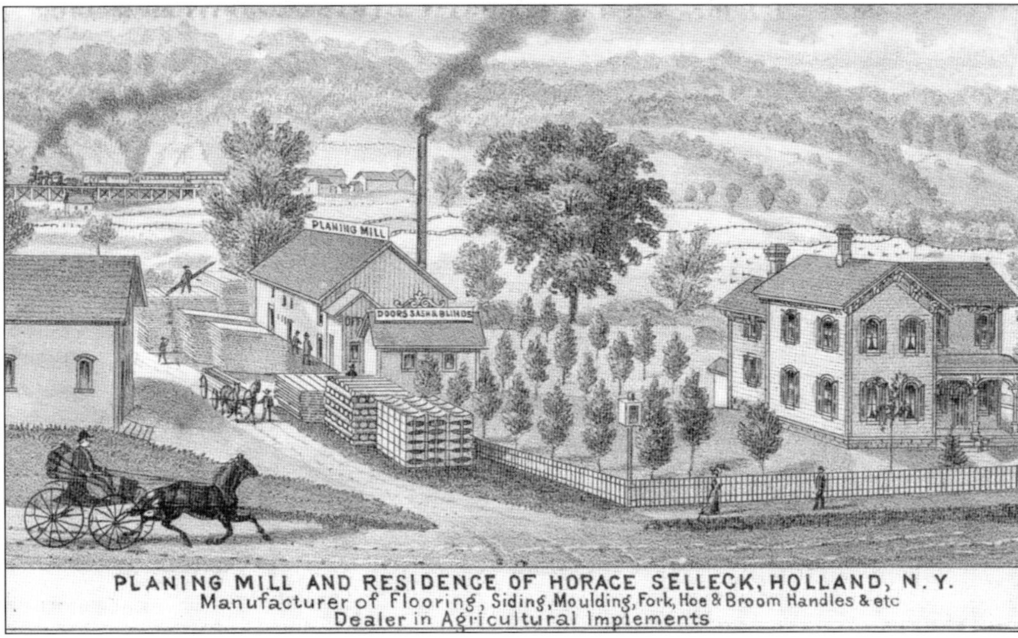

Horace Selleck built a planing mill in 1876 along with an establishment for the manufacture of farming implements. At least 10 workmen were employed by Selleck.

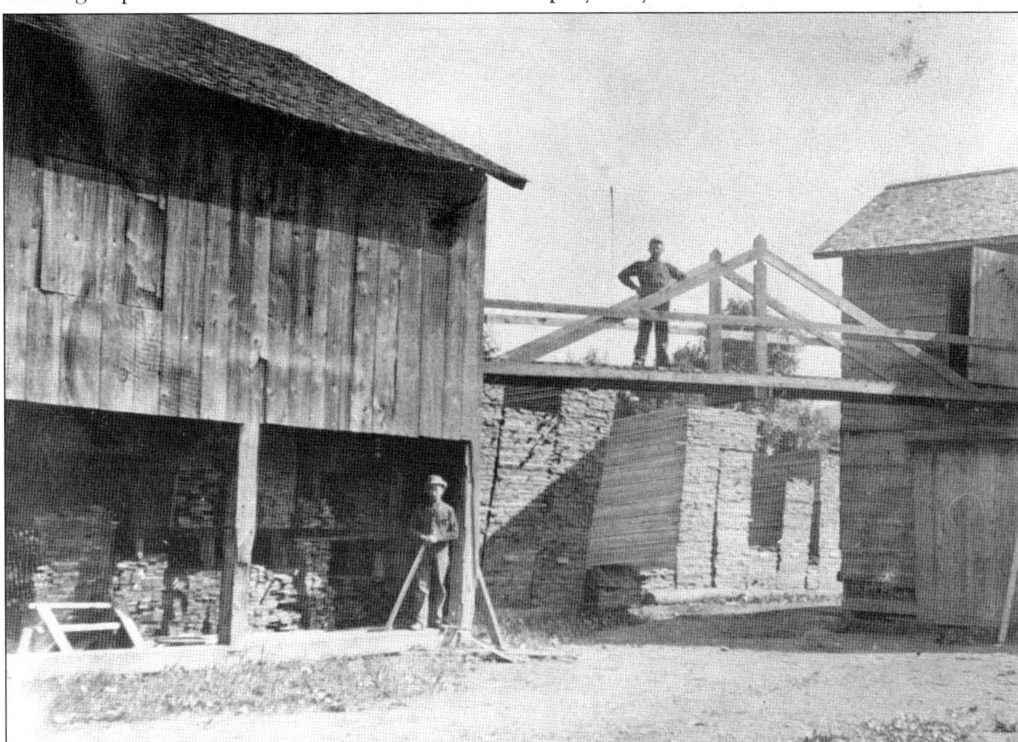

Two workmen are pictured with stacks of lumber at Horace Selleck's planing mill in the early 1900s. The mill was at the north end of Main Street and Rumsey Road, near the tannery.

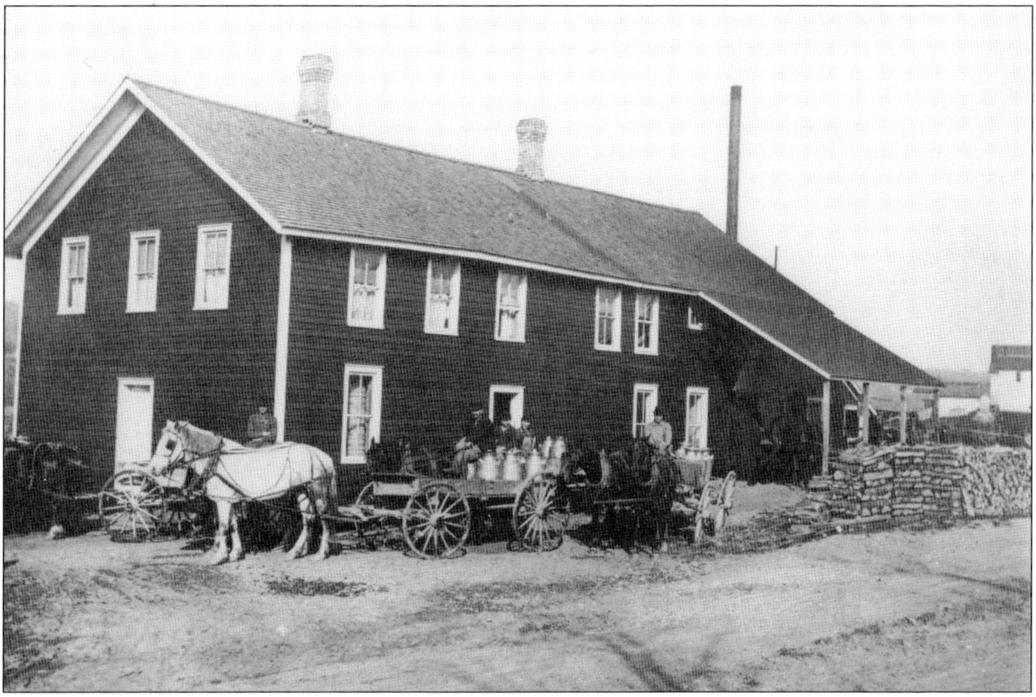

In this agricultural community, farmers needed a place to take their milk so it could be turned into cheese and butter. At this creamery on South Main Street near today's Lar's Garage, the cream was separated from the raw milk, and the whey was given back to the farmer, who was paid on the butter fat content and weight of the milk.

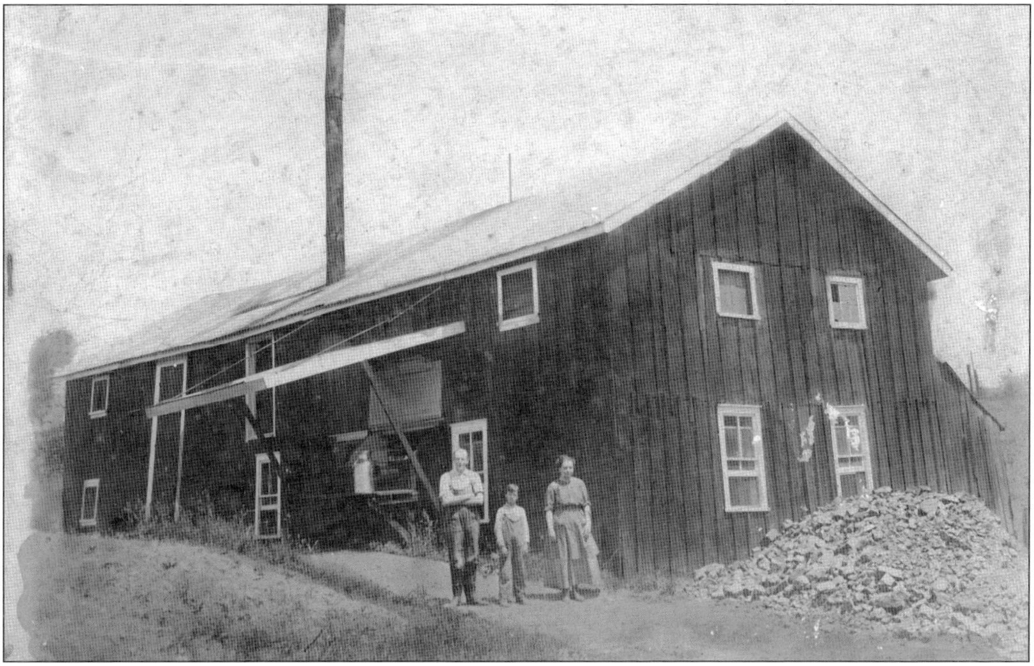

The Richardson-Beebee Company at one time operated 20 creameries in the Holland area. Walter and Edna Morey and their son Arthur Morey are pictured at a local cheese factory.

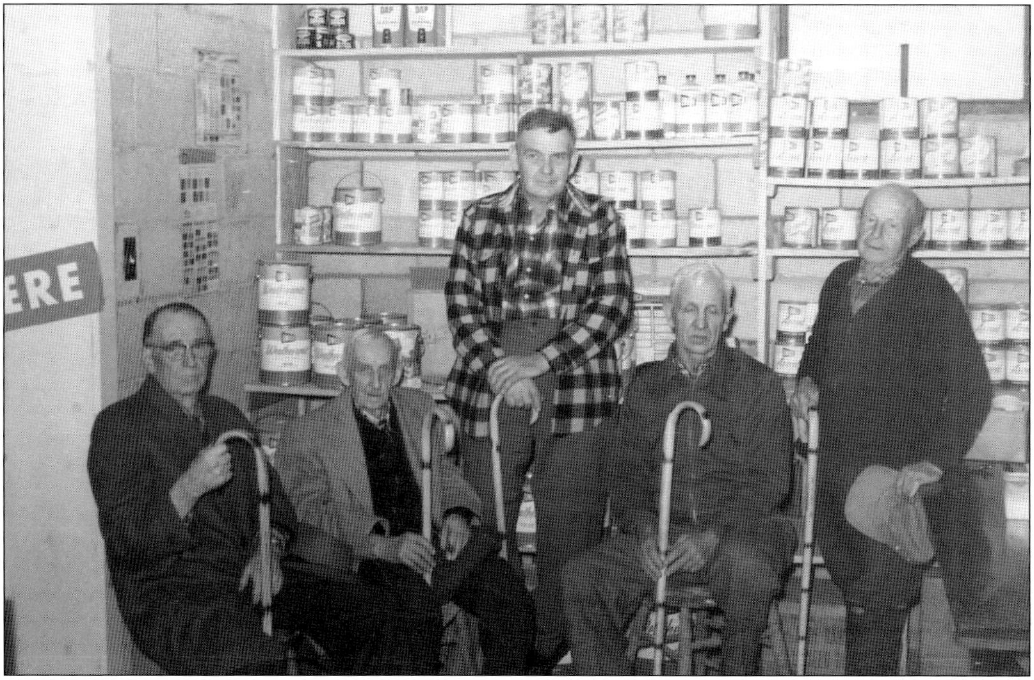

This picture of older men with their canes was taken in the spring of 1960 at the Grange League Federation (GLF) store in Holland. From left to right are Ralph Cooper, Burt Curtis, Robert Frew, Alexander Montgomery, and Floyd Taylor.

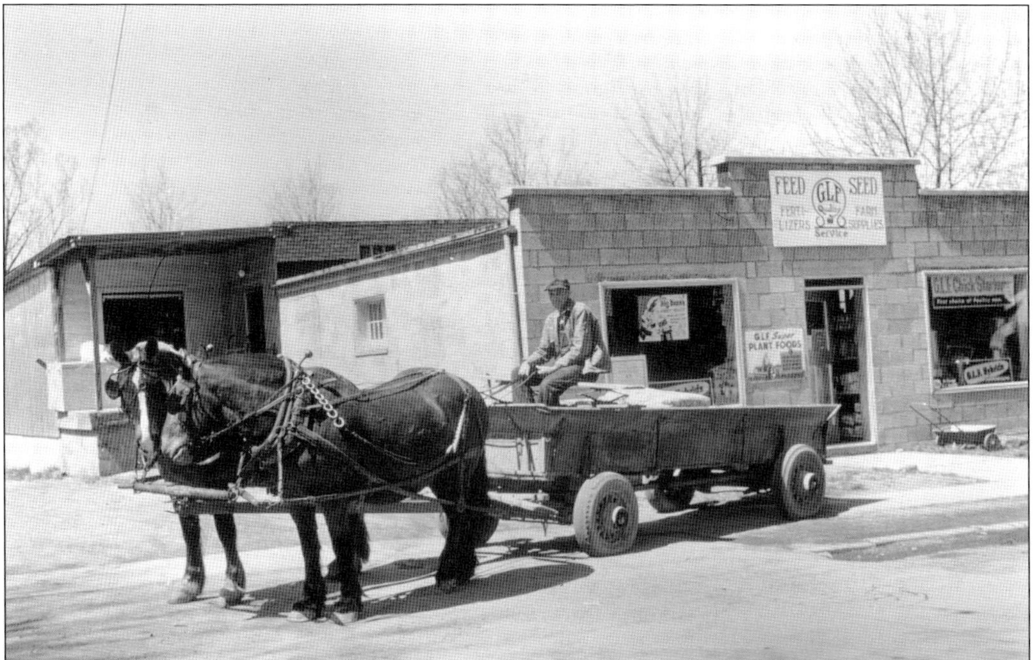

Millard Roth is shown with his team, Kit and Daisy, in front of Clarence Bush's GLF feed store on Pearl Street. They were one of the last teams of work horses in the area. The GLF building is now an apartment house.

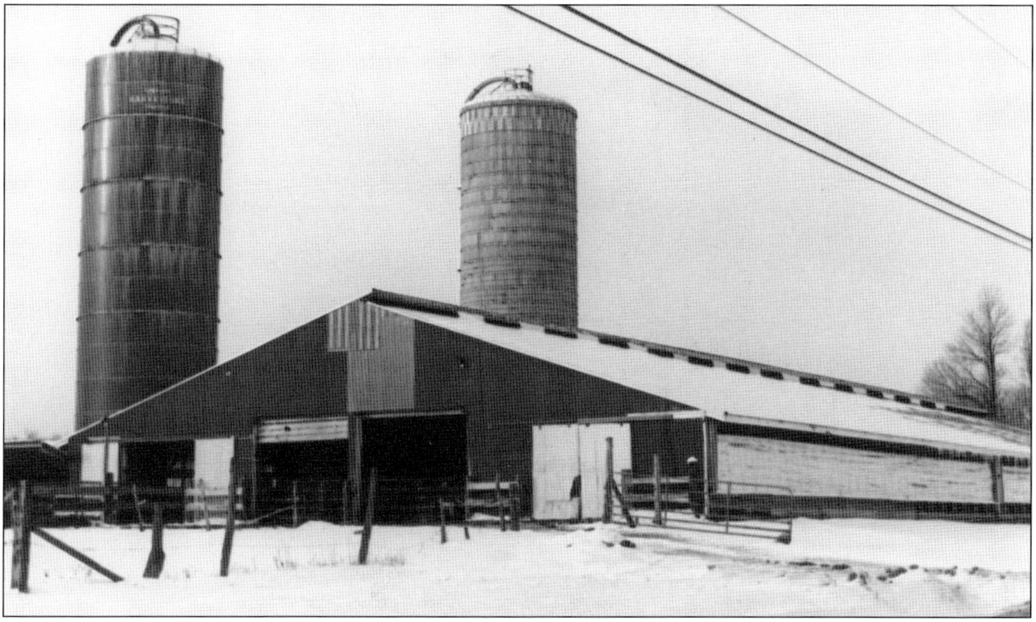

This dairy farm has been in the Kramer family since 1848, when John F. Kramer came from Switzerland and settled on Holland Glenwood Road. Always a working farm, it has been passed down through generations that included Cort, Hugh, and Robert Kramer. John F. Kramer's great-grandson John M. Kramer oversees farm operations today, which include milking nearly 550 of the 900 head of cattle, making it the largest dairy farm in Holland.

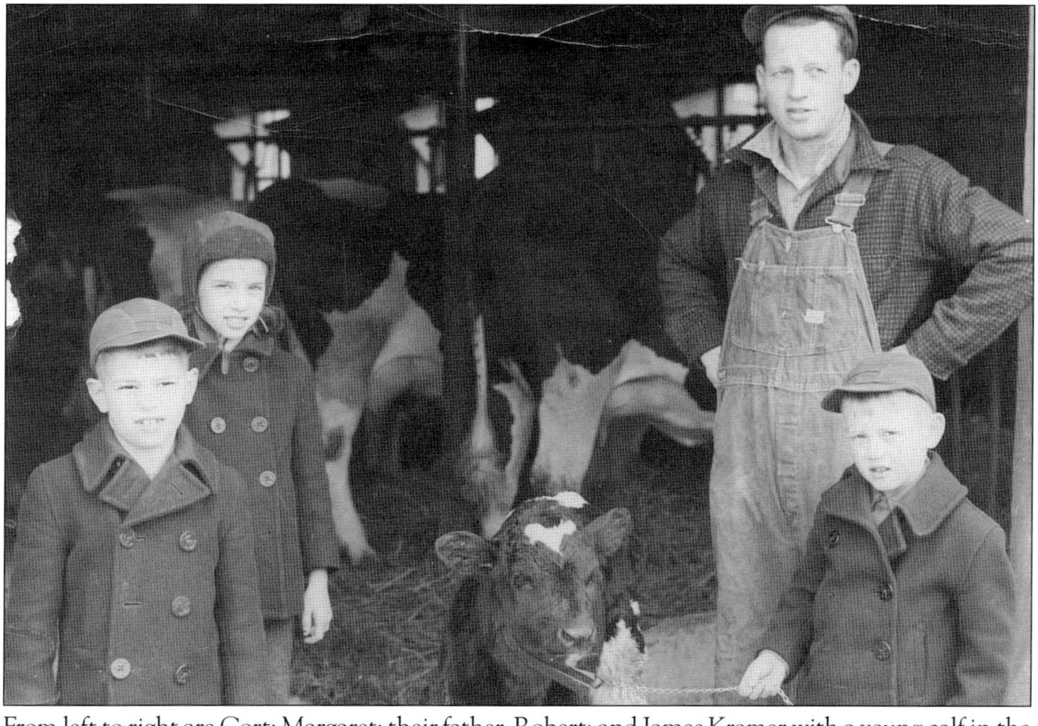

From left to right are Cort; Margaret; their father, Robert; and James Kramer with a young calf in the Kramer barn. The photograph dates from the early 1950s. (Courtesy of Margaret Kramer Baker.)

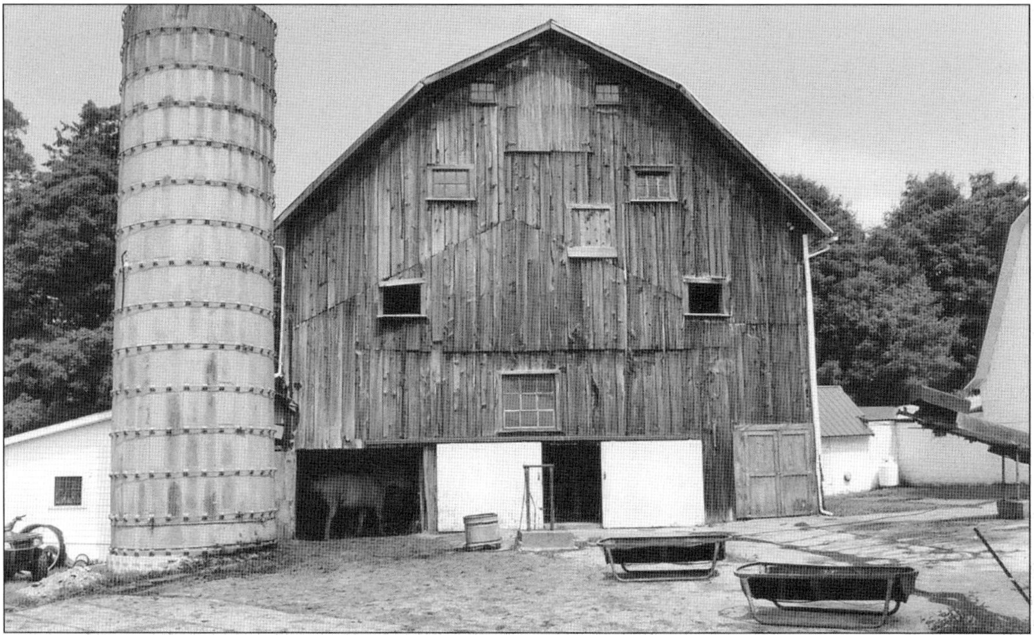

In 1939, William Bennett purchased 65 acres from Howard Bucknam for a farm with property on both sides of Olean Road. This working farm, now operated by William's son Norbert, has been in the Bennett family ever since. Pictured is one of the large barns on the property that was dismantled in 2005. (Courtesy of Norbert Bennett.)

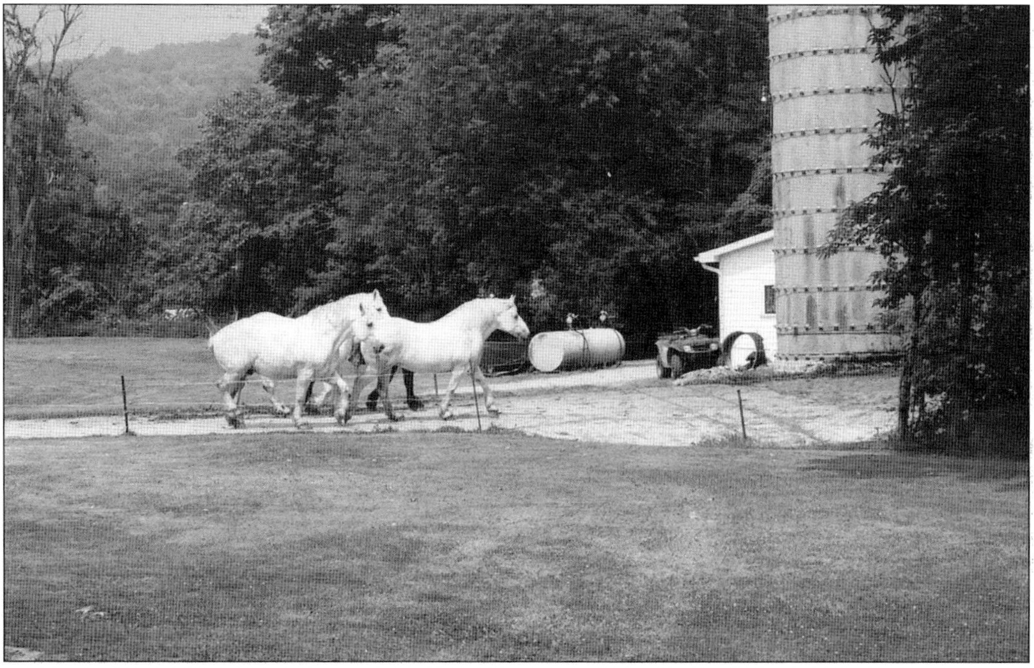

Horses have always been a part of Bennett's Pine Lawn Farms. These Percherons are used for work and pleasure driving. (Courtesy of Norbert Bennett.)

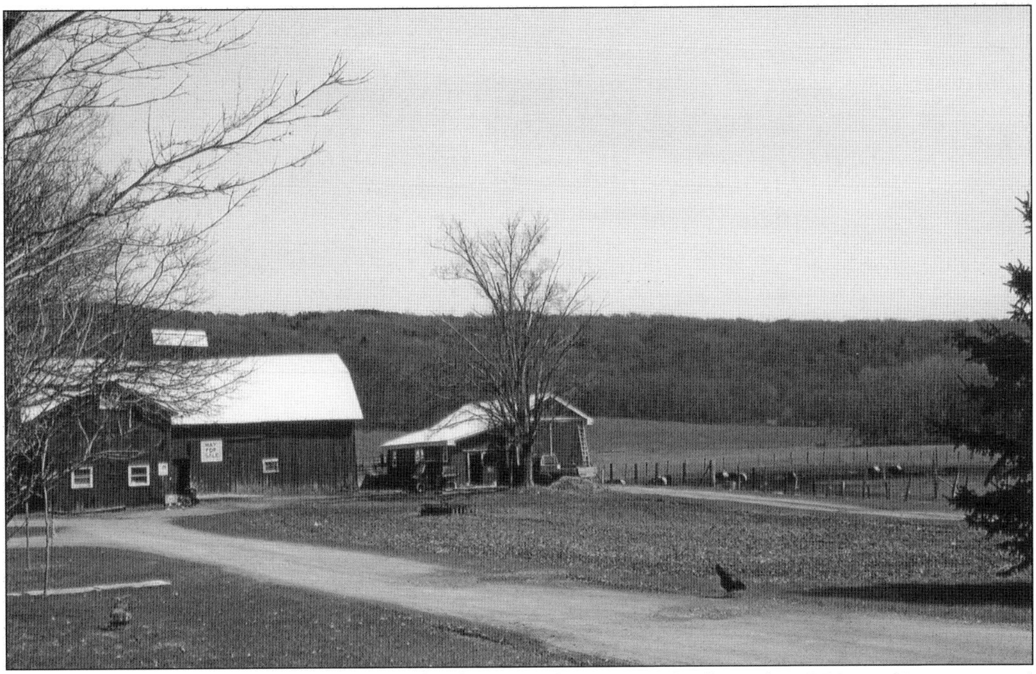

The barn on the Currier property, now Rickettson Farms, was built in the 1850s and is supported with hand-hewn beams made from lumber taken off the property. A well inside the original barn was built with stone laid by hand. The barn has been remodeled nearly every 20 years to keep current with its intended use.

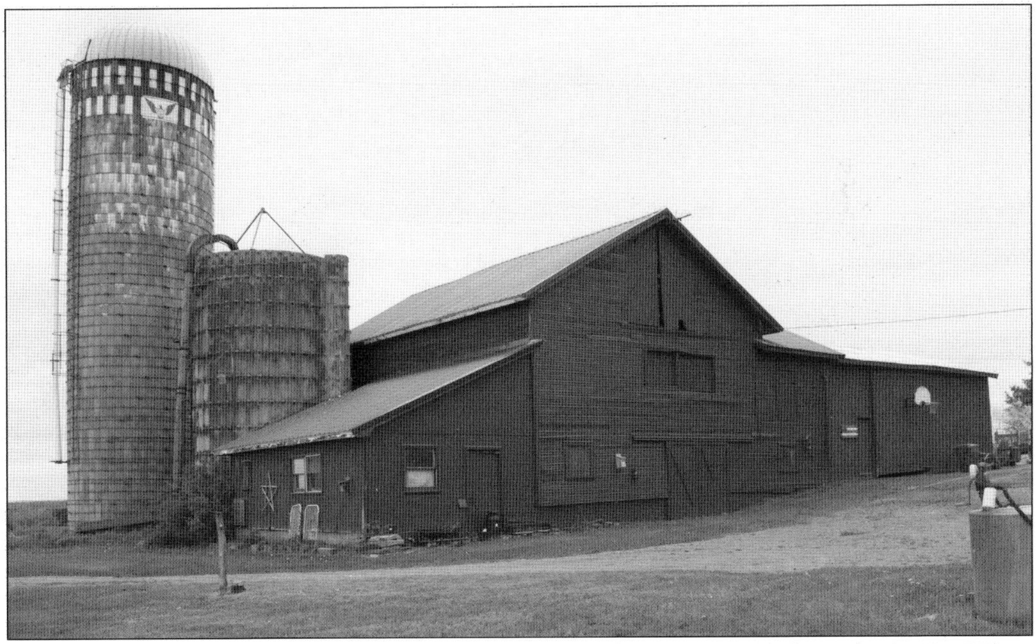

This farm on Whitney Road was deeded in 1830, and the barn was built in the 1880s. When owned by the Lingenfelter family, it was a dairy farm. The homestead has 130 acres and includes an orchard. Current owners Kenneth and Mary Major purchased the property in 1977 and raised beef and dairy cows until the late 1980s.

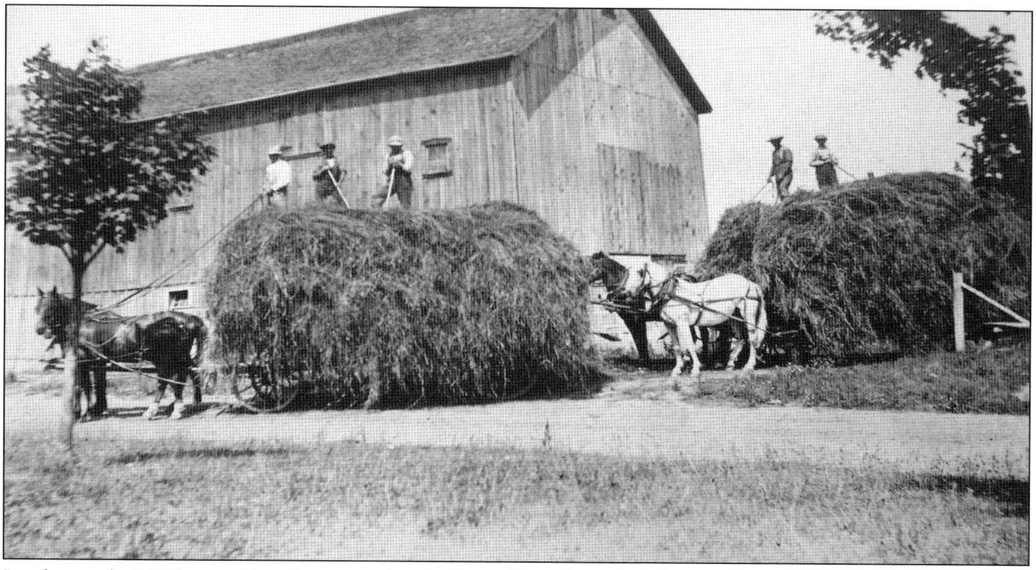

In the early 1900s, making hay involved a lot of hard work. This picture was taken around 1911 at the Colby-Fischer homestead on Vermont Hill Road. On top of the hay wagons are, from left to right, (first wagon) Chapin Colby, George Holloman, and Charles Camp; (second wagon) Hume Colby and Harold Lang. (Courtesy of Norma Fischer.)

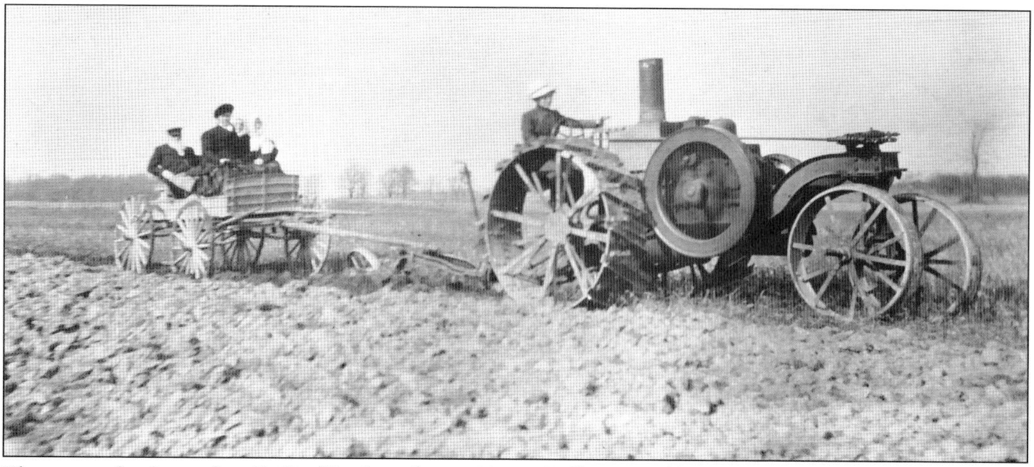

Photographed on the Colby-Fischer farm, Zina Colby Gould drives the tractor, most likely preparing for planting season. Lawrence Hawks and Katie are in the wagon that is hitched to the plow. (Courtesy of Norma Fischer.)

Four

Hotels and Transportation

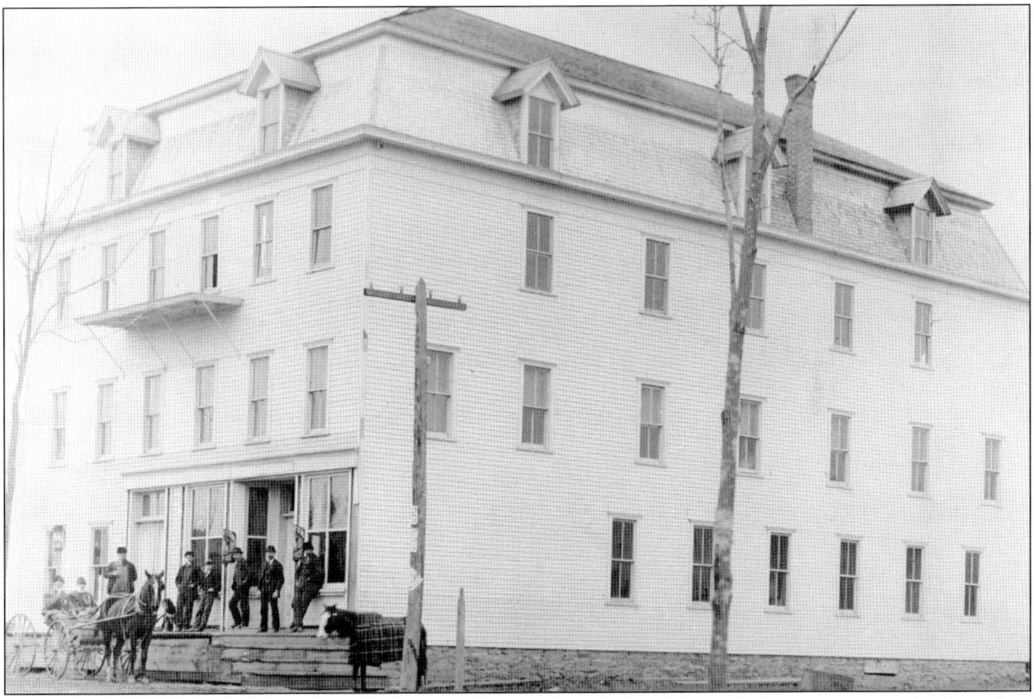

Joshua Barron opened the first tavern and hotel in Holland in 1815 and 1816, respectively. Another hotel was built in 1829; it was sold to Anson Norton, William Crook, Vinal Morey, and Abner Orr. The Holland House was built by Jonathan Paul, who was succeeded by his son David Paul and David's wife, Mary Ryder Paul, along with their partner, Seward H. Sears. The final owner was a Mr. Lenox, and the name changed to the Lenox Hotel. The three-story Lenox Hotel, one of the most important gathering spots in Holland, stood at the site now occupied by Upstate Automotive Group, 188 North Main Street. The third floor of this hotel was a ballroom. The building went unoccupied for a time and was destroyed by fire on February 2, 1915. Due to its size and color, it was nicknamed "the White Elephant."

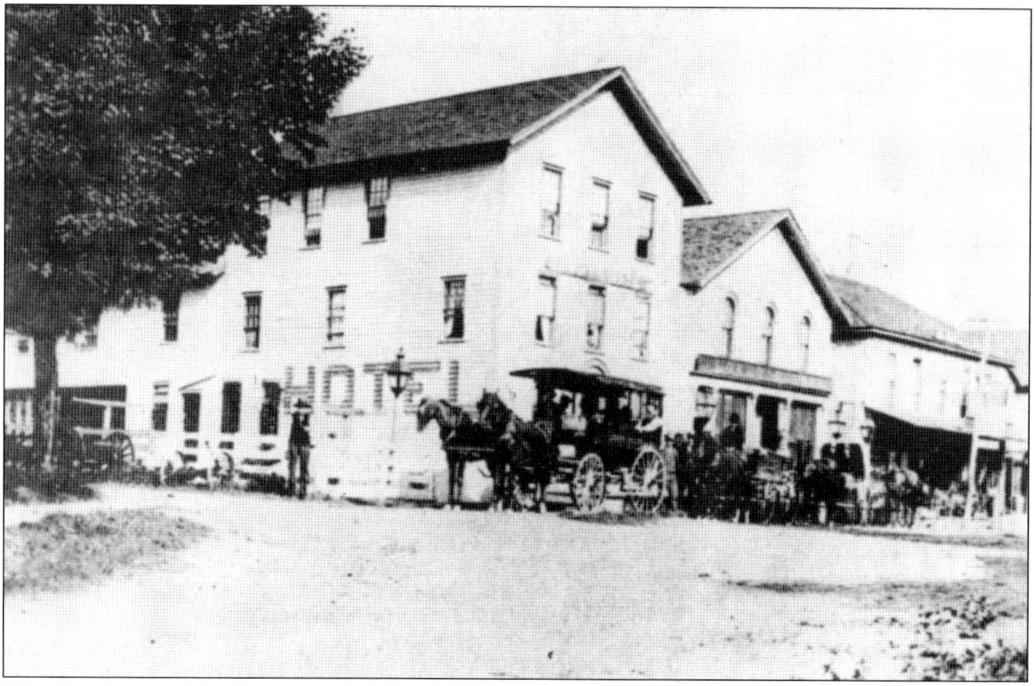

The first Lowry Hotel was on the east side of North Main Street, near the curve and bridge (across the street from Upstate Automotive Group), and was owned by Charles C. Lowry. This photograph dates from the late 1800s. This hotel and tavern were later destroyed by fire.

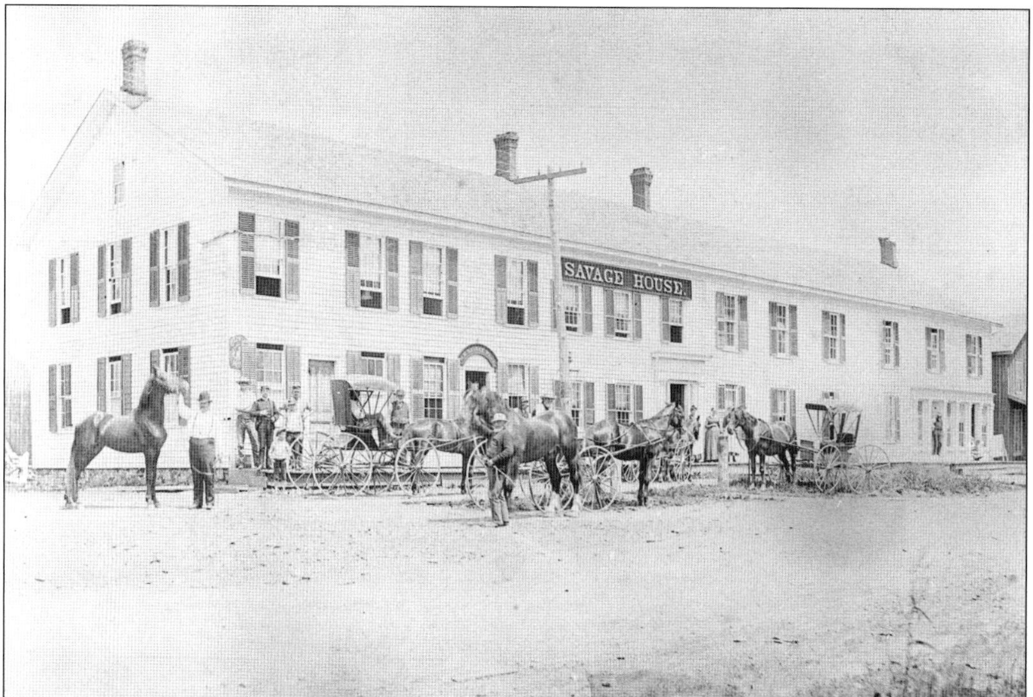

The Savage House was the first hotel built on the present site of the Holland Hotel. At the corner of Main and Pearl Streets, it was built in 1850 and was purchased by Charles C. Lowry in 1874.

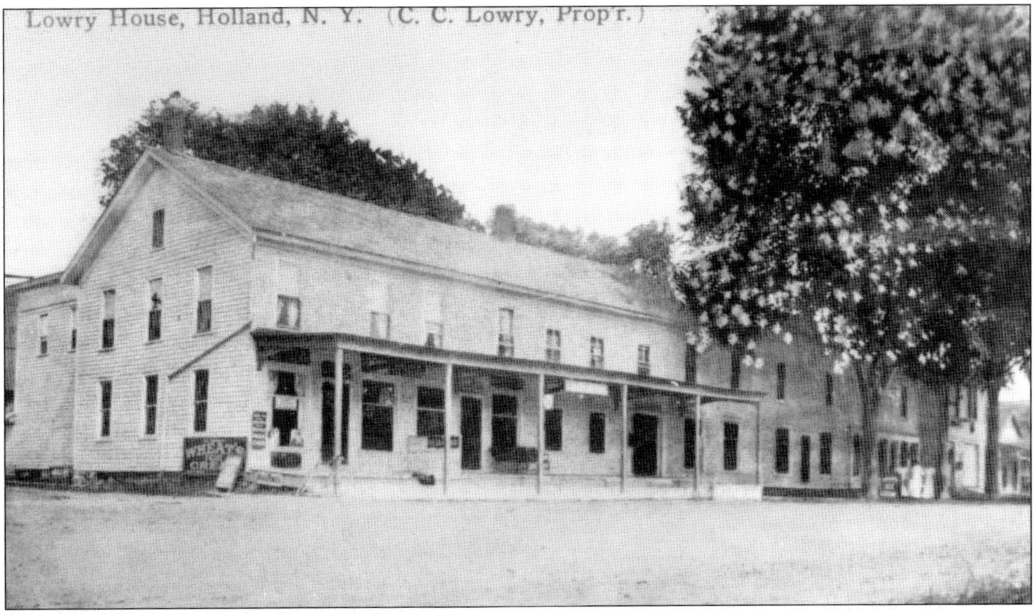

When Charles C. Lowry purchased the Savage House in 1874, he renamed it the Lowry House, and so it became known as the second Lowry House. Above is an early photograph of the Lowry House, and the picture below shows it remodeled. It burned in 1890, but new owner Frank Putnam rebuilt and reopened the hotel in 1914.

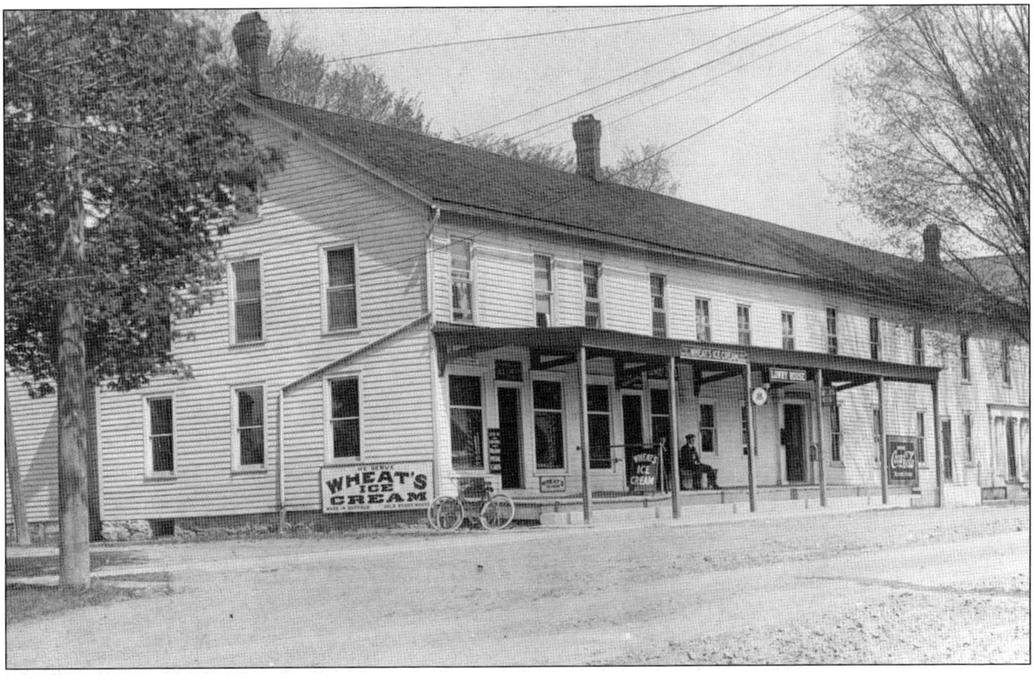

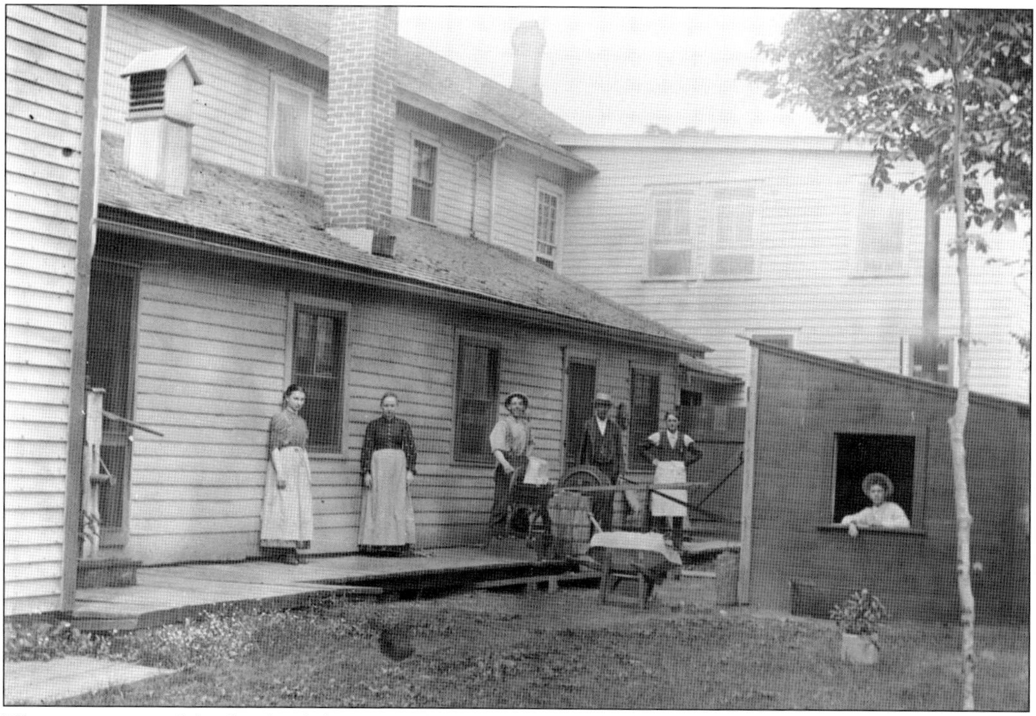

This is a view of the back of the second Lowry House, at the corner of Main and Pearl Streets. It appears to be wash day, as the hotel help is hand-cranking whites, while other items lie in the wheelbarrow. On the left end of the back porch is a hand pump for drawing water from the well. This picture is from the late 1880s.

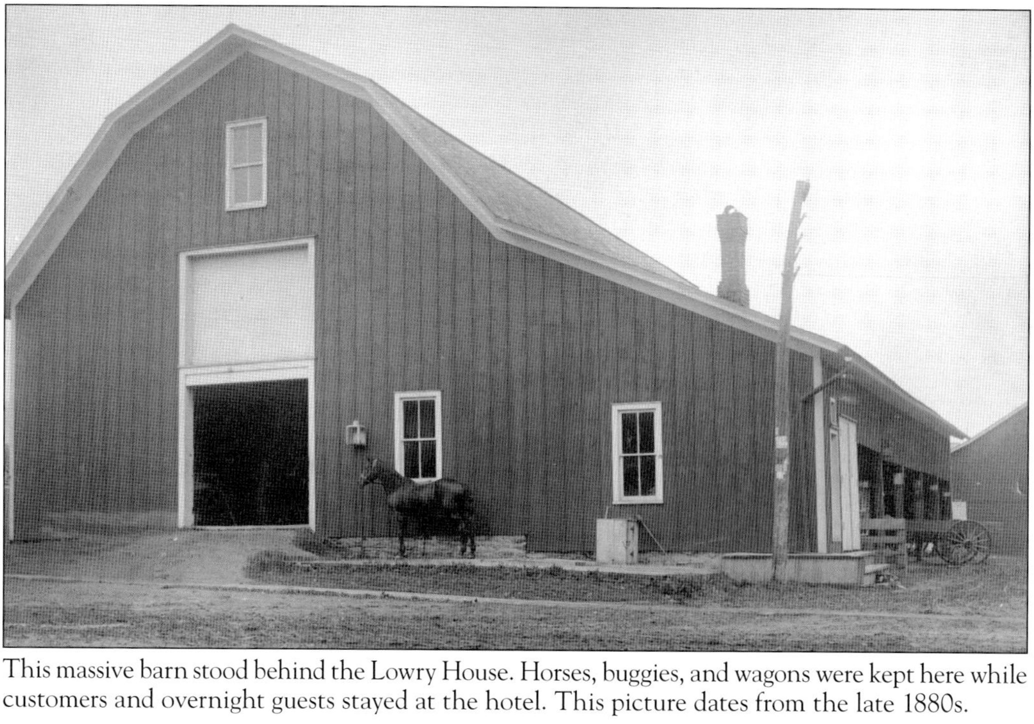

This massive barn stood behind the Lowry House. Horses, buggies, and wagons were kept here while customers and overnight guests stayed at the hotel. This picture dates from the late 1880s.

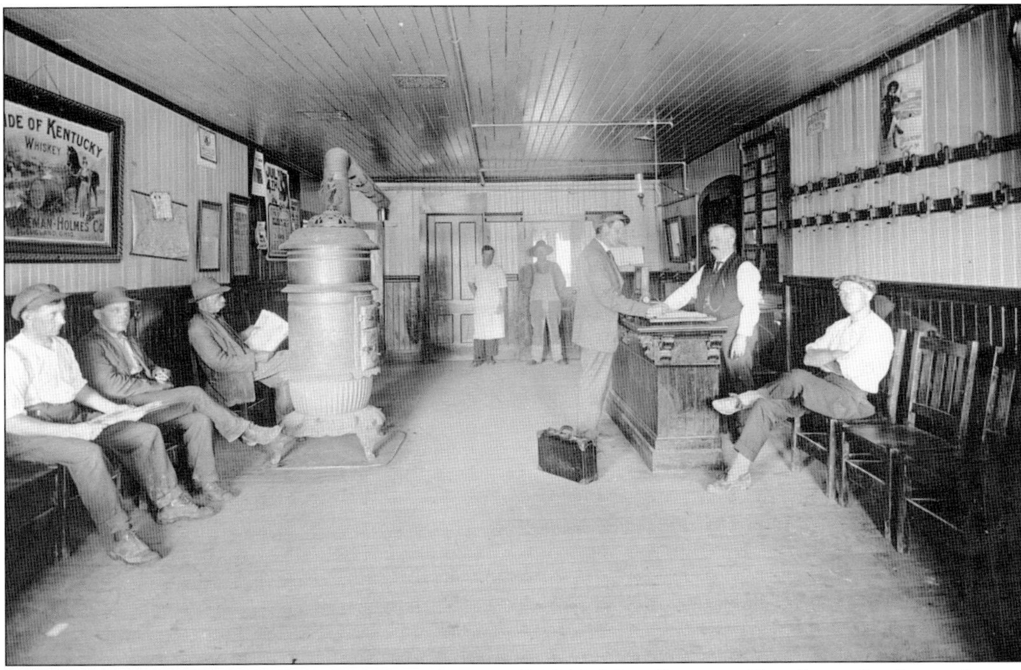

This is the interior of the Putnam Hotel around 1915. The Putnam Hotel was built on the site of the second Lowry House, which burned in 1890. Owner Frank Putnam is shown registering a guest while others wait in the lobby.

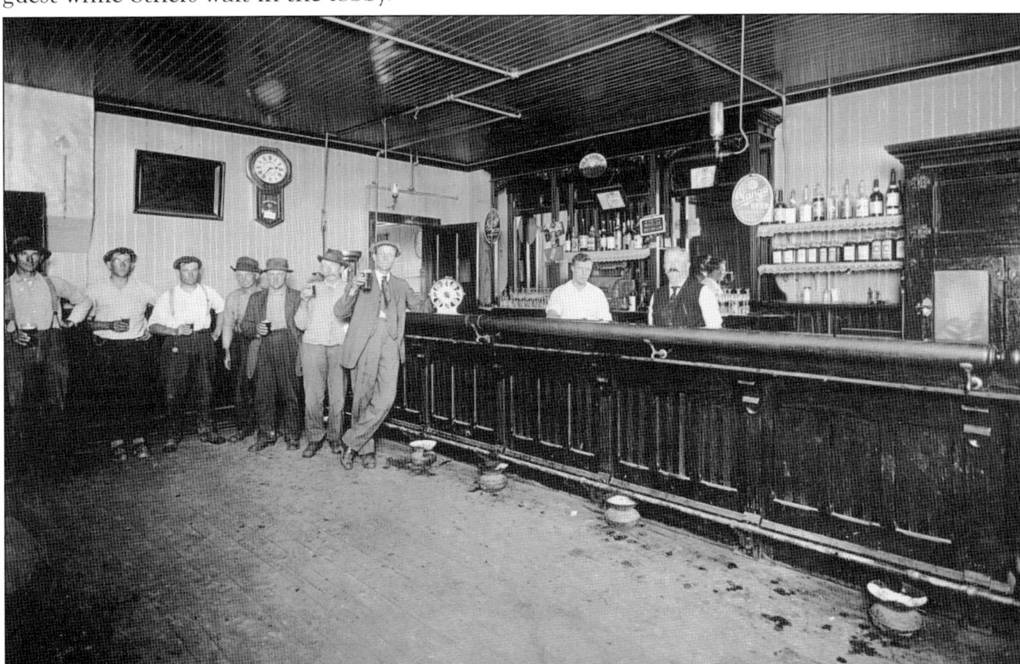

Frank Putnam and a bartender are pictured behind the bar at the Putnam Hotel while other men line up for the picture and raise a glass. Notice the spittoons and tobacco stains at the base of the extended bar. Many stopped here for a beer and to catch up on news and happenings.

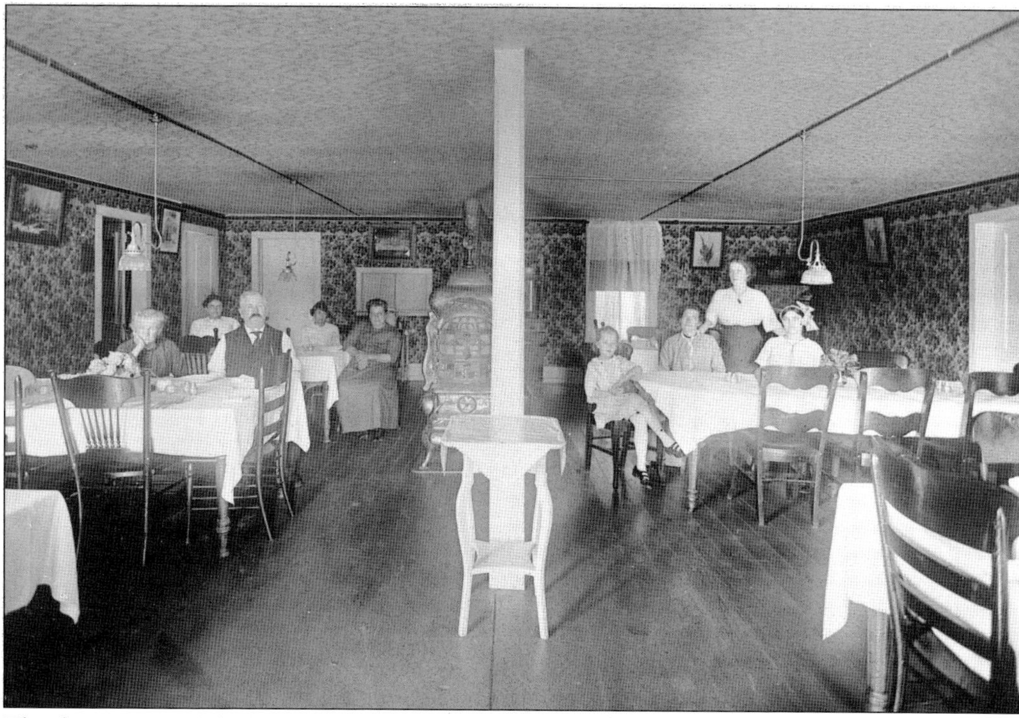

The dining area of the Putnam Hotel is seen here. Seated at the table on the left is owner Frank Putnam. The little girl seated on the chair at right is Putnam's daughter Gladys Putnam Miller. Seated next to Gladys is her mother, Mary Putnam. The photograph dates from 1915.

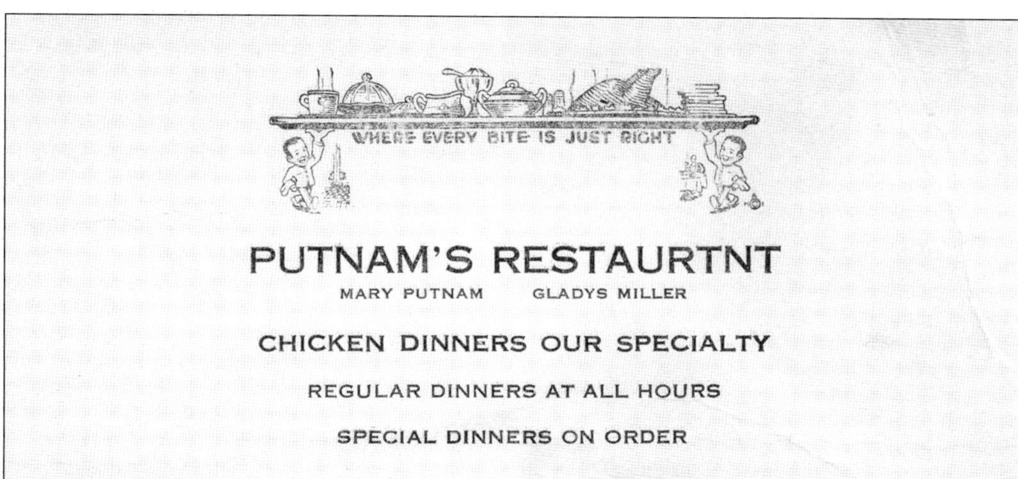

This is an advertising card for the restaurant in the Putnam Hotel before it burned in 1925. (Courtesy of James Miller, grandson of Frank and Mary Putnam.)

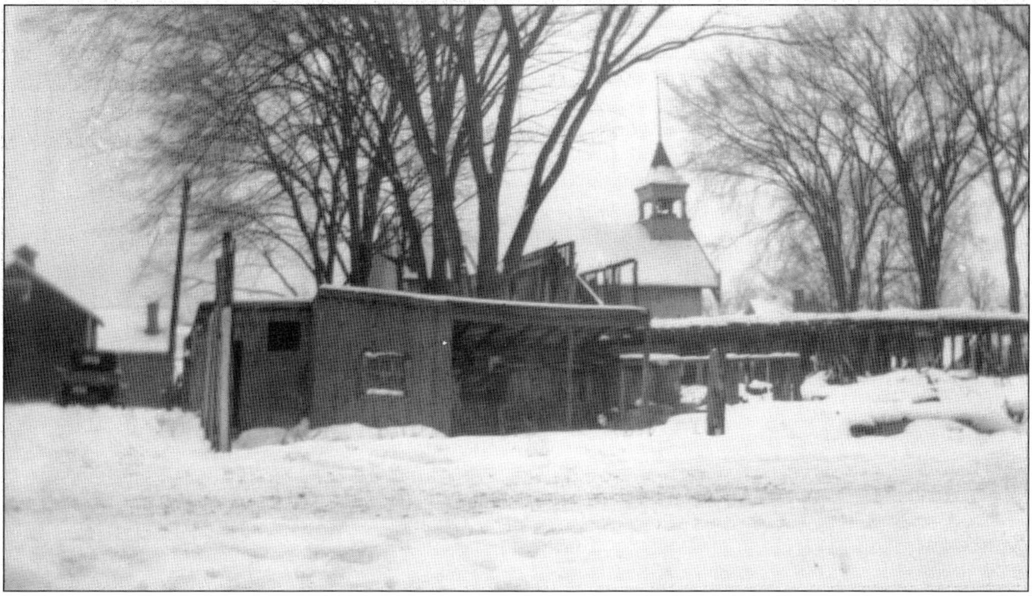

This is the aftermath of the Putnam Hotel fire in January 1925. The steeple on the Holland Fire Department's building can be seen in the background at far right above. Below is Mary Putnam, wife of owner Frank Putnam, at the site of the fire. The present Holland Hotel was later built here.

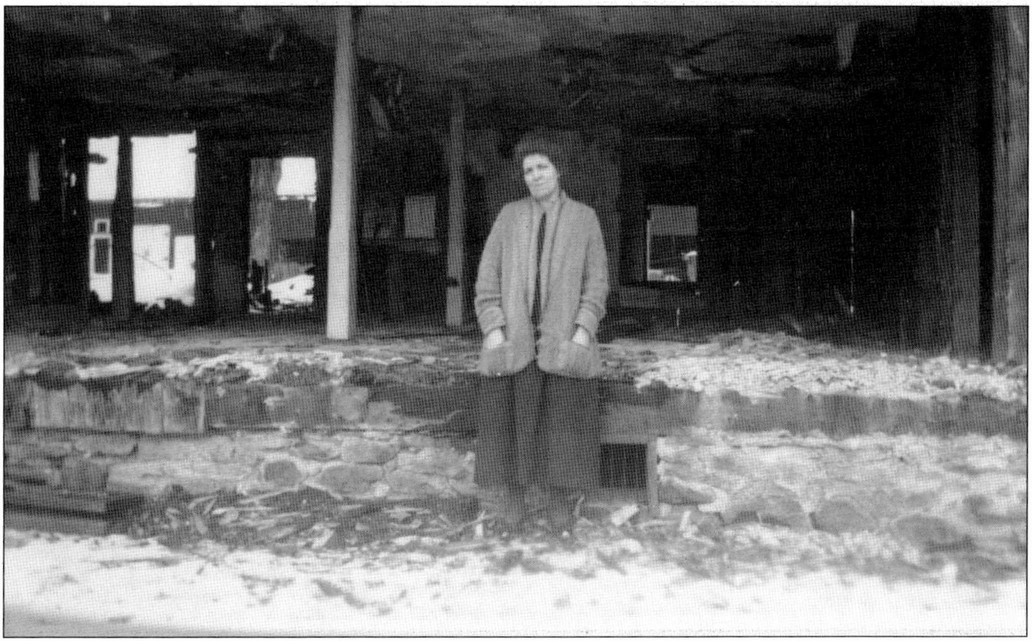

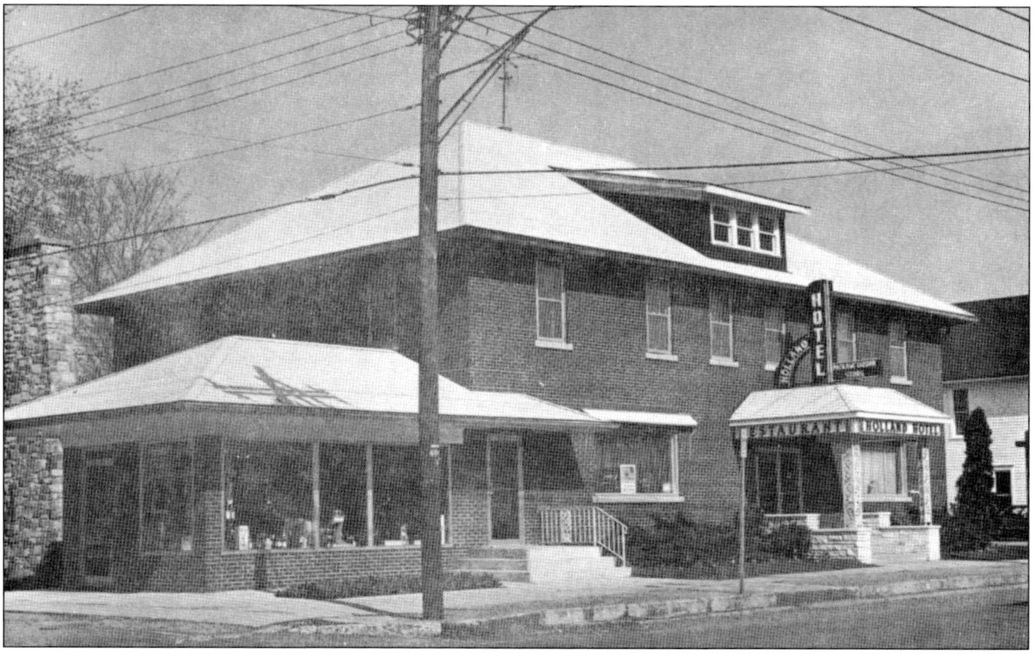

The Holland Hotel that currently stands at the corner of Main and Pearl Streets was built with brick by Anthony Chmielewski in 1934. In 1956, he sold it to John Hileman, who ran it as a family business. Richard and Mina Potts purchased the hotel in 1984 and successfully managed it until their retirement.

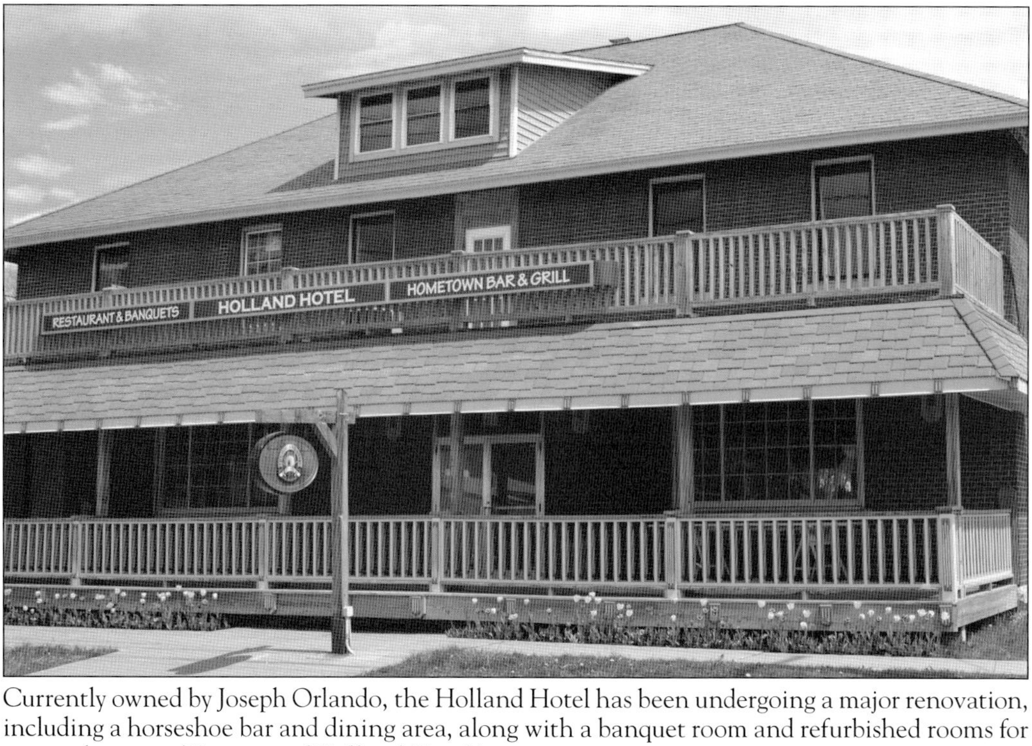

Currently owned by Joseph Orlando, the Holland Hotel has been undergoing a major renovation, including a horseshoe bar and dining area, along with a banquet room and refurbished rooms for overnight stays. (Courtesy of Holland Hotel.)

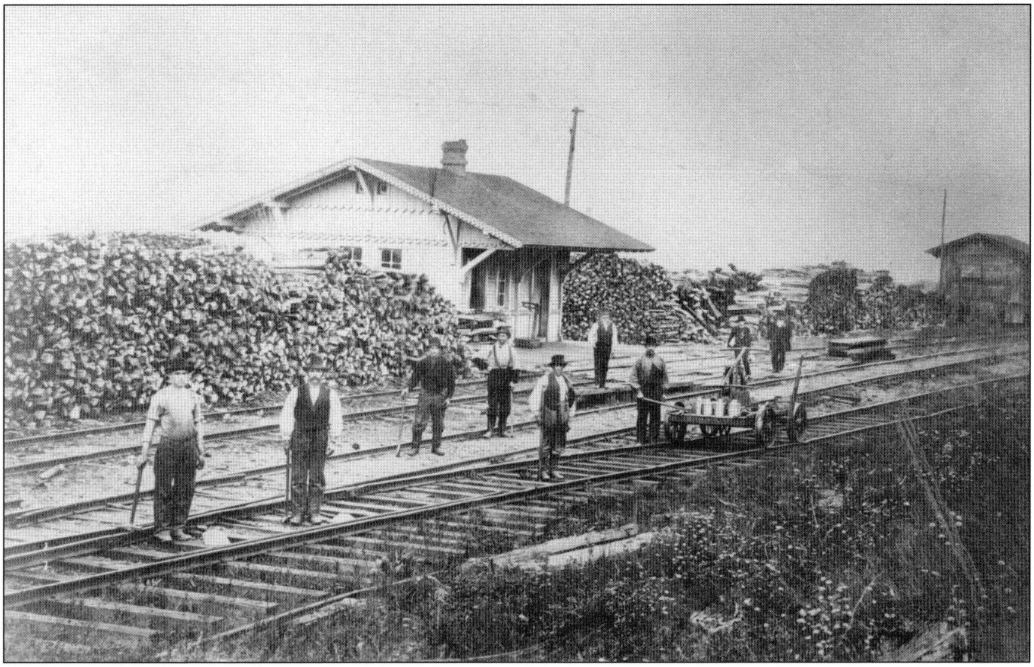

Shown here in the late 1890s is Holland's first depot, which was at the end of Rumsey Road. Piles of charcoal wood are ready for loading onto freight cars. Farmers in the area sent produce to Buffalo, and in turn, they were supplied with feed, lumber, and farm equipment. The track crew is also pictured.

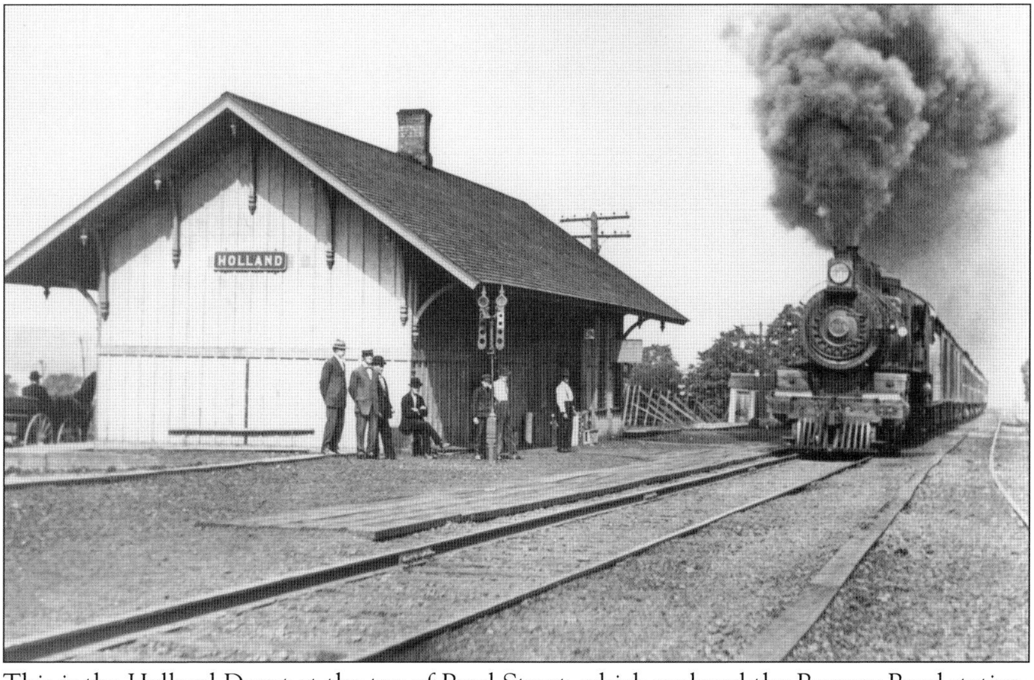

This is the Holland Depot at the top of Pearl Street, which replaced the Rumsey Road station. Now a Pennsylvania Railroad station, the new depot was in use for passenger travel. Local residents traveled to and from Buffalo for business or to attend schools. This photograph is dated 1905.

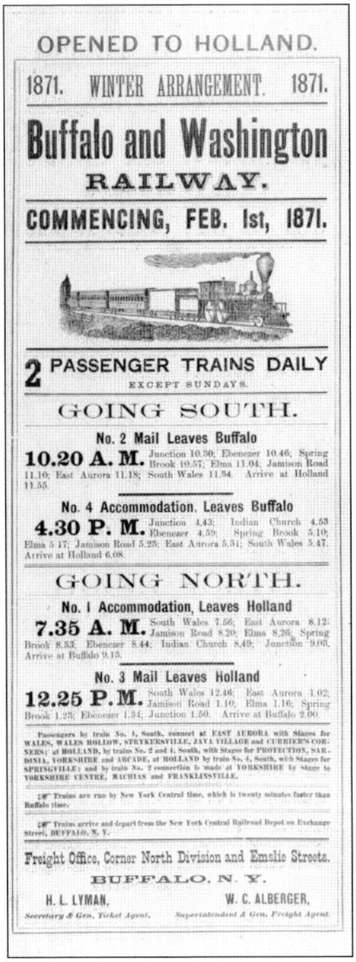

OPENED TO HOLLAND.

1871. WINTER ARRANGEMENT. 1871.

Buffalo and Washington

RAILWAY.

COMMENCING, FEB. 1st, 1871.

2 PASSENGER TRAINS DAILY

EXCEPT SUNDAYS.

GOING SOUTH.

No. 2 Mail Leaves Buffalo

10.20 A. M. Junction 10.30; Ebenezer 10.46; Spring Brook 10.57; Elma 11.04; Jamison Road 11.10; East Aurora 11.18; South Wales 11.34. Arrive at Holland 11.55.

No. 4 Accommodation, Leaves Buffalo

4.30 P. M. Junction 4.43; Indian Church 4.53 Ebenezer 4.59; Spring Brook 5.10; Elma 5 17; Jamison Road 5.23; East Aurora 5.34; South Wales 5.47. Arrive at Holland 6.08.

GOING NORTH.

No. 1 Accommodation, Leaves Holland

7.35 A. M. South Wales 7.56; East Aurora 8.12; Jamison Road 8.20; Elma 8.26; Spring Brook 8.33; Ebenezer 8.44; Indian Church 8.49; Junction 9.08. Arrive at Buffalo 9.13.

No. 3 Mail Leaves Holland

12.25 P. M. South Wales 12.46; East Aurora 1.02; Jamison Road 1.10; Elma 1.16; Spring Brook 1.23; Ebenezer 1.34; Junction 1.50. Arrive at Buffalo 2.00.

Passengers by train No. 1, South, connect at EAST AURORA with Stages for WALES, WALES HOLLOW, STRYKERSVILLE, JAVA VILLAGE and CURRIER'S CORNERS; at HOLLAND, by trains No. 2 and 4, South, with Stages for PROTECTION, SARDINIA, YORKSHIRE and ARCADE, at HOLLAND by train No. 4, South, with Stages for SPRINGVILLE; and by train No. 2 connection is made at YORKSHIRE by Stage to YORKSHIRE CENTRE, MACHIAS and FRANKLINSVILLE.

☞ Trains are run by New York Central time, which is twenty minutes faster than Buffalo time.

☞ Trains arrive and depart from the New York Central Railroad Depot on Exchange Street, BUFFALO, N. Y.

Freight Office, Corner North Division and Emslie Streets.

BUFFALO, N. Y.

H. L. LYMAN, *Secretary & Gen. Ticket Agent.*

W. C. ALBERGER, *Superintendent & Gen. Freight Agent.*

Pictured is an old railroad schedule when Holland was first opened as a stop on the Buffalo and Washington Railway. Rail service began on February 1, 1871. Passenger and mail trains left Buffalo heading south to Holland at 10:20 a.m. and 4:30 p.m. They arrived at the Holland station at 11:55 a.m. and 6:08 p.m. Going north to Buffalo, trains left Holland at 7:35 a.m. and 12:25 p.m. and arrived at the New York Central Railroad Depot on Exchange Street in Buffalo at 9:13 a.m. and 2:00 p.m. There were about eight depot stops on the Buffalo–Holland route.

Colby's Livery would meet the trains at the station and carry passengers to various parts of town. Sleigh runners replaced the wheels for winter use. Harry Colby is pictured with his coach.

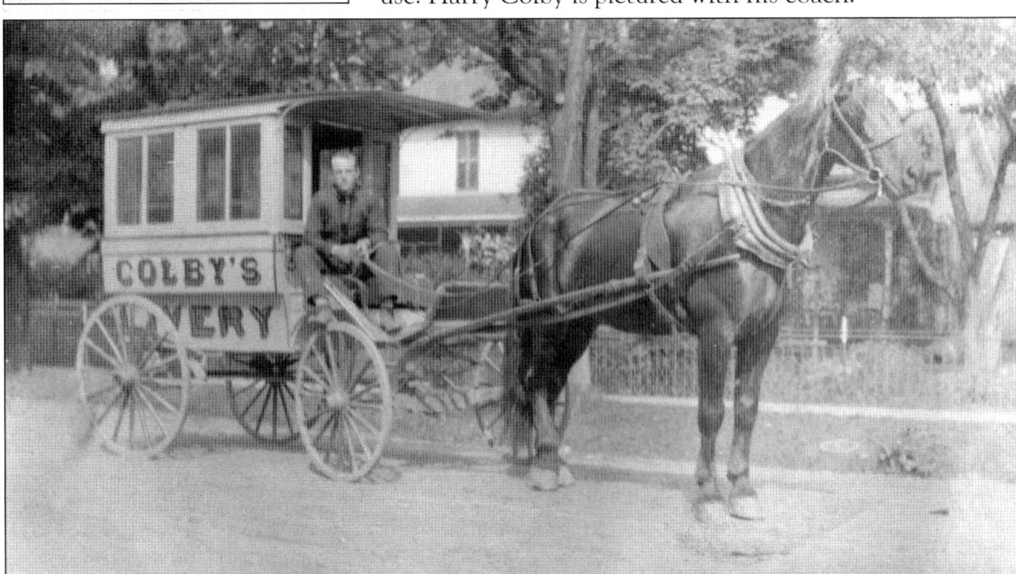

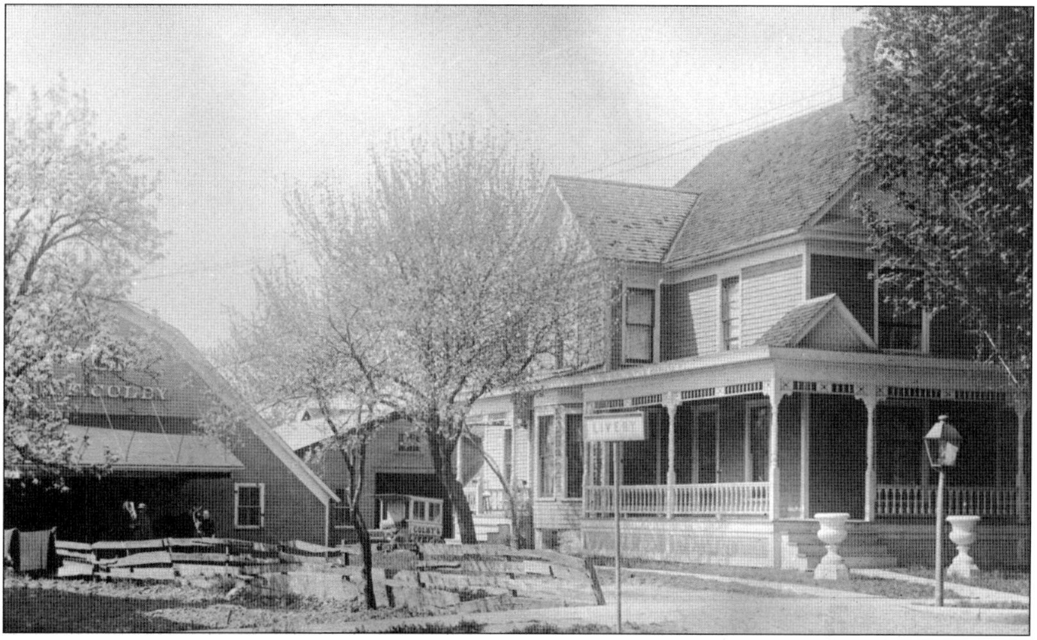

This is the home and business of Colby's Livery, near the corner of Park and Pearl Streets. It was destroyed by fire when the basket factory burned in 1929. The basket factory was around the corner from the livery on Park Street. The brisk wind that night spread the flames to neighboring houses, and many were lost.

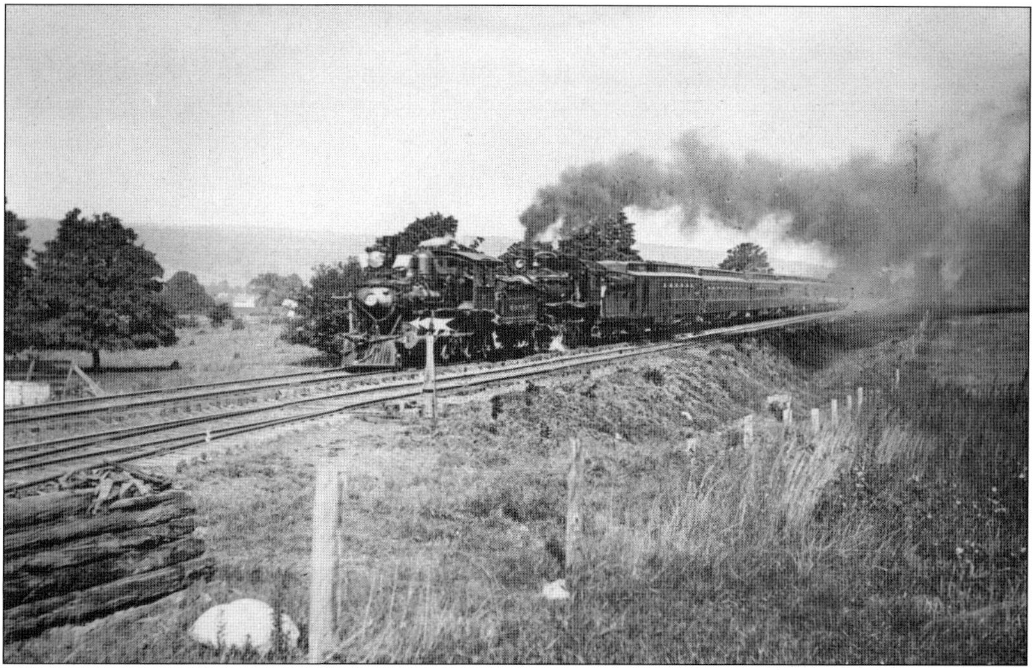

In 1901, Pres. William McKinley's funeral train passed through the Holland valley. Two passenger engines were used to pull the train from Buffalo to Washington, DC. The president was assassinated on September 6, 1901, inside the Temple of Music on the grounds of the Pan-American Exposition in Buffalo, approximately 30 miles north of Holland.

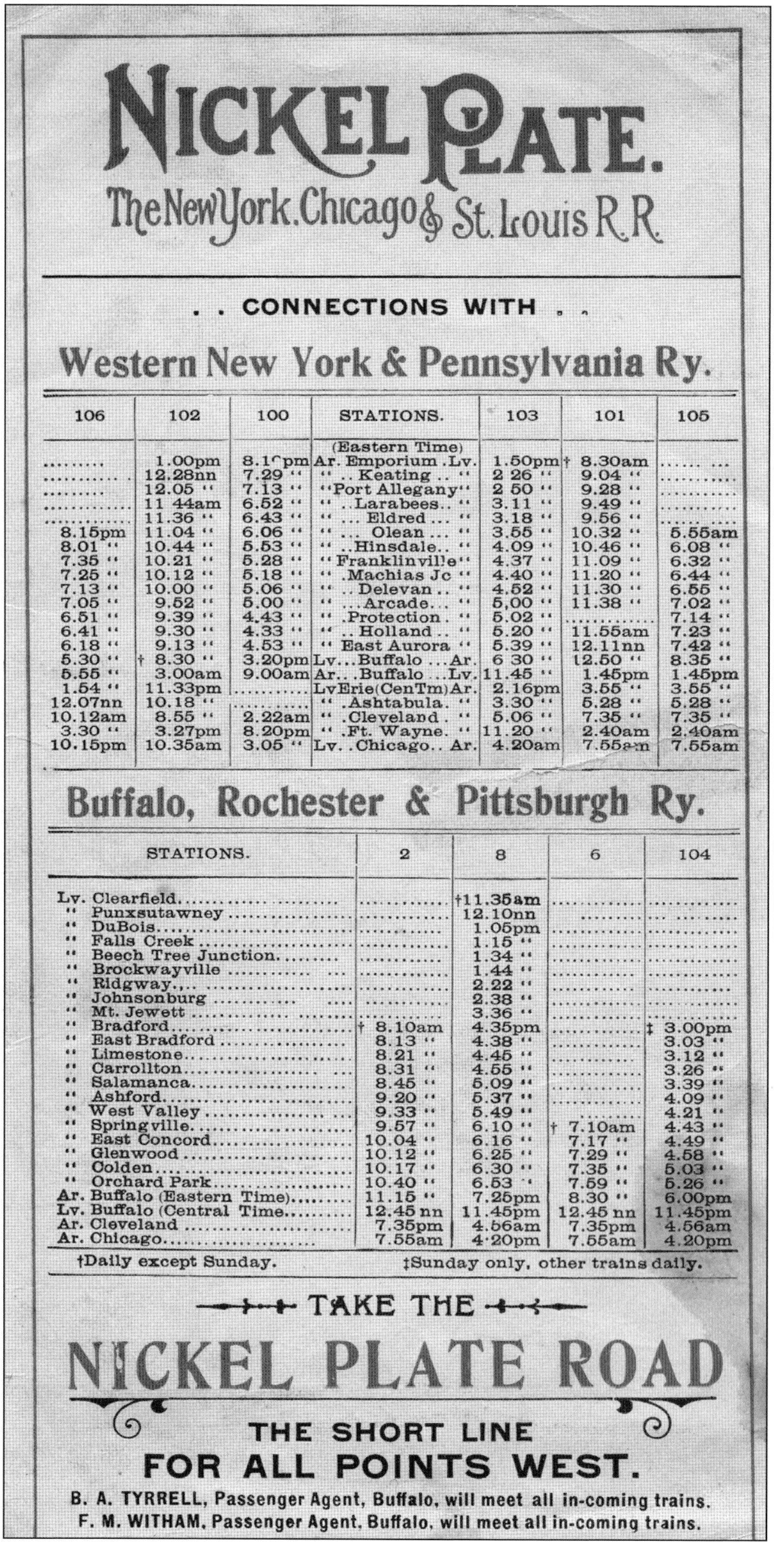

NICKEL PLATE.

The New York. Chicago & St. Louis R.R.

. . CONNECTIONS WITH . .

Western New York & Pennsylvania Ry.

106	102	100	STATIONS.	103	101	105
			(Eastern Time)			
....	1.00pm	8.1?pm	Ar. Emporium .Lv.	1.50pm	† 8.30am	....
....	12.28nn	7.29 "	" . . Keating . . "	2 26 "	9.04 "	....
....	12.05 "	7.13 "	"Port Allegany"	2 50 "	9.28 "	....
....	11 44am	6.52 "	" . . Larabees . . "	3.11 "	9.49 "	....
....	11.36 "	6.43 "	" . . . Eldred . . . "	3.18 "	9.56 "	....
8.15pm	11.04 "	6.06 "	" . . . Olean . . . "	3.55 "	10.32 "	5.55am
8.01 "	10.44 "	5.53 "	" . . Hinsdale . . "	4.09 "	10.46 "	6.08 "
7.35 "	10.21 "	5.28 "	"Franklinville"	4.37 "	11.09 "	6.32 "
7.25 "	10.12 "	5.18 "	" .Machias Jc "	4.40 "	11.20 "	6.44 "
7.13 "	10.00 "	5.06 "	" . . Delevan . . "	4.52 "	11.30 "	6.55 "
7.05 "	9.52 "	5.00 "	" . . . Arcade . . "	5,00 "	11.38 "	7.02 "
6.51 "	9.39 "	4.43 "	" .Protection . "	5.02 "	....	7.14 "
6.41 "	9.30 "	4.33 "	" . . Holland . . "	5.20 "	11.55am	7.23 "
6.18 "	9.13 "	4.53 "	" East Aurora "	5.39 "	12.11nn	7.42 "
5.30 "	† 8.30 "	3.20pm	Lv. . . Buffalo . . Ar.	6 30 "	12.50 "	8.35 "
5.55 "	3.00am	9.00am	Ar. . . Buffalo . . Lv.	11.45 "	1.45pm	1.45pm
1.54 "	11.33pm	....	LvErie(CenTm)Ar.	2.16pm	3.55 "	3.55 "
12.07nn	10.18 "	....	" .Ashtabula. "	3.30 "	5.28 "	5.28 "
10.12am	8.55 "	2.22am	" .Cleveland . "	5.06 "	7.35 "	7.35 "
3.30 "	3.27pm	8.20pm	" .Ft. Wayne. "	11.20 "	2.40am	2.40am
10.15pm	10.35am	3.05 "	Lv. . Chicago. . Ar.	4.20am	7.55am	7.55am

Buffalo, Rochester & Pittsburgh Ry.

STATIONS.	2	8	6	104
Lv. Clearfield........	....	†11.35am	....	....
" Punxsutawney	....	12.10nn	....	....
" DuBois........	....	1.05pm	....	....
" Falls Creek	....	1.15 "	....	....
" Beech Tree Junction........	....	1.34 "	....	....
" Brockwayville	....	1.44 "	....	....
" Ridgway.,........	....	2.22 "	....	....
" Johnsonburg	....	2.38 "	....	....
" Mt. Jewett	....	3.36 "	....	....
" Bradford........	† 8.10am	4.35pm	....	‡ 3.00pm
" East Bradford	8.13 "	4.38 "	....	3.03 "
" Limestone........	8.21 "	4.45 "	....	3.12 "
" Carrollton........	8.31 "	4.55 "	....	3.26 "
" Salamanca........	8.45 "	5.09 "	....	3.39 "
" Ashford........	9.20 "	5.37 "	....	4.09 "
" West Valley	9.33 "	5.49 "	....	4.21 "
" Springville........	9.57 "	6.10 "	† 7.10am	4.43 "
" East Concord........	10.04 "	6.16 "	7.17 "	4.49 "
" Glenwood	10.12 "	6.25 "	7.29 "	4.58 "
" Colden........	10.17 "	6.30 "	7.35 "	5.03 "
" Orchard Park........	10.40 "	6.53 "	7.59 "	5.26 "
Ar. Buffalo (Eastern Time)........	11.15 "	7.25pm	8.30 "	6.00pm
Lv. Buffalo (Central Time........	12.45 nn	11.45pm	12.45 nn	11.45pm
Ar. Cleveland	7.35pm	4.56am	7.35pm	4.56am
Ar. Chicago........	7.55am	4·20pm	7.55am	4.20pm

†Daily except Sunday. ‡Sunday only, other trains daily.

TAKE THE

NICKEL PLATE ROAD

THE SHORT LINE

FOR ALL POINTS WEST.

B. A. TYRRELL, Passenger Agent, Buffalo, will meet all in-coming trains.
F. M. WITHAM, Passenger Agent, Buffalo, will meet all in-coming trains.

This is a railway timetable for the Nickel Plate Railroad showing stops at Holland and other local stations. Local businessman Charles C. Lowry was a retired travel passenger agent for Nickel Plate. Lowry at one time owned the Lowry Hotel, a general store, and an ice cream and candy shop on Main Street.

Five

Education at Holland Central School

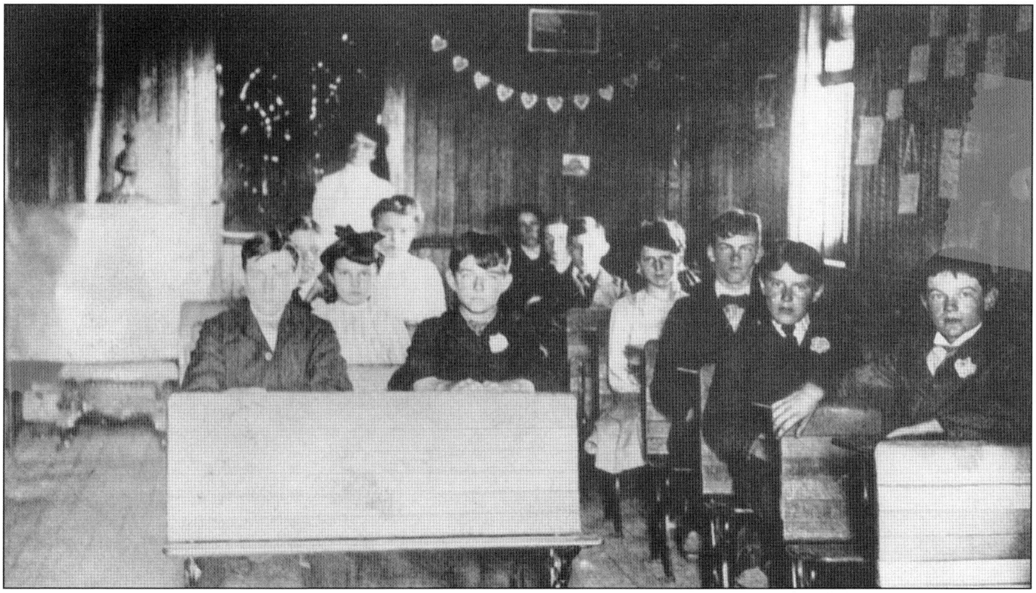

The first school in Holland was in the Humphrey area near the intersection of Blanchard Road and Route 16. It was built before the War of 1812, and Abner Currier taught there during the winter months. In the 1820s and 1830s, several additional one-room schoolhouses were built outside the village, accommodating 10 to 20 students from their immediate areas. This picture dates from the early 1900s.

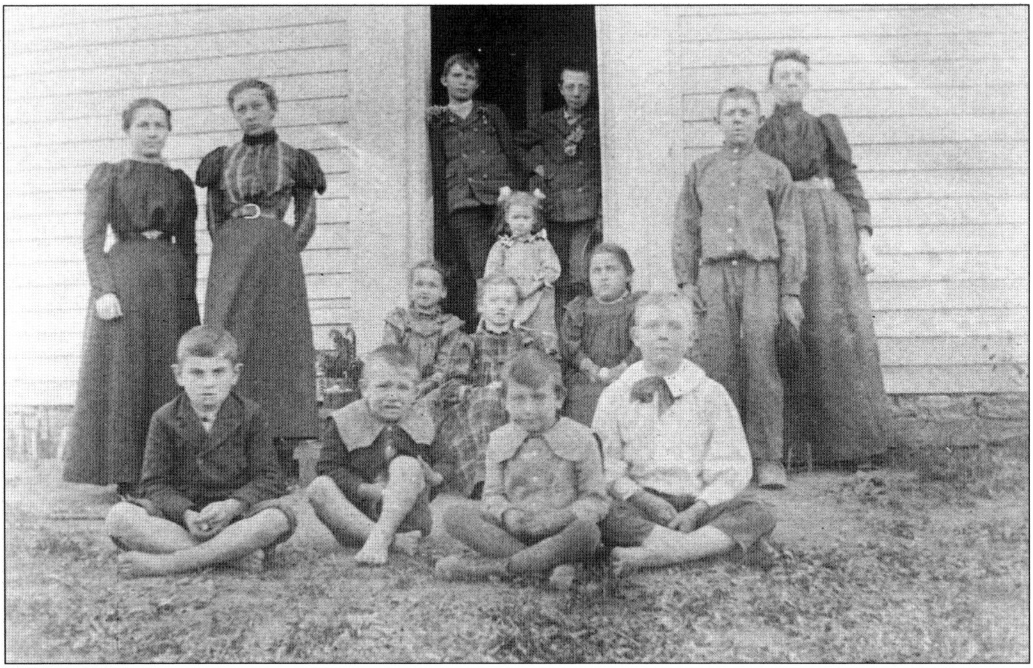

Holland's very first village school was at the end of Continental Avenue. School No. 3 held classes in an old house on this dead-end road. This was the forerunner of Holland Union School, Village District No. 3, which was built on the present town hall site. It is believed that Lodisa Orr or Sarah Stanton taught here. This picture dates from the mid-1850s.

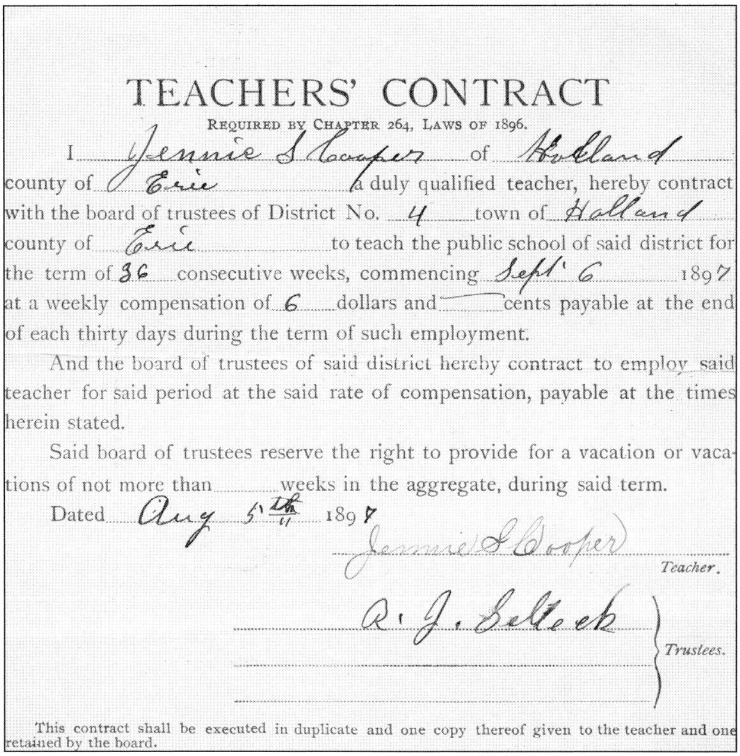

TEACHERS' CONTRACT

REQUIRED BY CHAPTER 264, LAWS OF 1896.

I Jennie S Cooper of Holland county of Erie a duly qualified teacher, hereby contract with the board of trustees of District No. 4 town of Holland county of Erie to teach the public school of said district for the term of 36 consecutive weeks, commencing Sept 6 1897 at a weekly compensation of 6 dollars and —— cents payable at the end of each thirty days during the term of such employment.

And the board of trustees of said district hereby contract to employ said teacher for said period at the said rate of compensation, payable at the times herein stated.

Said board of trustees reserve the right to provide for a vacation or vacations of not more than ...... weeks in the aggregate, during said term.

Dated Aug 5th 1897

Jennie S Cooper Teacher.

R. J. Selleck Trustees.

This contract shall be executed in duplicate and one copy thereof given to the teacher and one retained by the board.

Shown is a typical teacher's contract from 1897 between teacher Jennie S. Cooper and Randall Jay Selleck, a member of the school's board of trustees. Cooper taught at District School No. 4, the Humphrey/Olean Road District.

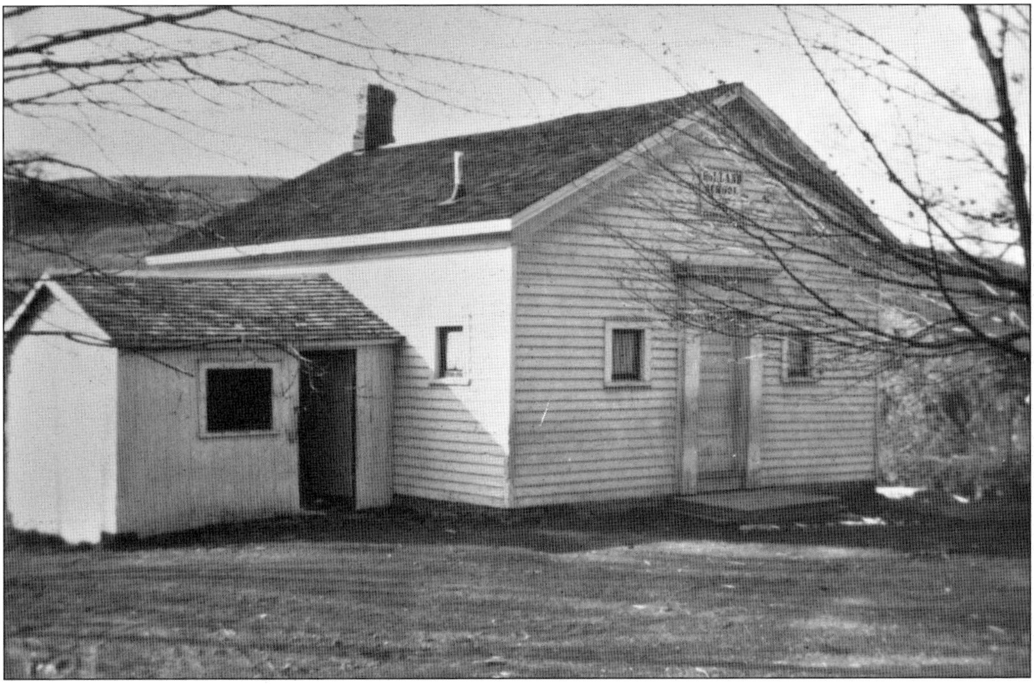

School District No. 5 was known as the Savage Road District. Part of this schoolhouse is still attached to the present home owned by the Vella family. Students who attended this school are, from left to right below, (first row) William Vogt, Marion Heitman, Beulah Heitman, Eleanor Morrell, Norma Hiller, and Sayer Wales; (second row) Jay Morrell, Elizabeth Hartenstein, Albert Hattler, and James Schickler; (tall boy in the back) Leland Heitman.

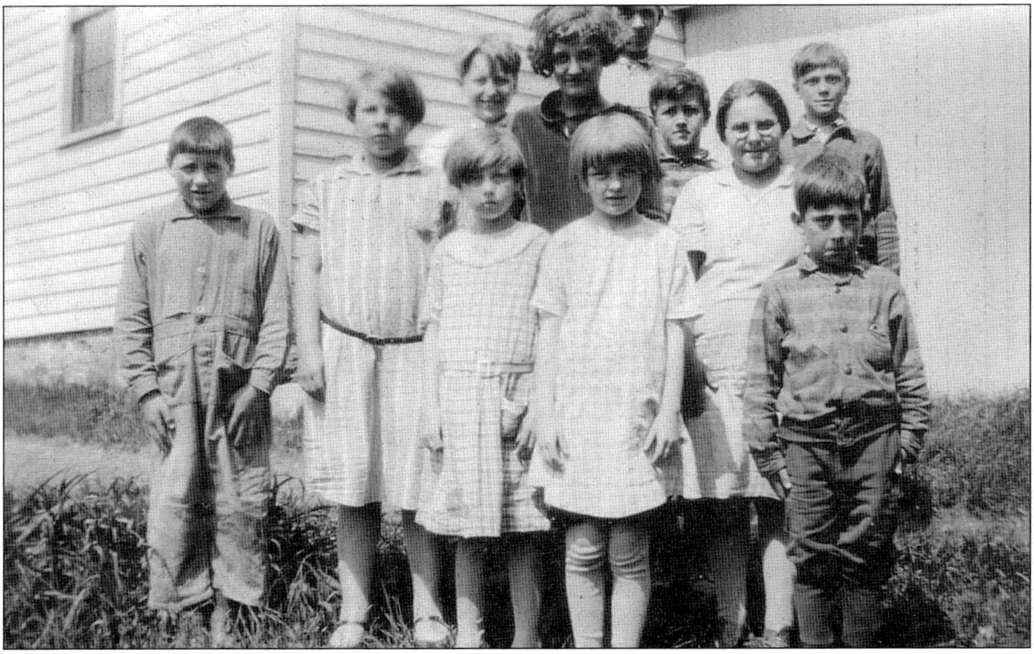

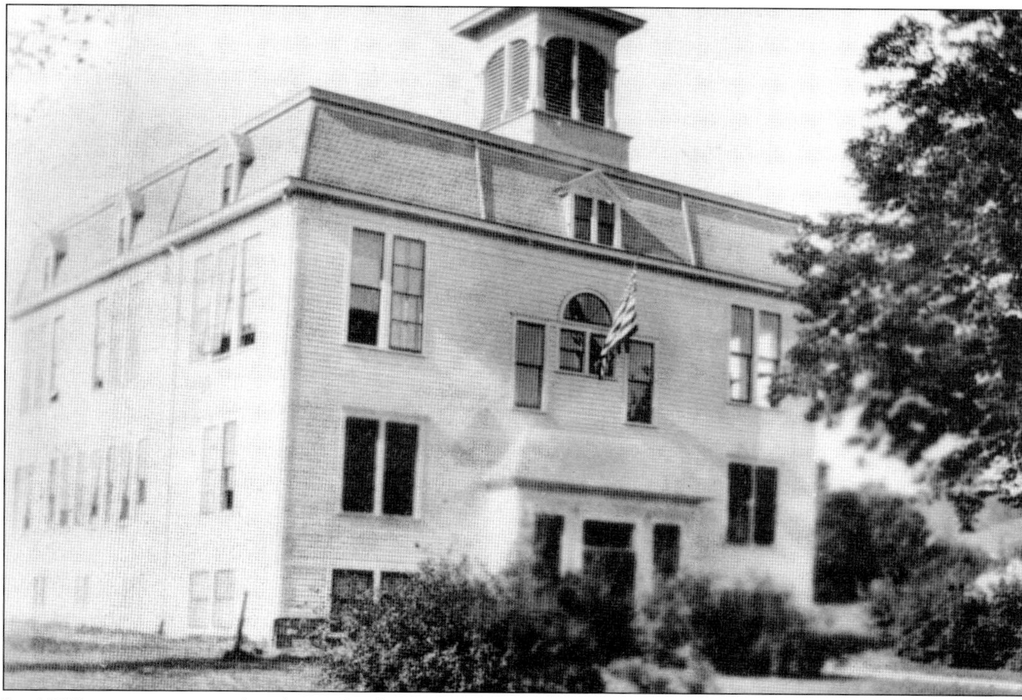

In 1887, a two-story school was built on Pearl Street where the Holland Town Hall now stands. This was Holland Union School, Village District No. 3. In this building were seven classrooms and a library. During its use, the school was remodeled and changed three times. The school year consisted of four quarters, starting in late August and ending in late June. Tuition was charged to students living outside the village district: $2 for primary students, $2.50 for intermediate, and $3 for academic (high school) students. Two high school majors were offered, classical and scientific. Students could also take four years of German, French, Latin, and Greek. Courses such as "Fruit Growing" and "Poultry Raising" were available, too. After the central school was built, this building was used for the Holland Town Hall until it burned in 1934.

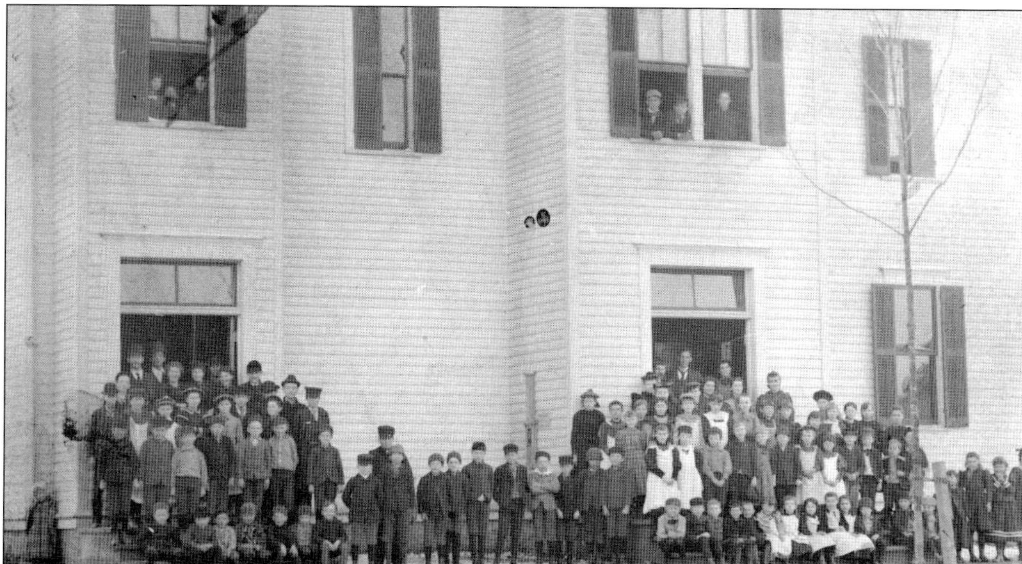

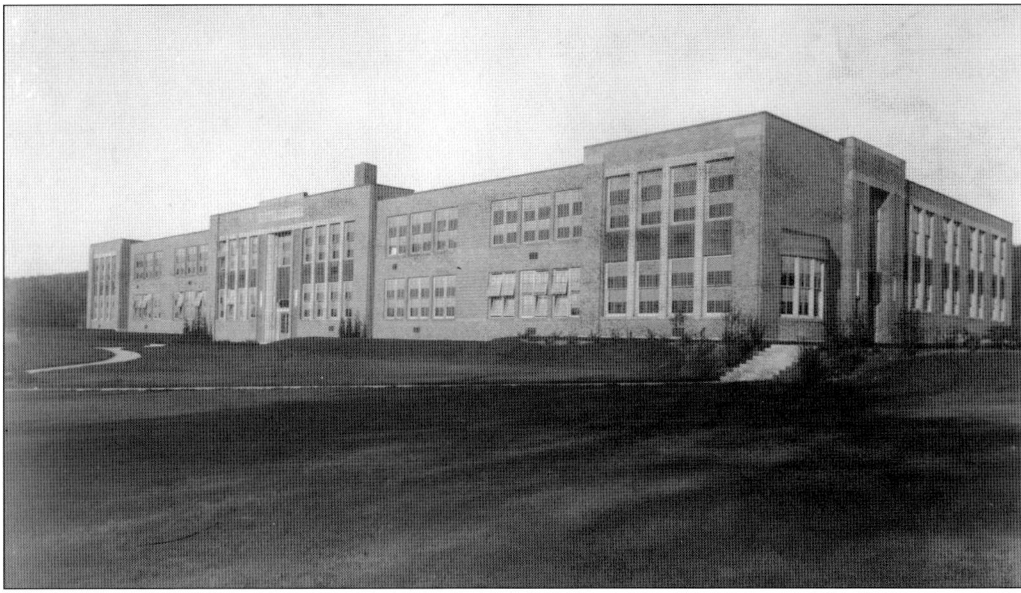

The campaign for the establishment of a central school in Holland began in 1928 under district superintendent William Bensley and Principal Harold Brumsted. After many public meetings and pro-centralization petitions, the community overwhelmingly voted to centralize the village and eight rural districts on June 12, 1931. It became the first community in Erie County to establish a central school district when Holland Central School was formed. This early picture of the school was taken around 1933. The entire cost for the new school project was $200,000, a tremendous sum at that time.

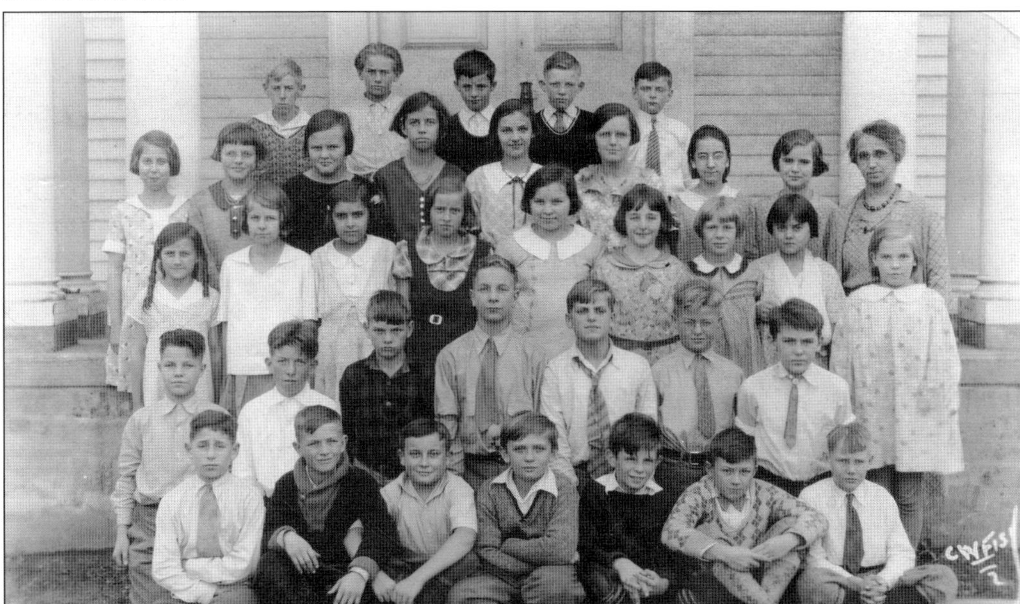

This group photograph is from the 1932–1933 school year. It shows students in grades five and six from Nora Kanner's classroom. These children were still at the village school on Pearl Street and moved into the new central building after Christmas vacation, in January 1933. (Courtesy of Robert White.)

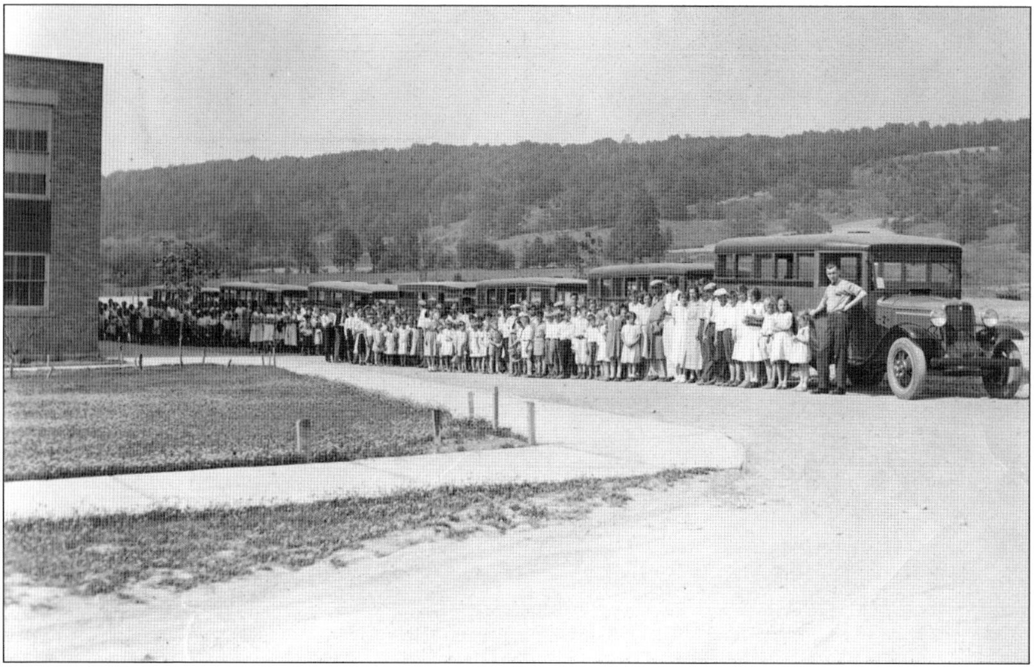

After the completion of the new central school building, the rural schools that were part of the central district were closed, and students were gradually integrated into the classes and grades in the new central building. Buses were needed for the first time. The fleet of seven buses was contracted from Ross Brown, a local businessman. The district did not own its own fleet for almost 10 years. Above is a lineup of buses at dismissal time in 1933.

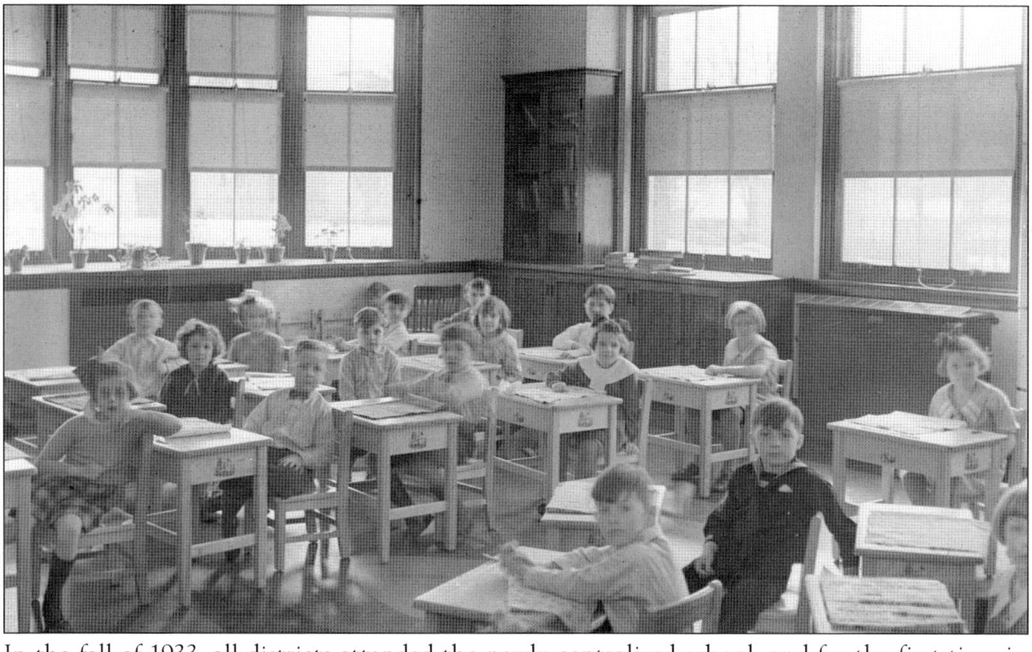

In the fall of 1933, all districts attended the newly centralized school, and for the first time in their lives, rural children had a full course of music, art, shop, home economics, and physical education. Pictured are young students in their new classroom setting.

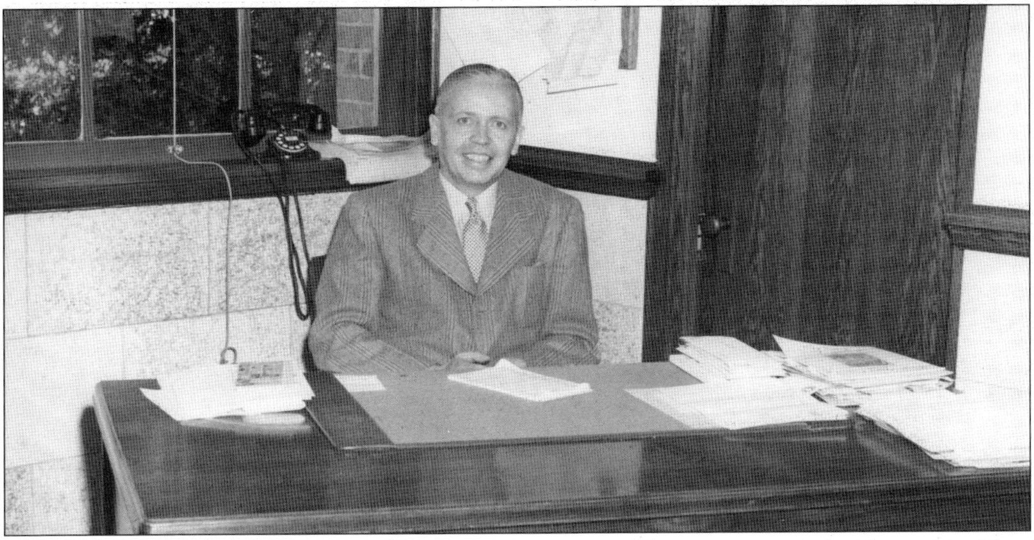

Harold O. Brumsted (1901–1981) was the primary organizer and longtime principal and superintendent of the Holland Central School District. He began at the Holland Village School as principal in September 1926. Brumsted was quick to sense the total inadequacy of both the building and the curriculum of the old school and decided that centralization offered the only solution. For nearly three years, he worked tirelessly for the cause, aided by Superintendent William E. Bensley. In June 1931, centralization was achieved. Brumsted's greatest contribution was the enrichment of lives of the boys and girls who attended Holland Central School. He retired in 1968 and was a beloved figure in the Holland community.

Ever dedicated to Holland Central School, business manager Beverly C. Beardsell (1915–1981) served the district for 40 years. She was a 1938 graduate of Cornell University, began as secretary to Principal Harold Brumsted in 1940, and was later named business manager. Beardsell's role extended beyond attentive business manager, as she held a great concern for the students. She established many after-school service clubs, held lessons for class officers on how to best perform their duties, and in general helped shape career choices. She was a key figure in the success of Holland Central School from the 1940s to 1970s.

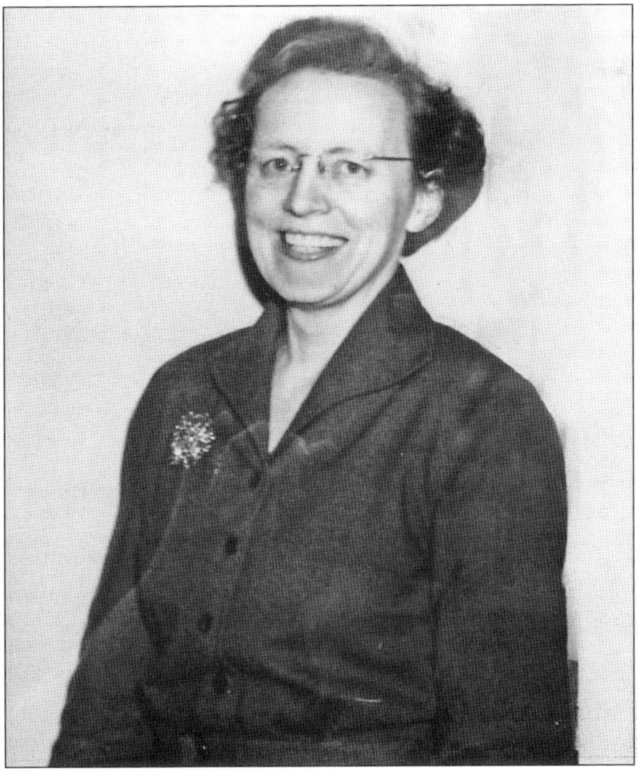

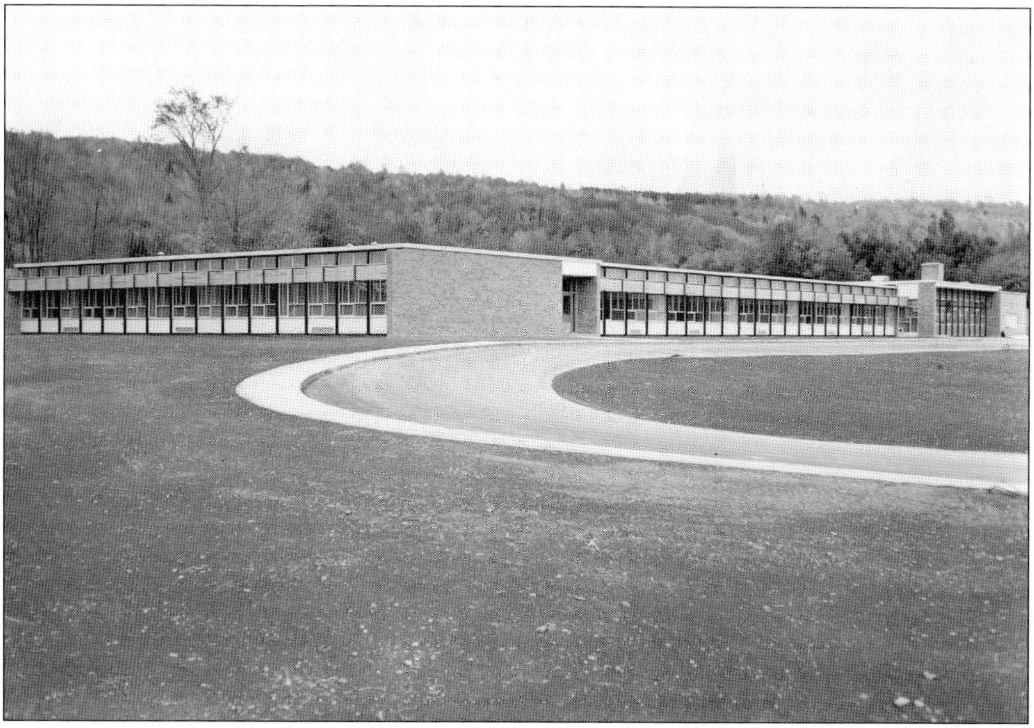

As enrollment continued to grow in the 1950s, it was soon clear that more classroom space was needed. In June 1959, voters approved funding for a new elementary school. The school opened its doors to students in 1960 and was aptly named Harold O. Brumsted Elementary School. This building was modern and large, but additional classrooms and a bus garage had to be added in the late 1960s.

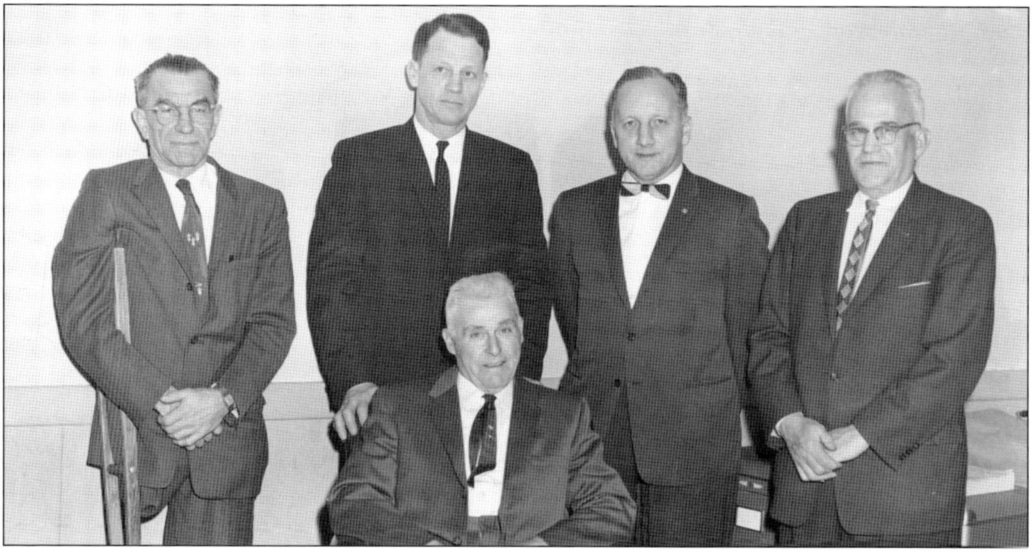

The Holland Central School Board of Education is shown in the early 1960s. Standing from left to right are Wesley Richards, Robert Kramer, Earle Persse, and Clarence Bush. Edward Rickettson is seated. Members of the first board of education, elected in 1931, included Frank Carroll, Cort Kramer, Everett Sleeper, George Wangelin, and Paul Wurst.

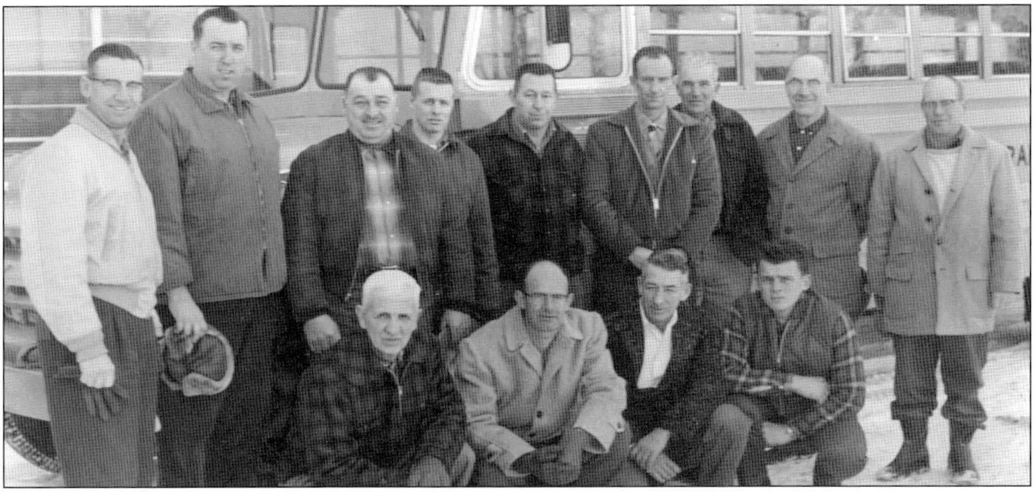

Pictured are the school's bus drivers for 1961. From left to right are (first row) Allen Montgomery, David Custard, Charles Stevens, and Jerald Zywiczynski; (second row) Sheridan Geer, Melvin Bucknam, Benny Zywiczynski, George Sechrist, Robert Wells, Orson Cooper, Gordon Hessel Sr., Stephen Custard, and Medford Savage. In a rural district that experiences all four seasons, their sturdy driving skills were often put to the test.

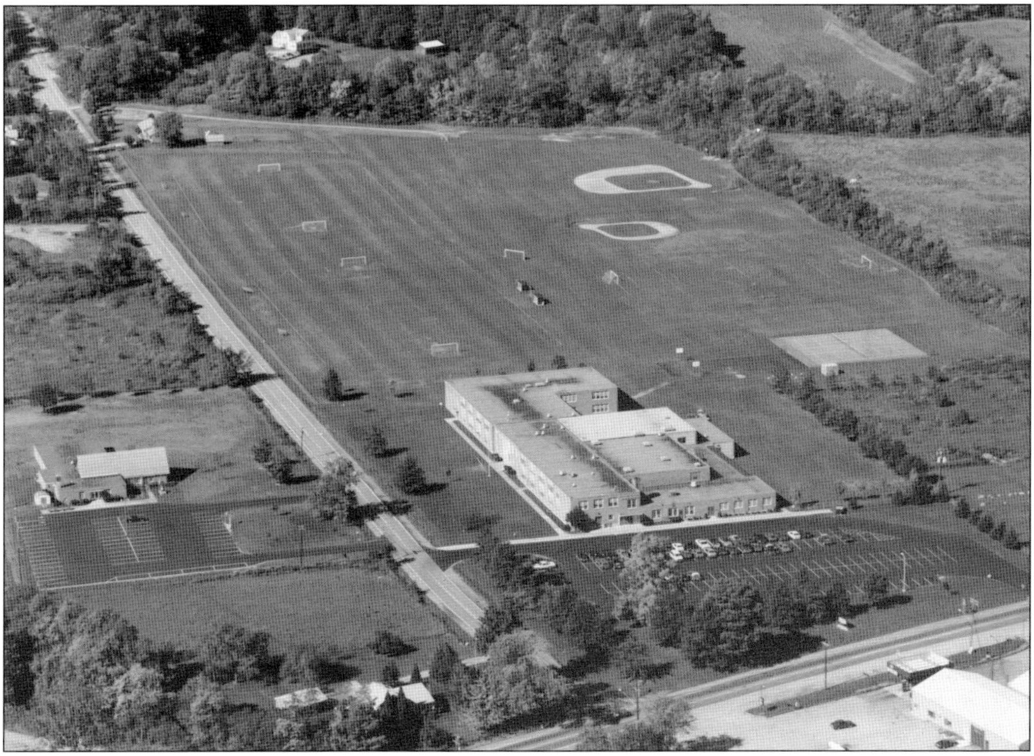

Construction of a middle school was approved in June 1970, and just over 17 acres were purchased at the corner of Route 16 and Partridge Road for this new building. A community-driven project provided outdoor lighting for the school's soccer field, and a volunteer-built concession stand complimented the new athletic fields. However, due to declining enrollment, the middle school was eventually closed in June 2012.

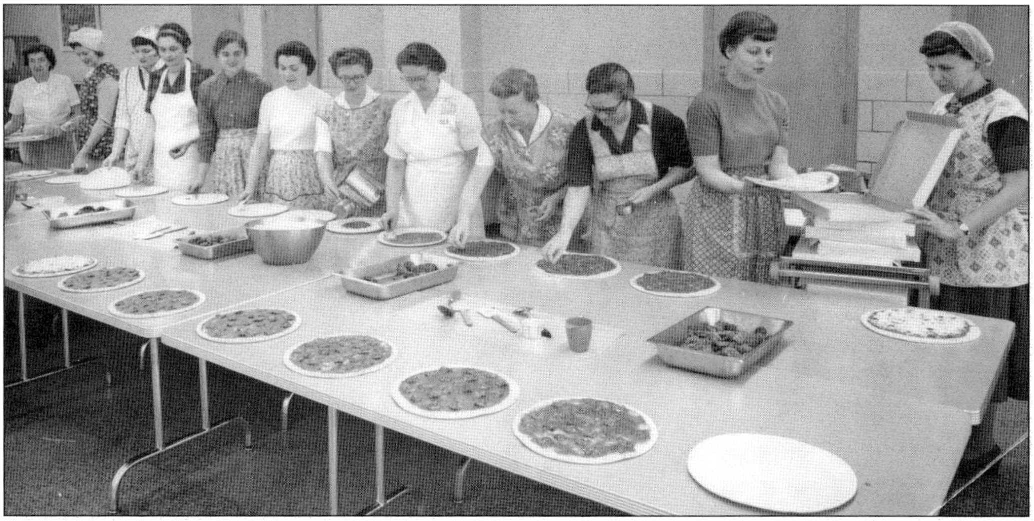

Holland has always been a community where residents lend a helping hand wherever needed. This picture shows women in the community who gathered yearly to work a pizza sale benefitting the school's American Field Service (AFS) Club. Volunteers in the early 1960s included, from left to right, Muriel Schwenke, Charlene Phelps, Mary Lou Fischer, Genevieve Bush, Miss Antunes (AFS advisor), unidentified, Kay Geer, Doris Savage, Anne Geer, Jane McArthur, Mary Strong, and Mildred Valenti.

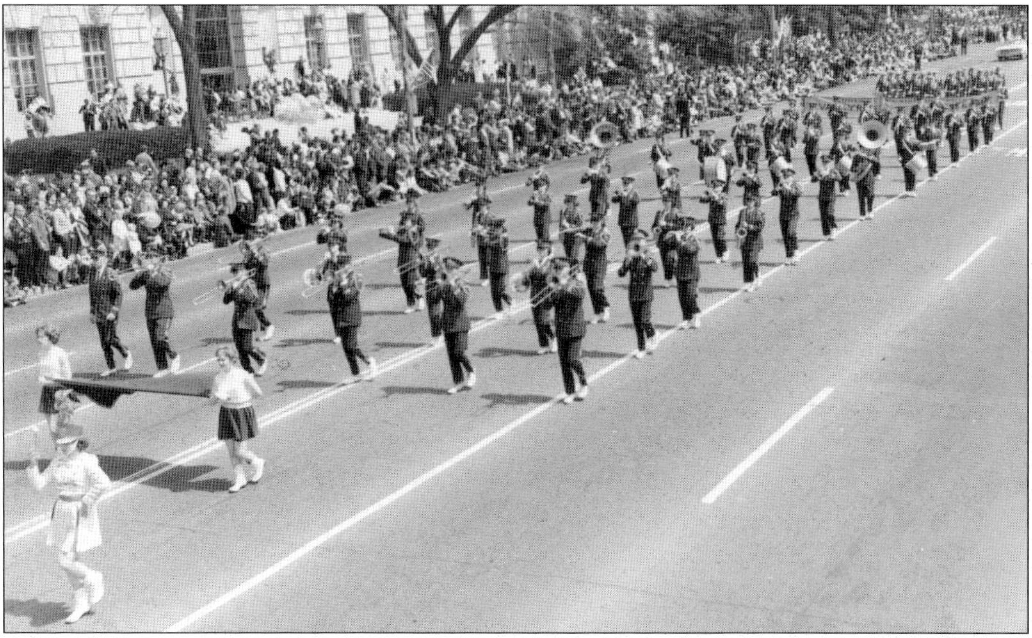

On April 10, 1965, eighty boys and girls from Holland Central School marched in the annual National Cherry Blossom Festival parade representing New York State. Band members, drum majors and majorettes, and the all-girl color guard paraded along Pennsylvania Avenue in Washington, DC, along with bandleader Barry Haywood. This was a band of distinction; in 1963, it represented New York State in the annual Thanksgiving Day Parade in Philadelphia, and in 1964, it served as the official band of Pres. Lyndon B. Johnson during his campaign visit to the Buffalo area. (Courtesy of Richard White.)

Six

Military Service and Fire Rescue

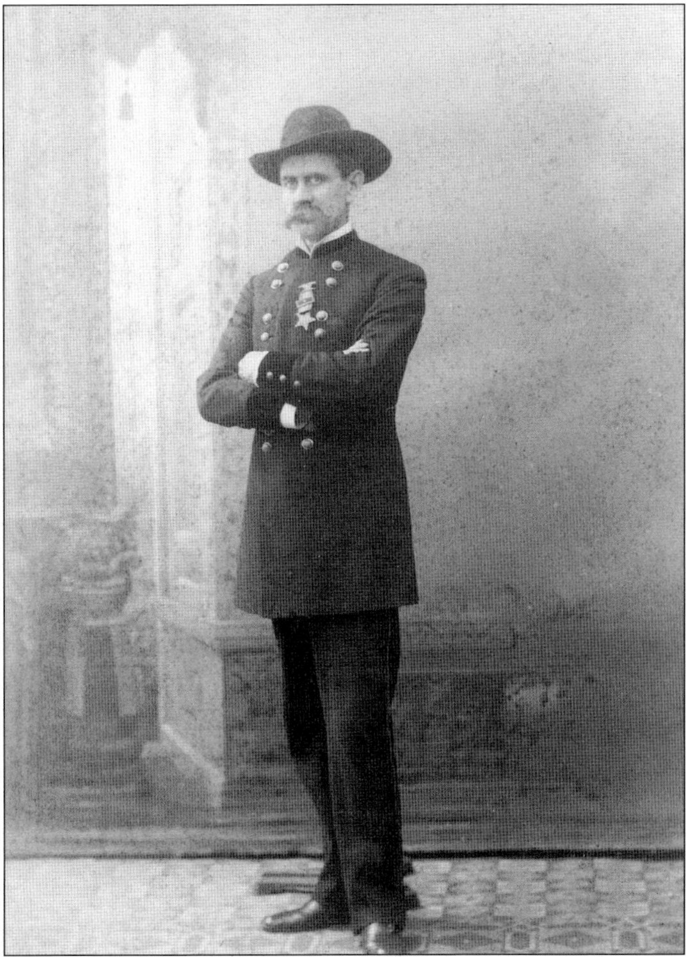

Born in Holland, New York, 16-year-old Charles Alvin Orr enlisted in the Union army (Company G, 187th New York Volunteer Infantry) in 1864, and within three weeks, he faced the South at the Battle of Hatcher's Run in Virginia. After the war, on March 22, 1898, Orr was awarded the Congressional Medal of Honor for his actions. His citation reads, "This soldier and two others, voluntarily and under fire, rescued several wounded and helpless soldiers." Charles Orr returned to his home in Holland and was in the milling business with his father.

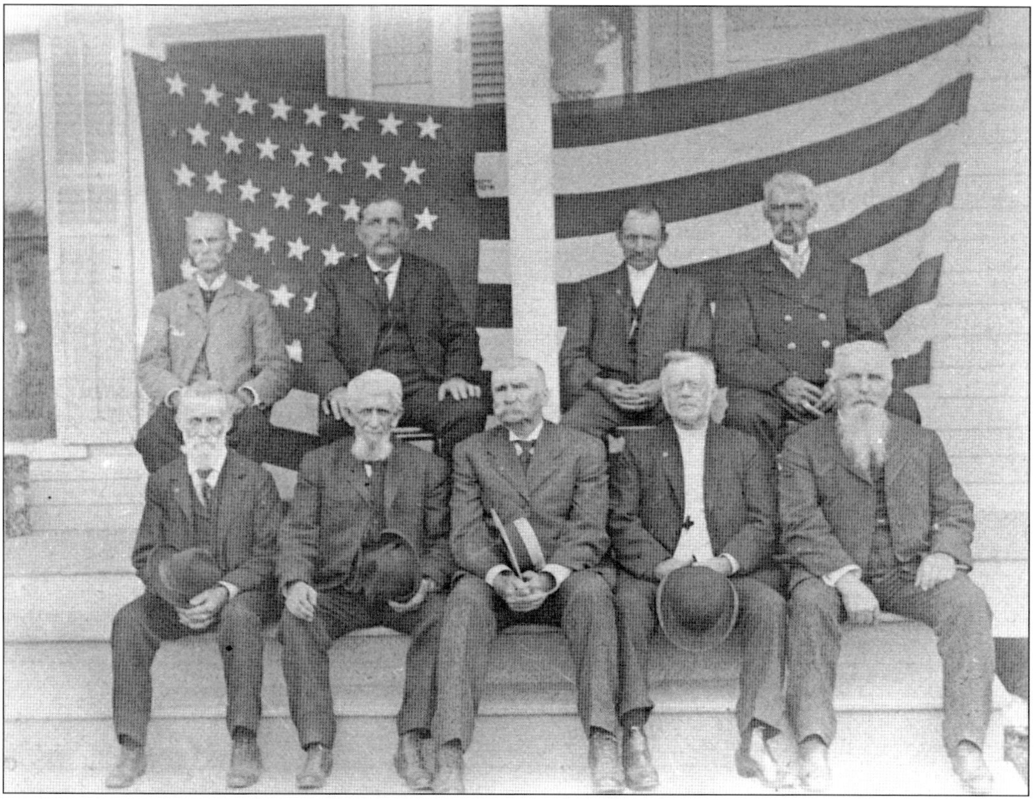

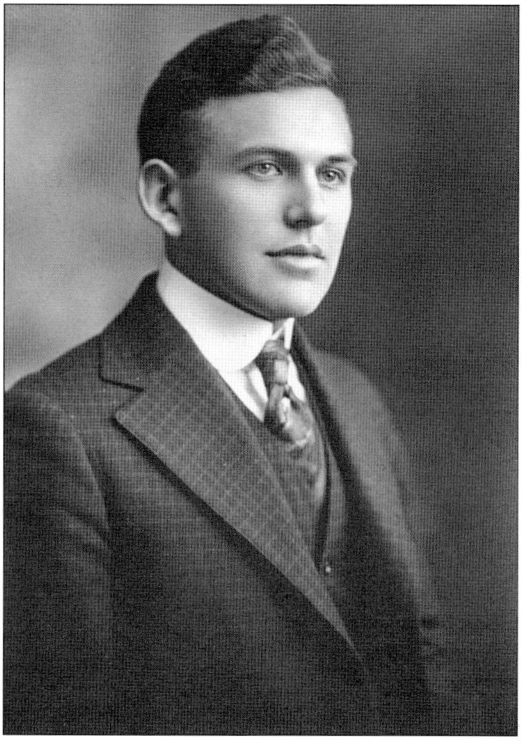

Many young men from Holland volunteered for the Civil War. One of the local men killed was Sgt. Robert Orr, brother of Charles Orr. Robert was killed in action at Fredericksburg, Virginia, and buried on the battlefield by his comrades. After the war, a GAR post was formed in Holland and was named the Robert Orr Post No. 553. Several members of Holland's GAR post are shown in this picture, including William H. Burnett, Horace Selleck (with long beard), and William H. Burlingham, who was the longtime commander.

In the fall of 1917, Frank H. Brink was the first Holland citizen to be drafted into World War I. He was also the first to lose his life. A dispatch rider, Brink was killed in action by a bomb while carrying his first message to the front in the Argonne Forest in France. The Holland American Legion Frank H. Brink Post No. 607 is named in his honor.

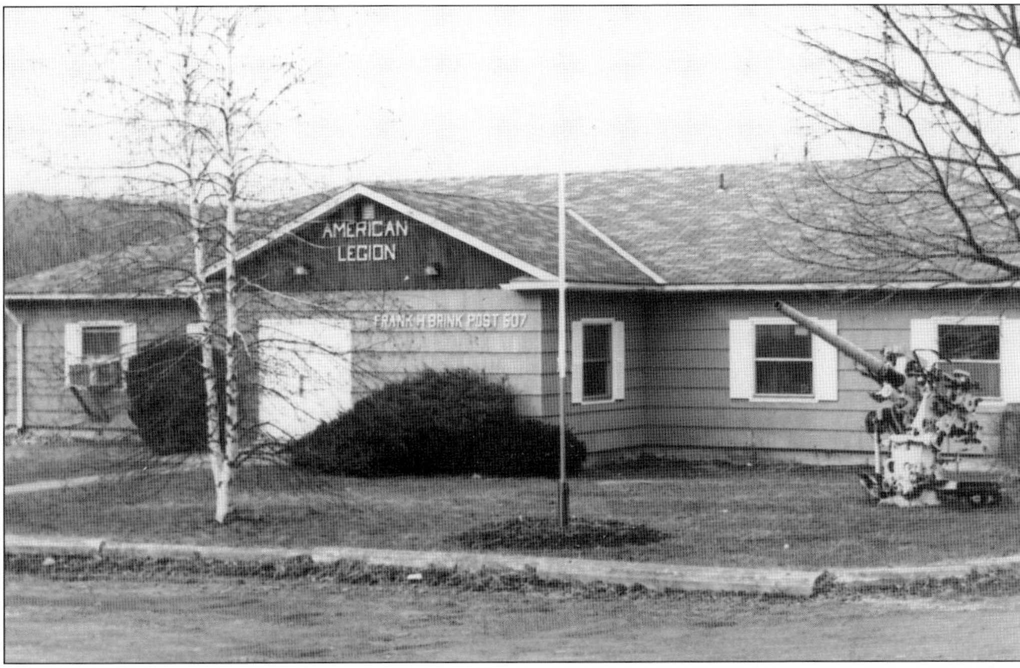

Early in 1919, returning veterans of World War I started meeting, and soon, over 16 men assembled and requested an American Legion charter. The charter for the American Legion Frank H. Brink Post No. 607 was granted on August 1, 1920. This is the Legion post that was built in 1962 and is still used today.

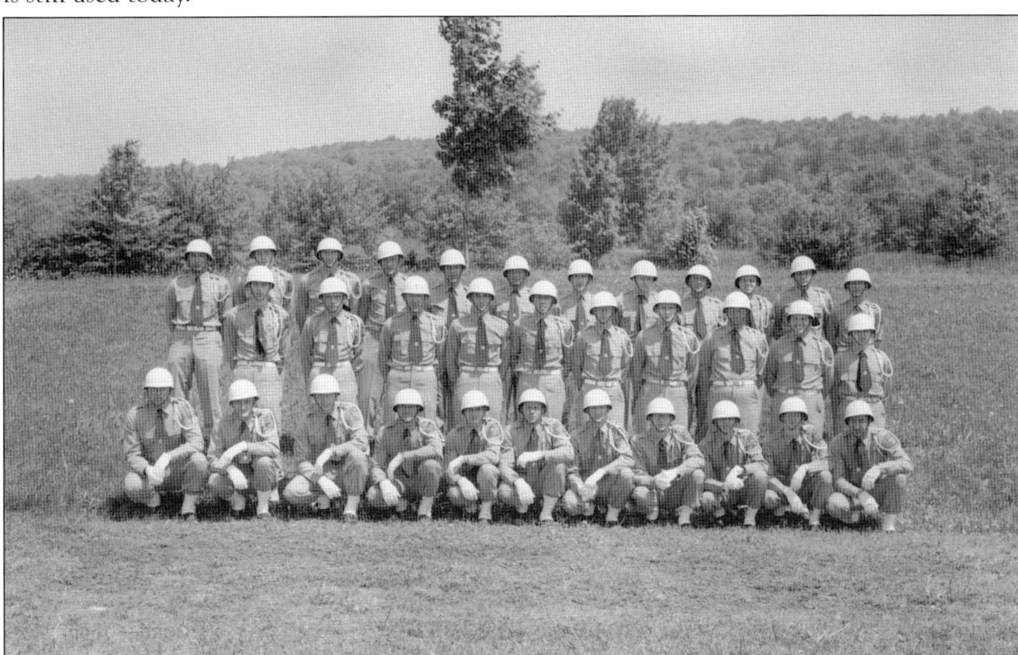

Shown here is the Frank H. Brink Post No. 607 parade unit on Memorial Day 1948. During its 16-year existence, the 60-man marching unit captured many awards at American Legion conventions and local parades.

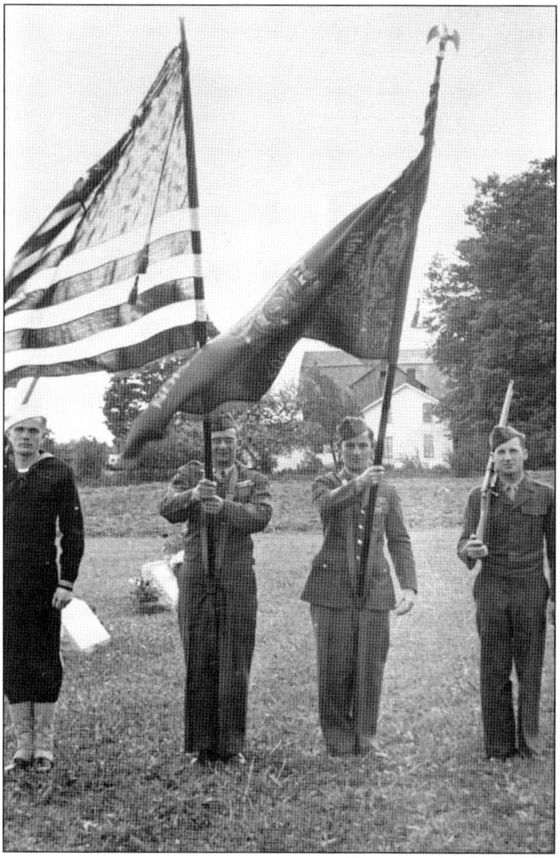

Pictured is Holland's American Legion Post 607 color guard unit on Memorial Day 1946. The members are, from left to right, Kenneth Tanner, Francis Schott, Joseph Piedmont, and William Pratt.

Members of the American Legion post's rifle squad are, from left to right, David Custard, Eugene Jackson, Theodore Bucknam, Frank Cook, Thomas Morrell, Charles Preston, and Eugene Renfro. This photograph was taken on Memorial Day 1946.

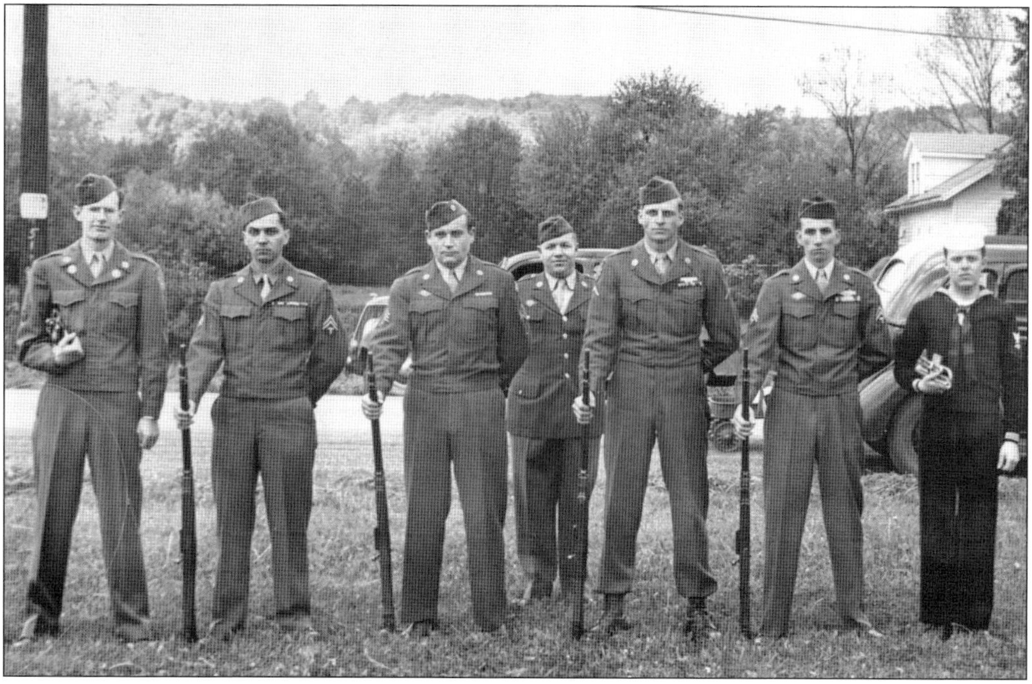

The Holland Hometown Heroes display was dedicated on Memorial Day 2011. Present at the ceremony were Boy Scouts from Troop 507, members of American Legion Post 607, Holland Kiwanis Club members, and many residents of the community. Maintained by the Boy Scouts, the display recognizes and supports the military service of those from Holland.

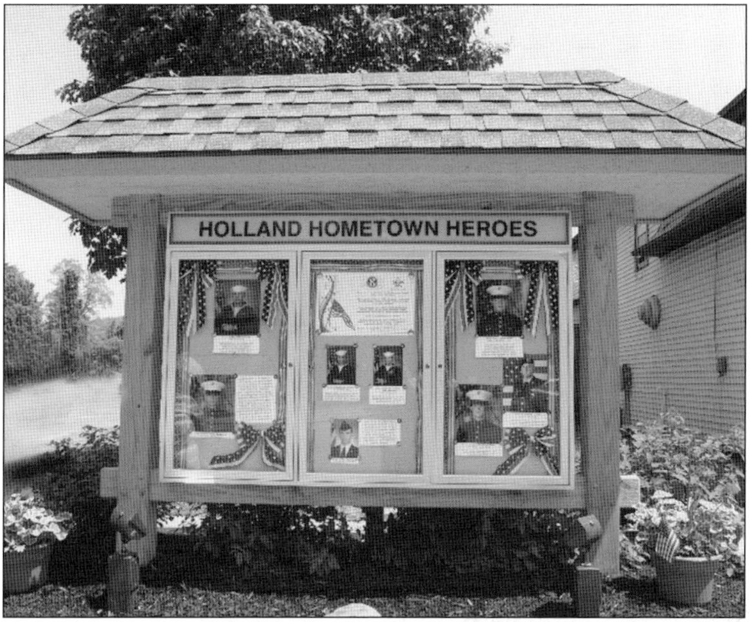

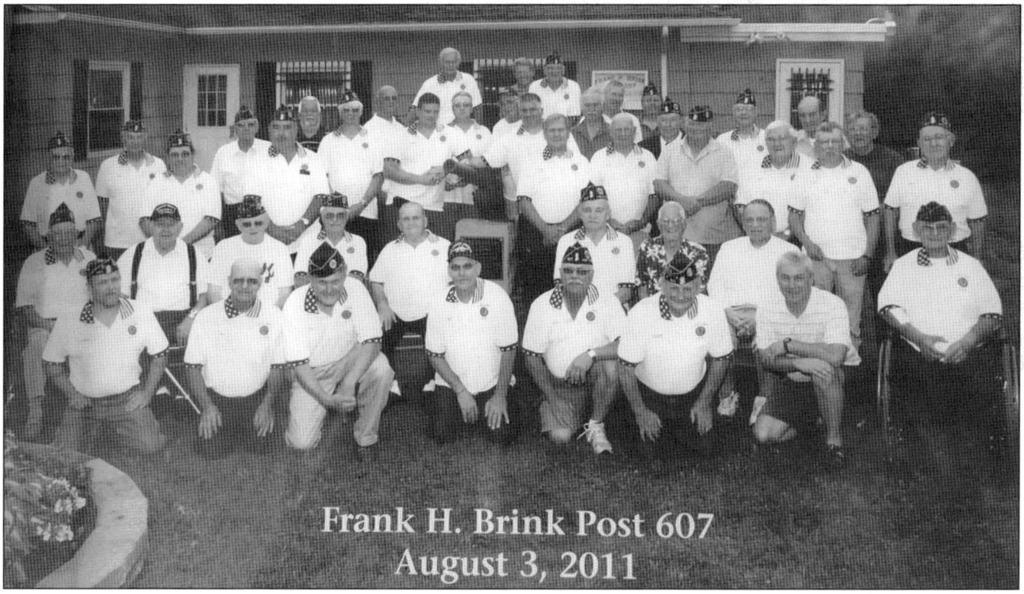

Members of Holland's American Legion Frank H. Brink Post No. 607 gather for a group photograph on August 3, 2011. The last group picture of post members was taken nearly 40 years ago. From left to right are (first row) Adrian Herr, William Neischel, Paul Draper, Michael Lester, Keith Johnson, Robert Pajonk, Timothy Van Splunder, and Alfred Kalinowski; (second row) James Van Splunder, John Allen, Paul Allen, John Rickettson, Bud Bohadlo, Tony Snaza, William Pratt, and Charles Root; (third row) William Miller, Merritt Smith, Gary Kingston, Jerry Pietraszek, Harris Evans, Roy Charles, Richard Sheehan, Howard Gardner, and Matthew Kalinowski; (fourth row) Michael Doyle, Lyle Giesler, Robert Yount, Shawn Janer, Joseph Levesque, Terry Lynch, Robert Herget, John Inglis, William Hack, and Joseph Fridman; (fifth row) Herbert McArthur, David Sears, Gerald Husman, Robert Urban, James Radford, and Jeremy Barron; (sixth row) Paul Ruminski, Richard Springer, and Lee Duerr.

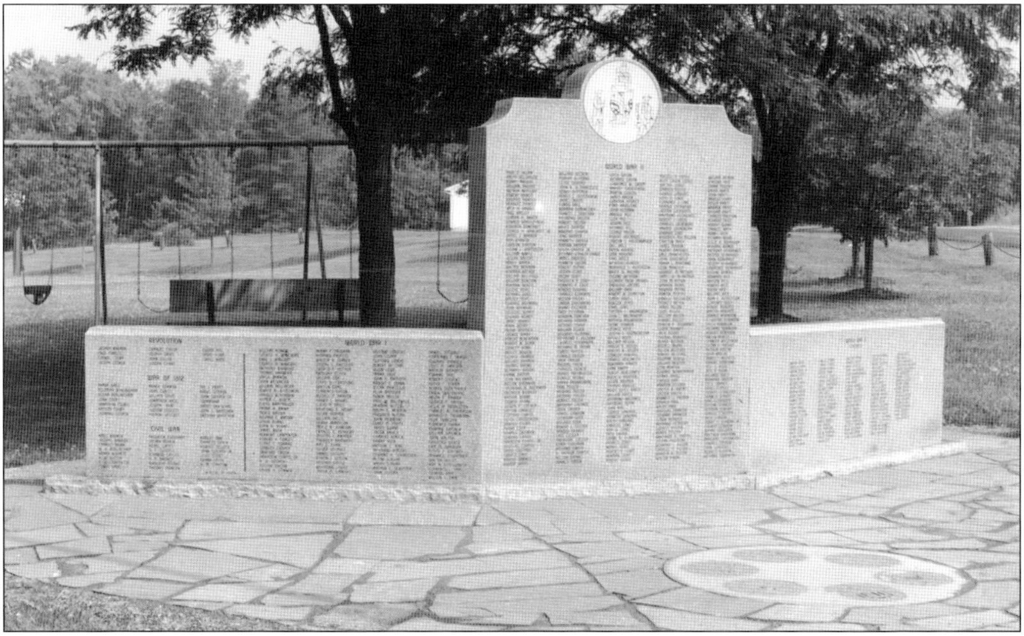

A veterans memorial for Holland was the idea of Richard Draper, who saw a monument dedicated to the veterans of a small town while traveling in Maine with his nephew, Robert Draper. Money was raised for the monument through local American Legion fundraisers, grants, and donations from individuals, town organizations, and businesses. Several hundred people attended Holland's Memorial Day observance and monument dedication in 2001. The monument is located on Legion Drive at Holland's Town Park.

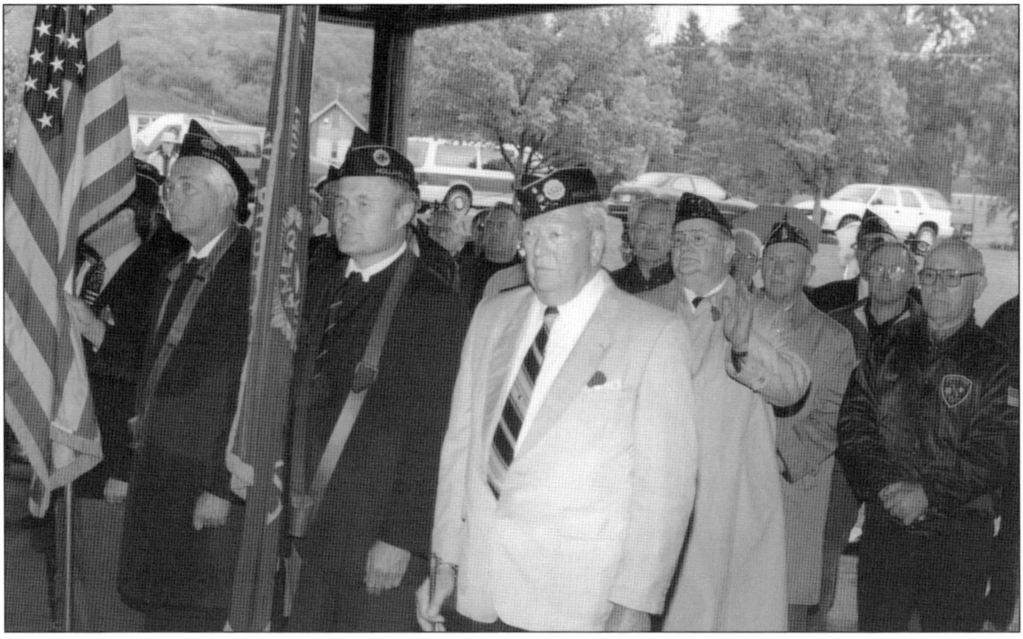

Pictured is the color detail unit at the Holland veteran's memorial dedication. They are, from left to right in the first row, Robert Draper (behind US flag), Joseph Fedus, Paul Draper, and Richard Draper.

The Holland Fire Department was organized in 1893 with 10 charter members: John Bolender, Wesley Bucknam, P.N. Cullen, Albert Griggs, Henry Spaulding, William Spaulding, Dana Tanner, James Templeton, Robert Templeton, and Paul Wurst. This is the original fire hall, which was completed in 1896 in a central part of the town's Main Street and business area. The building featured an intricate gable and bell tower. Henry Spaulding was elected fire chief and Dana Tanner first assistant chief. The first floor of this building is now home to the Holland Historical Society; the second floor provides a meeting place for the volunteer firemen.

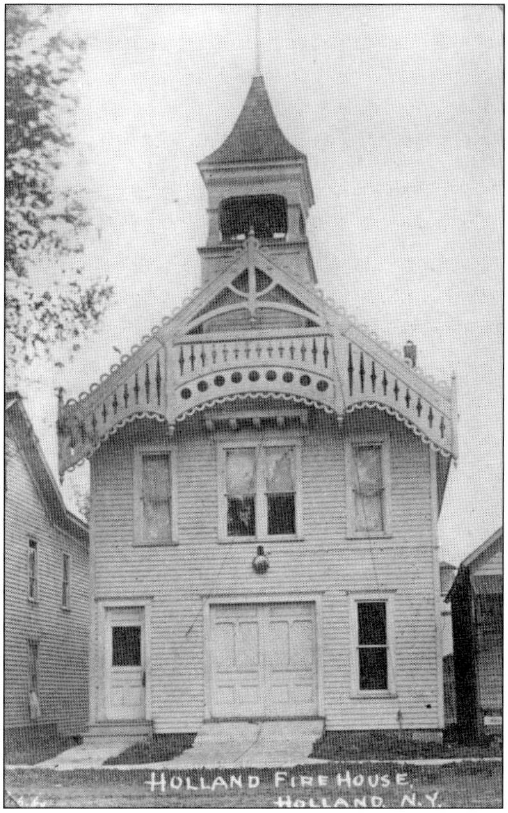

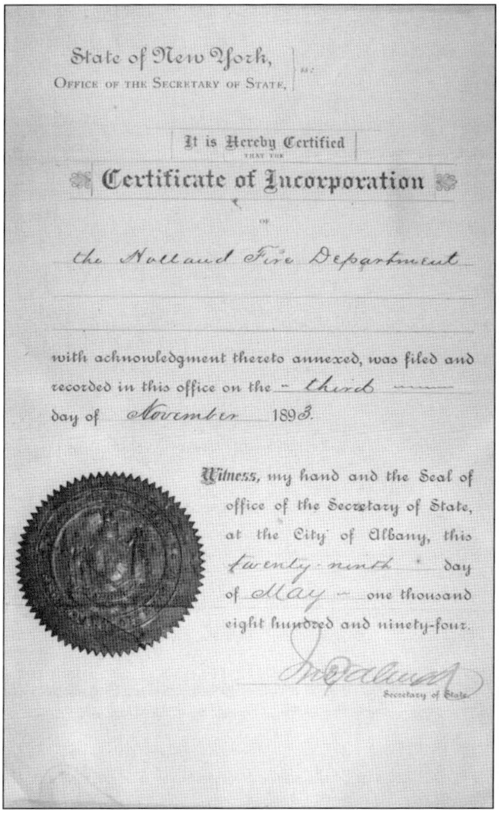
State of New York,
Office of the Secretary of State,

It is Hereby Certified
that the
Certificate of Incorporation
of
the Holland Fire Department

with acknowledgment thereto annexed, was filed and recorded in this office on the - third - day of November 1893.

Witness, my hand and the Seal of office of the Secretary of State, at the City of Albany, this twenty-ninth day of May — one thousand eight hundred and ninety-four.

Secretary of State.

The official certificate of incorporation of the Holland Fire Department was filed and recorded with New York State on November 3, 1893. The fire department was officially chartered on May 29, 1894. It remains a volunteer fire department to this day, serving the Holland community.

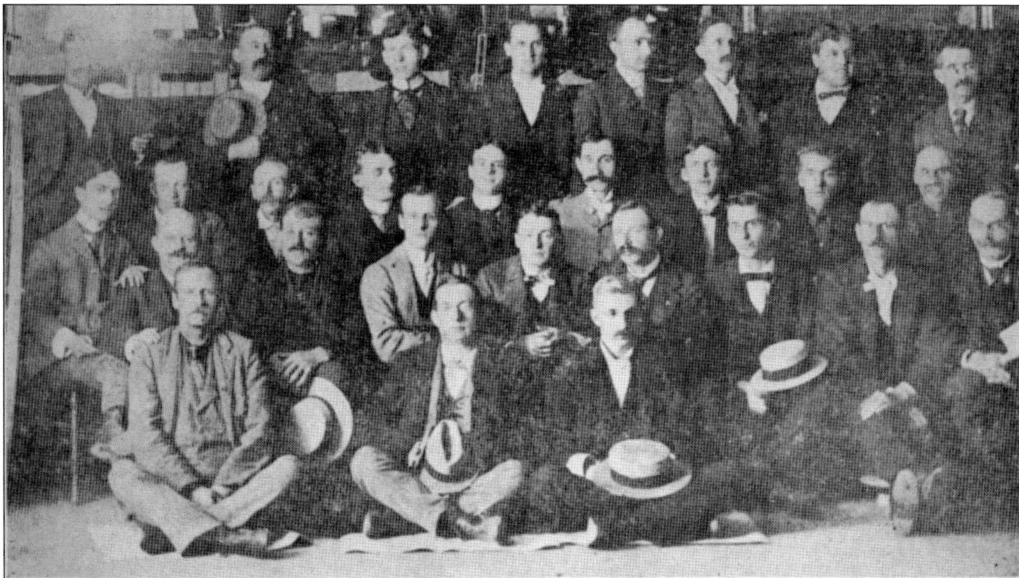

HOLLAND FIRE COMPANY, 1895. Left to right, first row: Henry Spaulding, Dana F. Tanner, George Merill; Second row: John Bolender, Joseph Schlum, William Spaulding, Philip Riley, Lawrence Button, Robert Templeton, Henry Miller, ——; Third Row: Albert Bangert, Albert Griggs, James Andrews, ——, ——, William Jackson, Florest Fuller, ——; Fourth Row: Herbert Bucknam, ——, ——, ——, Paul Wurst, Charles Sill, George Keller, Wesley Bucknam. Compliments of Ross E. Brown.

This picture taken in 1895 shows the original members of the Holland Fire Department.

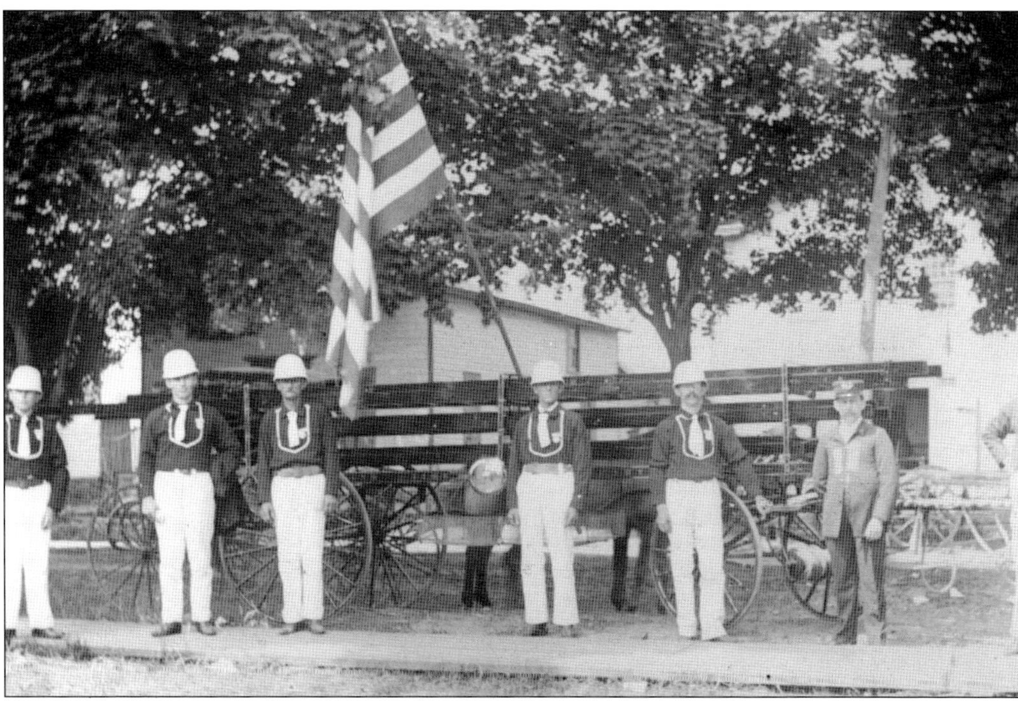

Shown in front of their hook and ladder truck are the original fire department officers in their new uniforms. From left to right are Dana Tanner (assistant chief), Robert Templeton (treasurer), Henry Spaulding (fire chief), Albert Griggs (hook and ladder crew), Lawrence Button (pipe man), and James Andrews (fireman).

An invitation to the fire department's second annual ball (1895) is shown here. These dances were most likely the social event of the year in Holland, drawing entertainment from Rehorn's Band of Buffalo. During these and other dances, the firemen would place a plank from the upper fire hall window to an upper window of the hotel next door and walk back and forth between the buildings.

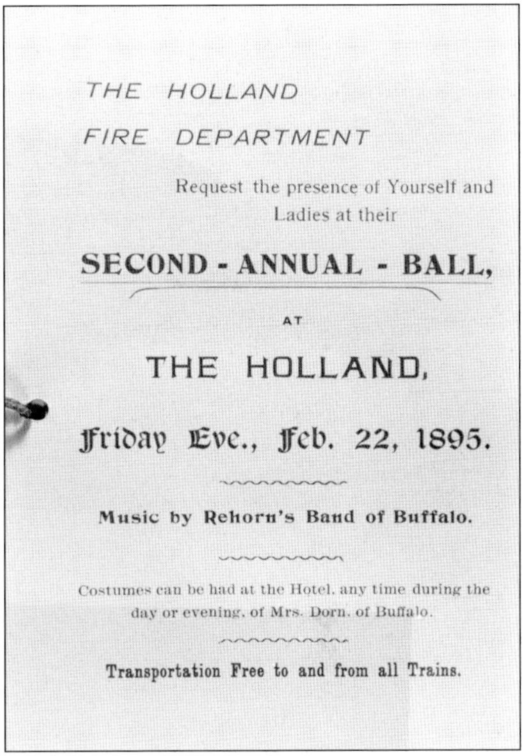

THE HOLLAND
FIRE DEPARTMENT

Request the presence of Yourself and Ladies at their

SECOND - ANNUAL - BALL,

AT

THE HOLLAND,

Friday Eve., Feb. 22, 1895.

Music by Rehorn's Band of Buffalo.

Costumes can be had at the Hotel, any time during the day or evening, of Mrs. Dorn, of Buffalo.

Transportation Free to and from all Trains.

An early group of Holland firemen are pictured in their original uniforms around 1894.

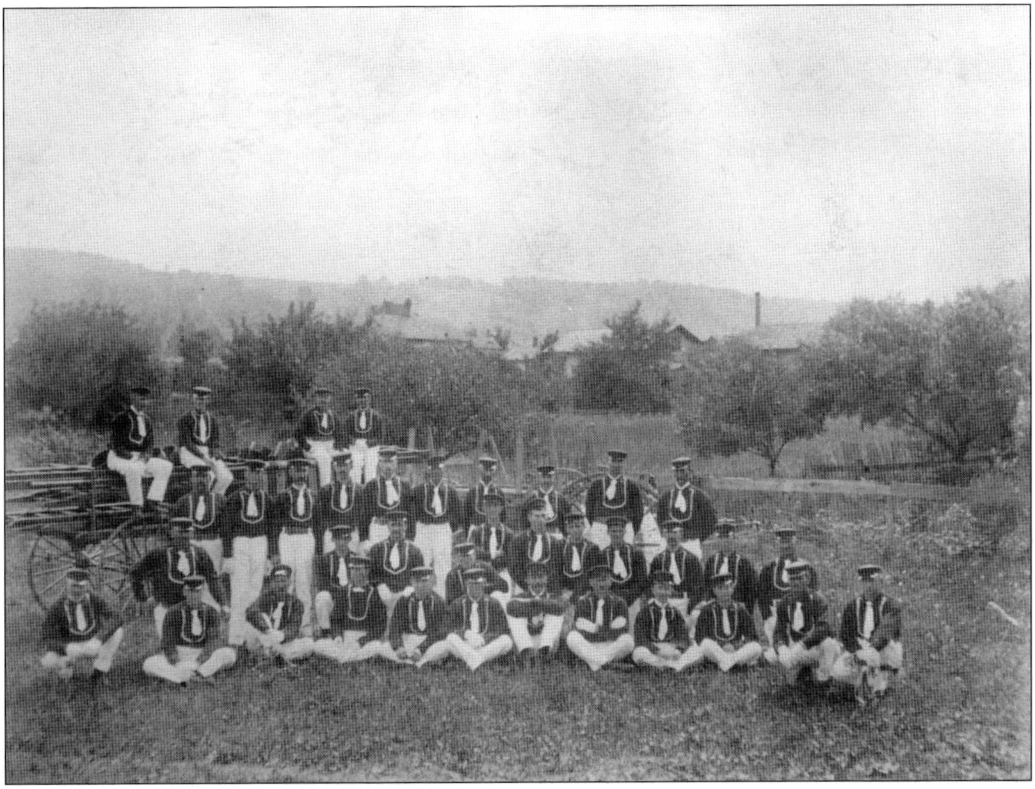

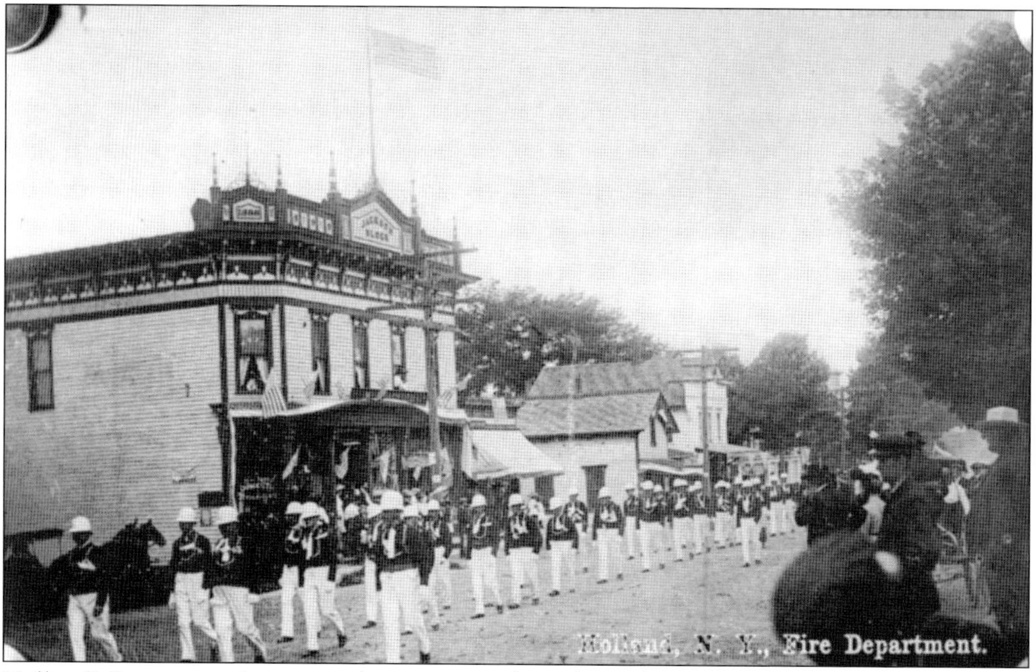

Holland's firemen are shown marching in a parade in the early 1900s. This photograph was taken as they passed the Jackson Block at the corner of Main and Mill Streets (now Capitol Heights).

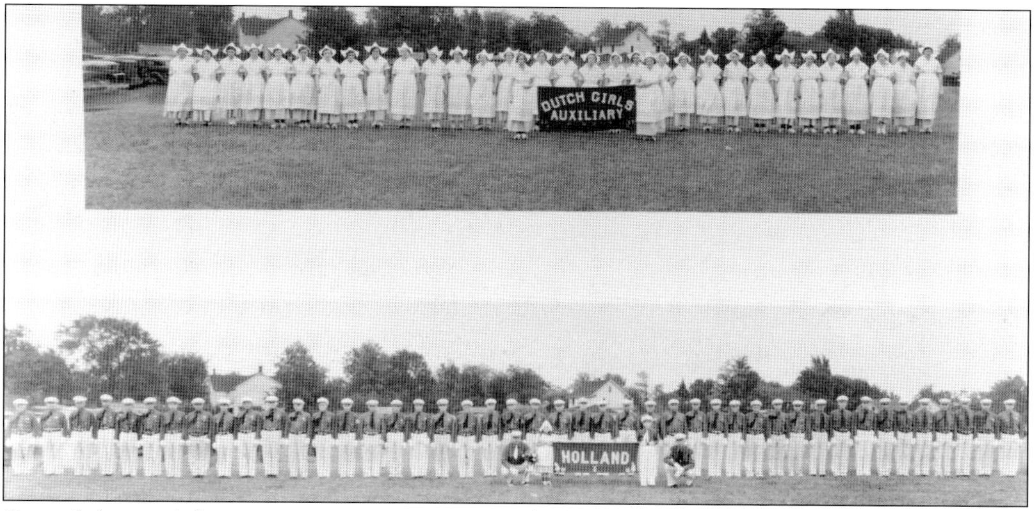

One of the area's best-appearing, prize-winning drill teams was organized by the Holland Fire Department. The parade unit of about 50 members, under the command of drillmaster Minor Miller, was organized around 1928. The department also formed a "Dutch Girls Auxiliary;" nearly 40 women, dressed in Dutch costumes complete with wooden shoes, shared the parade honors. One of the many highlights took place in the mid-1930s, when they took first prize at Hamburg Fair's Firemen's Parade. The units appeared in at least 30 parades each year.

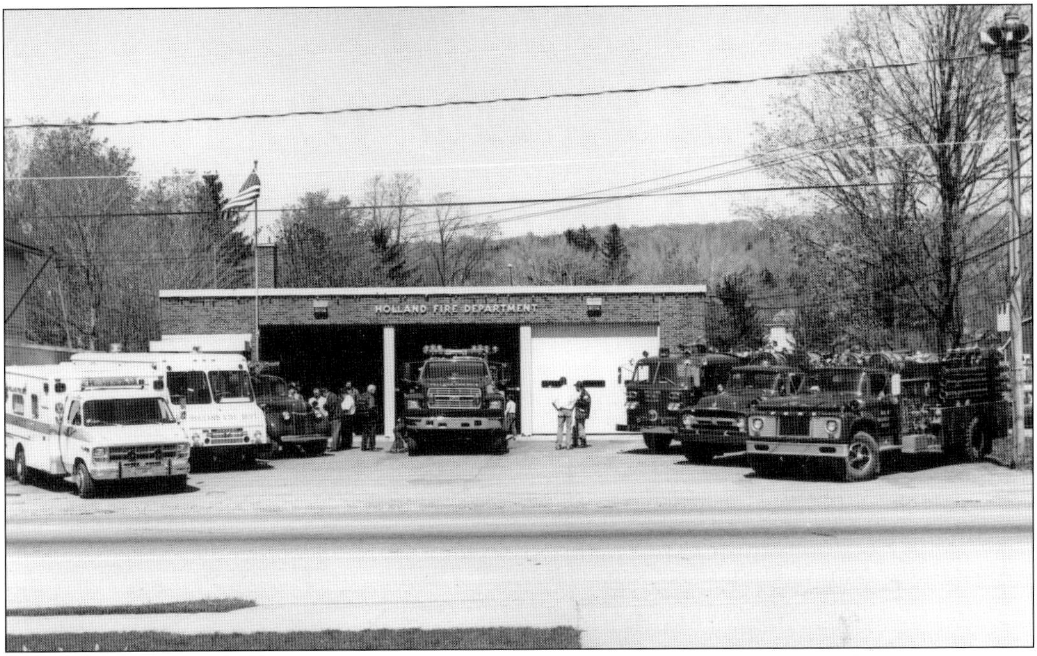

Holland's need for a new fire hall became evident in the early 1970s. A new fire station was built on Main Street next door to the original fire hall in 1974. This 1987 photograph shows the new fire station and its rescue vehicles. An additional fire station was built in 1996 on Hunters Creek Road.

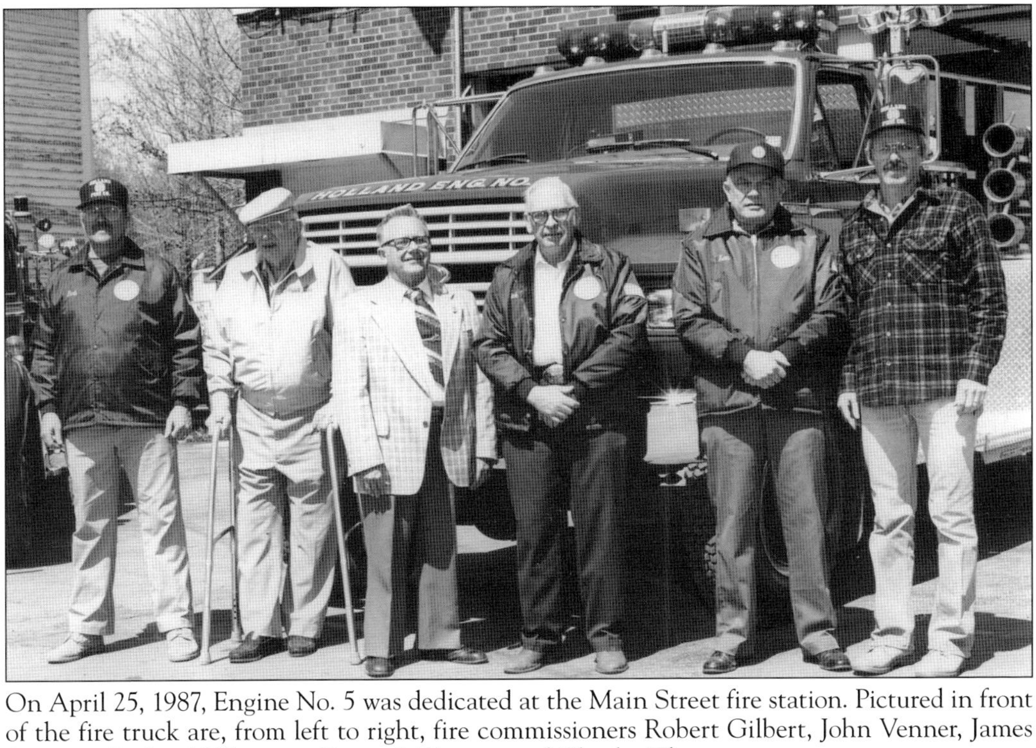

On April 25, 1987, Engine No. 5 was dedicated at the Main Street fire station. Pictured in front of the fire truck are, from left to right, fire commissioners Robert Gilbert, John Venner, James Rossette, Richard Wheaton, Kenneth Tanner, and Charles Thum.

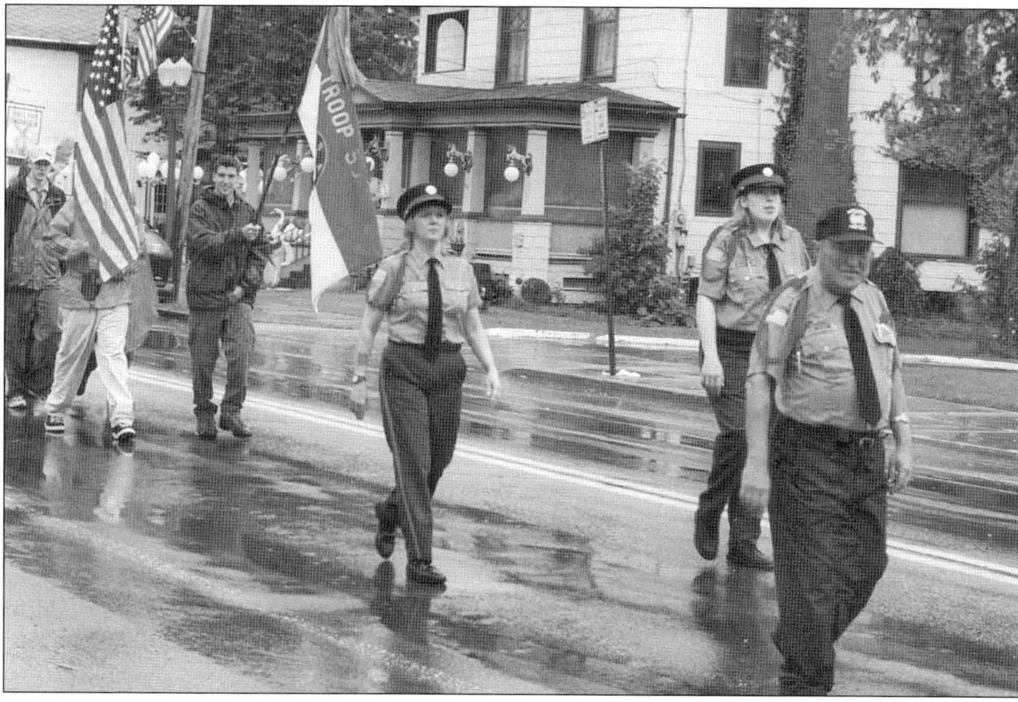

James "Jim" Jackson is shown leading Holland's Memorial Day Parade in 2001. Jim was a town favorite and participated in every local activity, whether school, Kiwanis, or fire company.

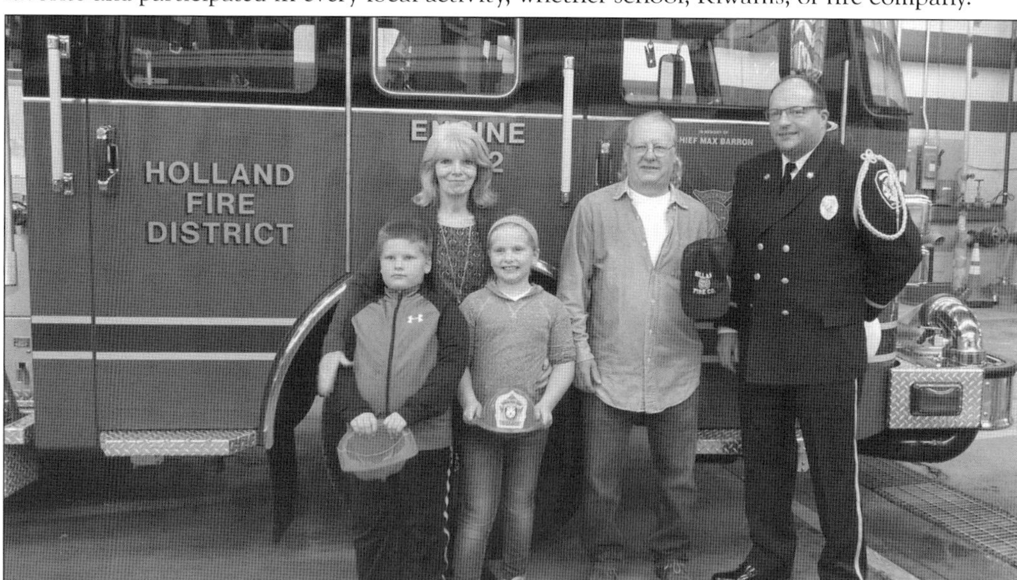

Members of the Holland Fire Department dedicated their new truck, Engine No. 2, on October 9, 2016, in memory of longtime member and past fire chief Max Barron. Barron joined the fire department in 1950, and during his many decades of service, he gave not only his time and talents but his knowledge and experience, too. Pictured from left to right are Tristan and Riana Barron, great-grandchildren of the late Max Barron; Max's daughter-in-law and son, Claudia and Jerry Barron; and fire chief Geoff Hack.

Seven

Religious Life

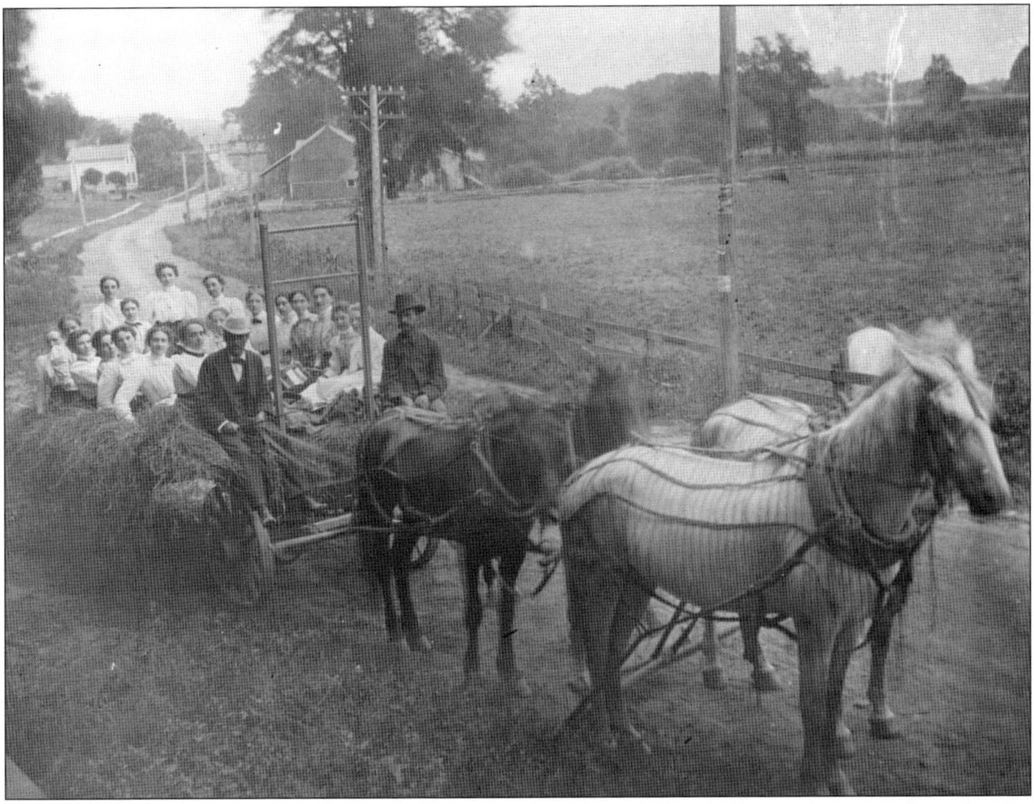

Churches were often the social center of the community. The back of this photograph reads "On their way to a Sunday school picnic." This country hayride appears to have taken place sometime between 1900 and 1915. Note the fly nets on the lead team of white horses. They were made of rawhide strips to help keep the bugs away.

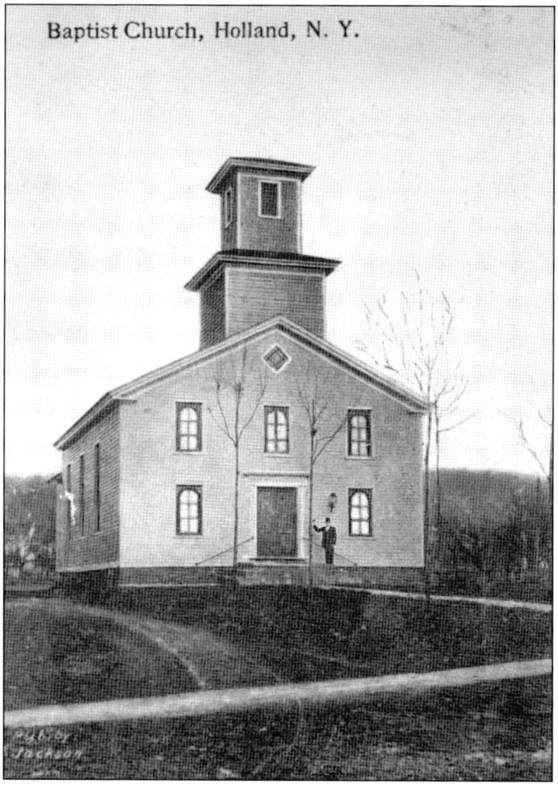

Organized in 1829, the Baptist church was the first church established in Holland. Rev. Elias Harman served as moderator and Lyman Clark as clerk for the 26 members of this church. The building was completed in 1844 and also served the community as a meeting hall. It hosted graduation ceremonies, guest speakers, and community gatherings. For approximately 16 years, the Baptist church was the only church in Holland.

A large crowd gathers for a photograph in front of the Baptist church on Main Street. The anchor on the building reads "Welcome," most likely for an important speaker. Many of the women are wearing blouses featuring leg-of-mutton sleeves, dating this picture to the 1890s.

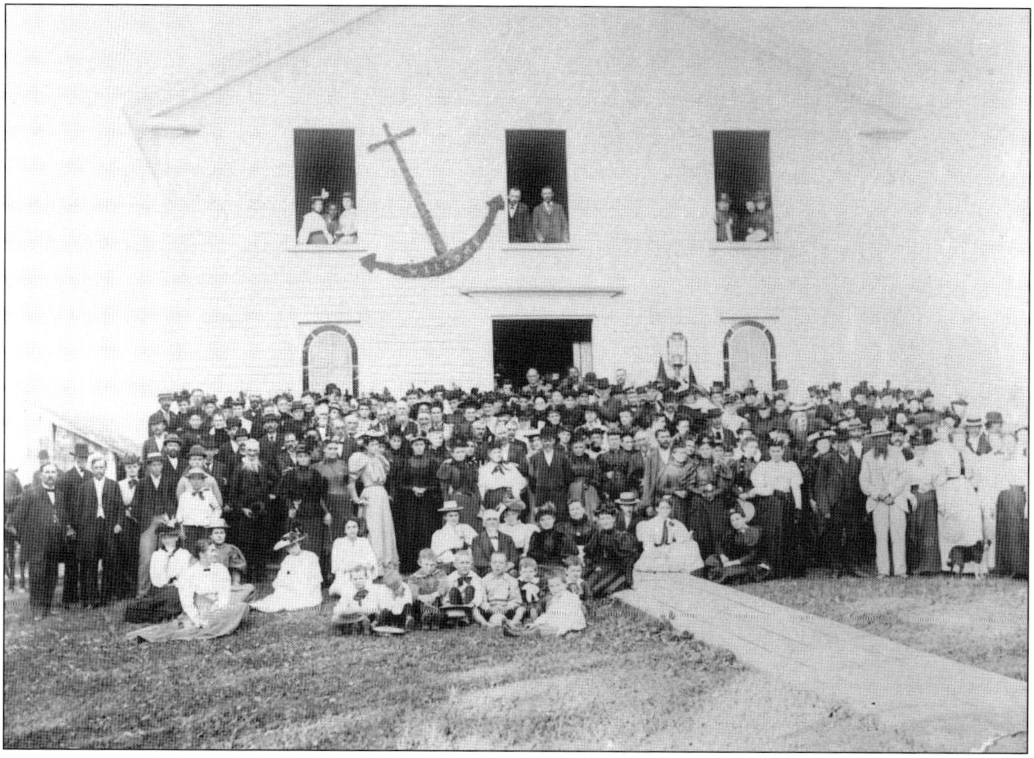

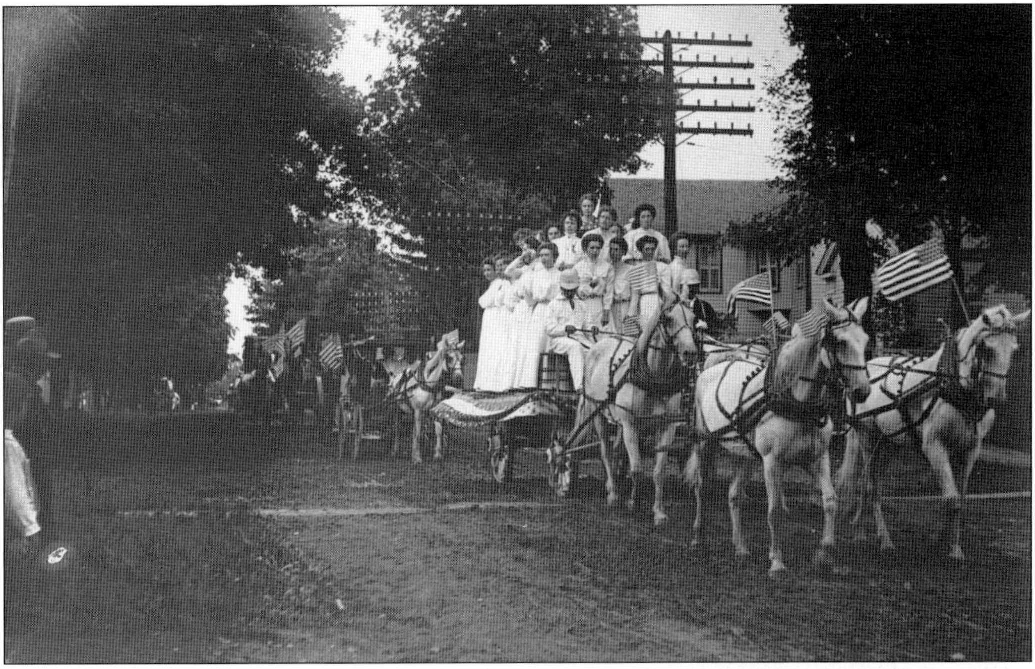

Pictured is the Baptist church float that took part in the Calithumpian Parade. Old Home Day, a fundraiser for the Baptist Church Repair Fund, was held on Saturday, July 24, 1909.

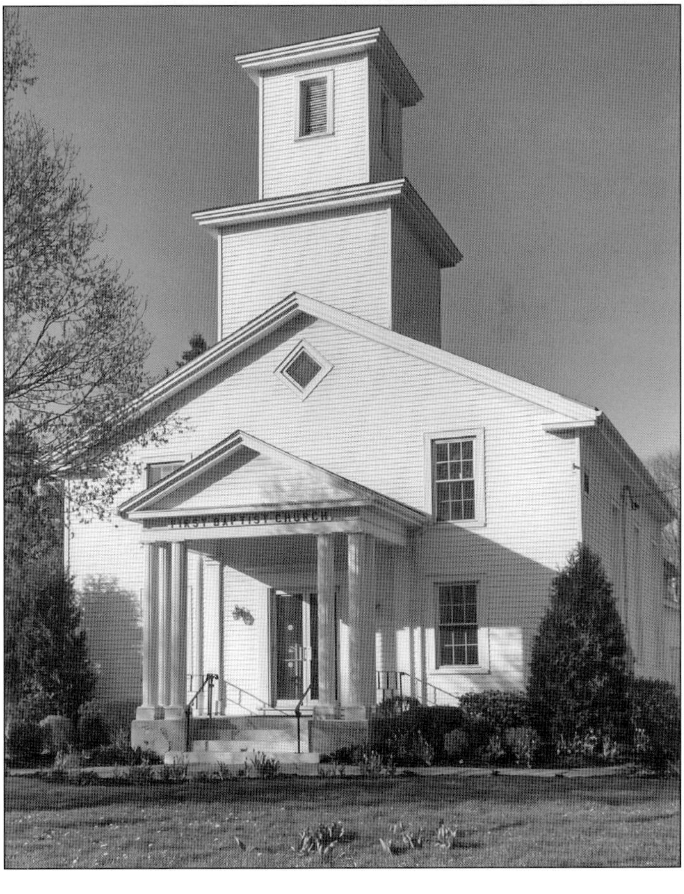

The Baptist church is one of the few original churches in town still utilized by its congregation. Improvements to the original structure were made in 1872, and a parsonage was added in 1876. A pipe organ was installed in 1928, followed by a recital given by Prof. William Gomph of Buffalo; the entry fee was 50¢. Pictured is the church as it looked in recent years.

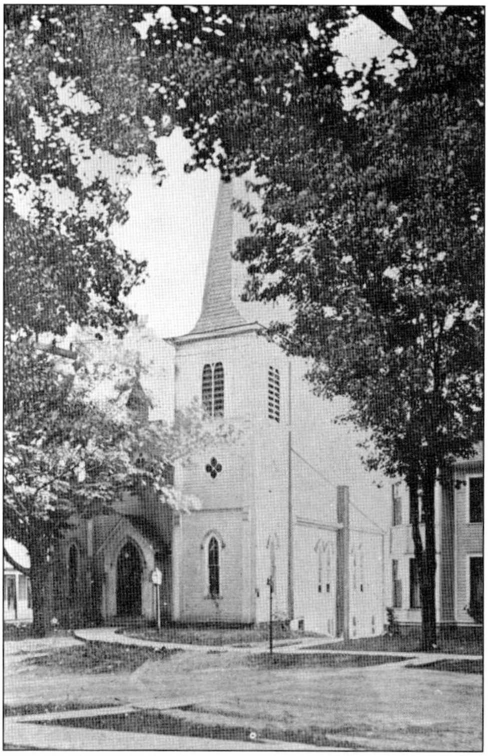

Incorporated in 1830, Holland's Methodist Episcopal congregation met in various settings, including the District No. 11 schoolhouse, the Baptist church, and the Charles Orr residence. In 1871, a handsome Gothic church edifice was erected at 51 South Main Street on land donated by Alvin Orr. The new church cost about $4,000. It was dedicated by Bishop Jesse T. Peck on February 7, 1872. A parsonage was added in 1895 on land donated by Jacob Wurst.

This is the Methodist church prior to being used as Holland's Boys and Girls Club. The original, taller steeple was damaged by lightning and replaced with a shorter steeple. The Boys and Girls Club purchased the property in 1972.

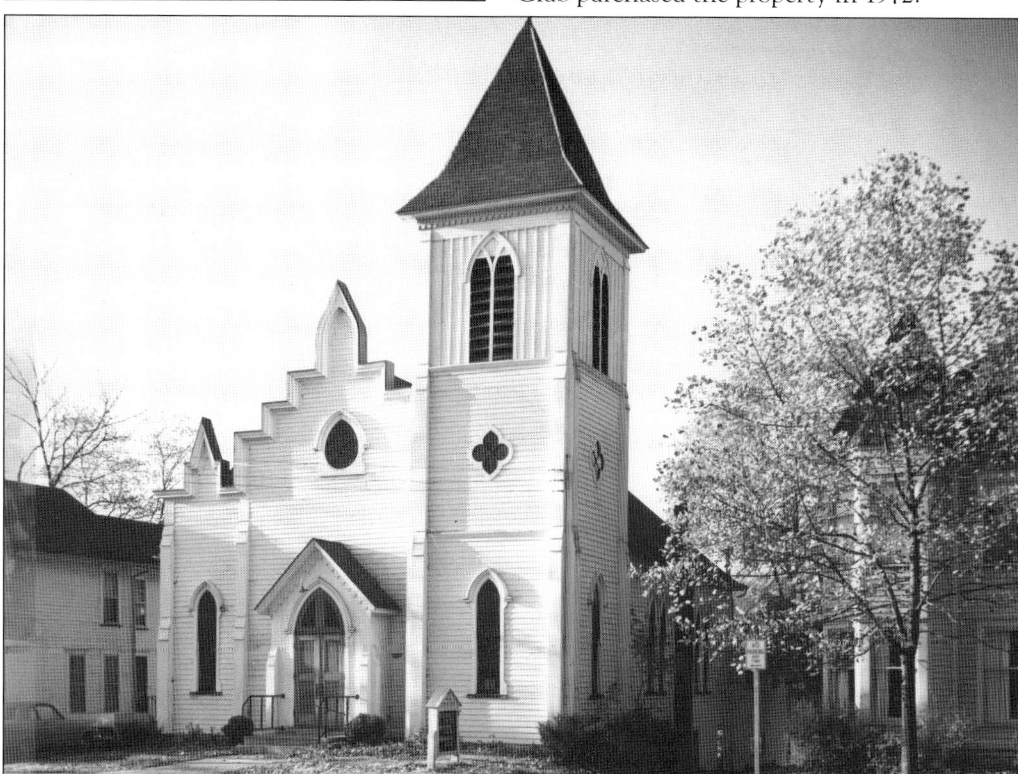

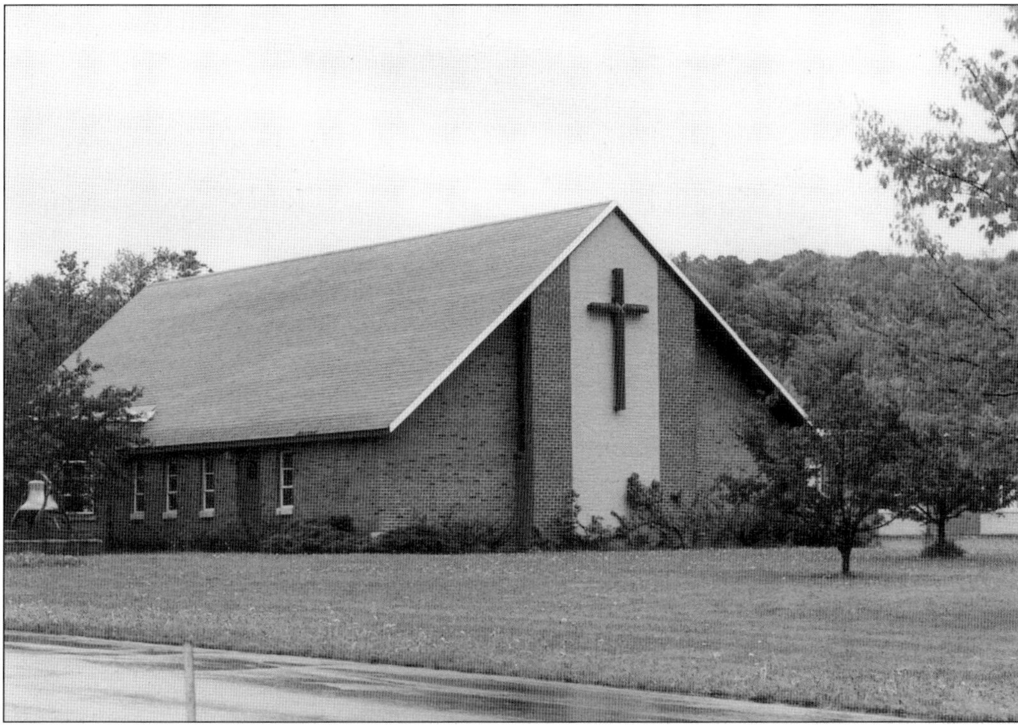

As membership continued to grow, a new Methodist church was built at 11699 Partridge Road. Madeline Roth donated the land in 1966. The first service in the new church was held on March 5, 1971; Rev. William Bailey officiated.

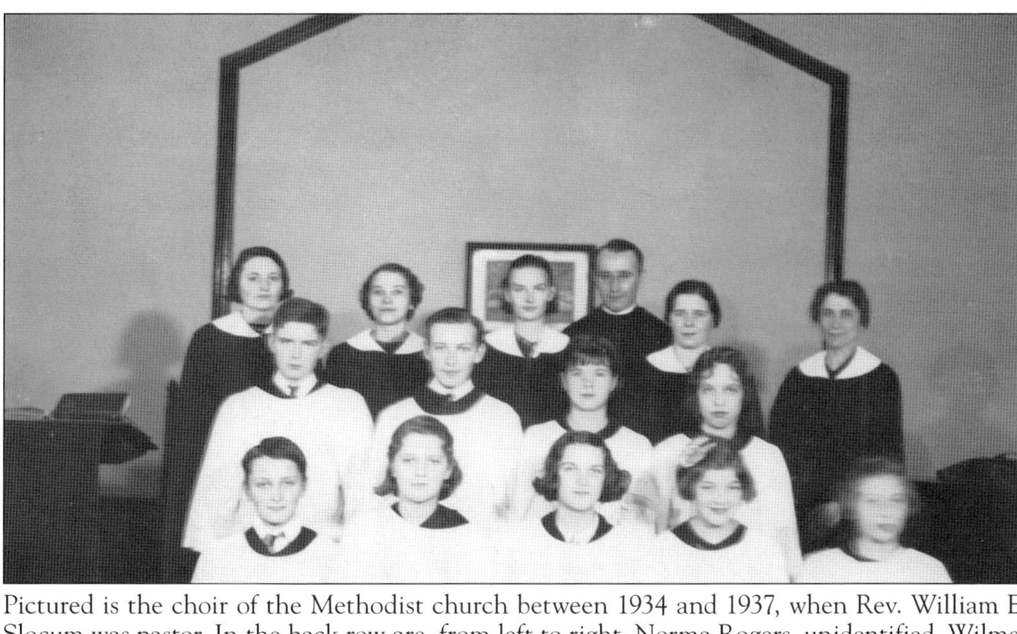

Pictured is the choir of the Methodist church between 1934 and 1937, when Rev. William E. Slocum was pastor. In the back row are, from left to right, Norma Rogers, unidentified, Wilmet Newton Liddle, Reverend Slocum, Bernice Savage Guenther, and L. Grace Slocum. The first and second rows are unidentified.

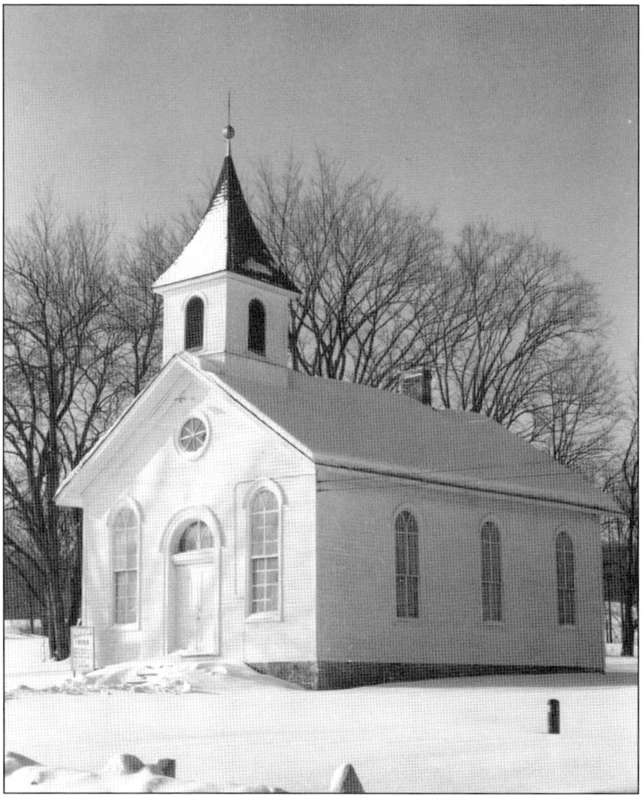

Hunters Creek Bible Baptist Church, at the corner of Hunters Creek Road and Church Street, was dedicated on August 24, 1867. The church was built in response to the need for a place of worship to accommodate the large number of German Baptists who settled in that area. Services were offered in German until the 1920s. This picture dates from the 1950s.

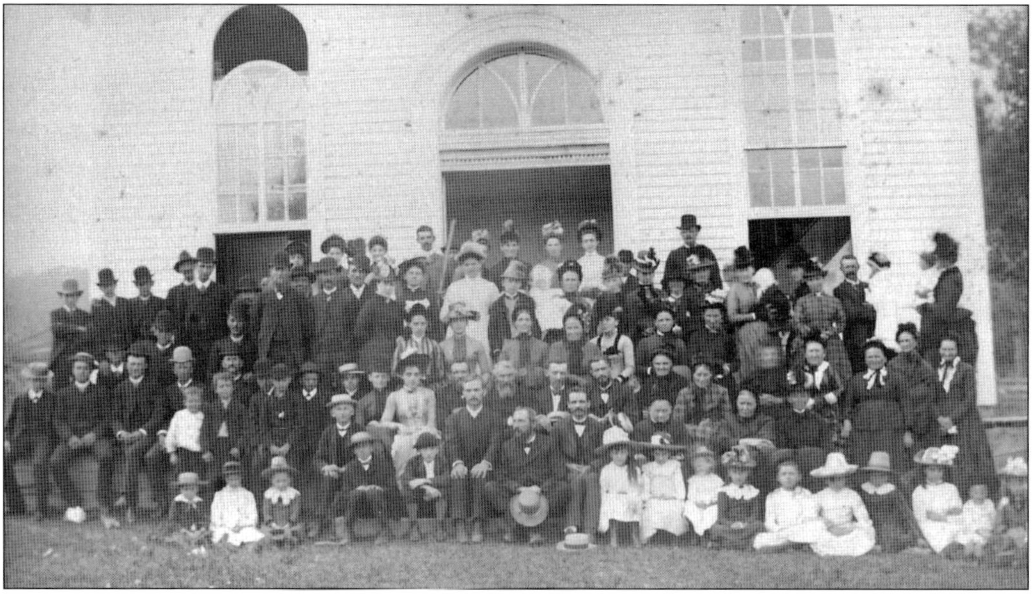

Dressed in their Sunday best, families gather in front of the Hunters Creek Bible Baptist Church in 1882. These people had originally worshiped in a small house on Philip Fisher's land on Fish Hill Road in the Town of Wales. John and Julian Sleeper deeded a three-quarter-acre lot to the First Society of the German Baptist Church (as it was originally named) when the need for a larger building became evident. (Courtesy of Hunters Creek Bible Baptist Church.)

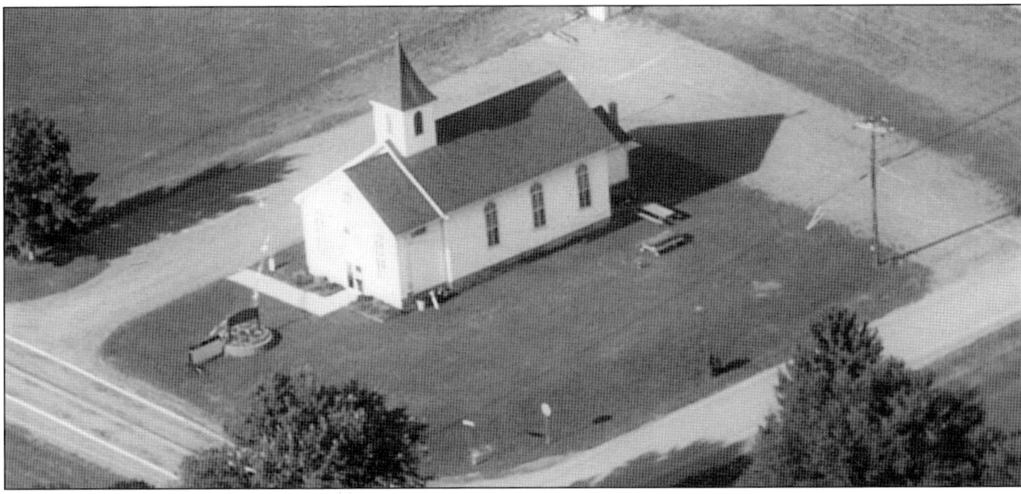

The Hunters Creek Bible Baptist Church celebrated its 150-year anniversary in 2017. It is still located at 7184 Hunters Creek Road. (Courtesy of Hunters Creek Bible Baptist Church.)

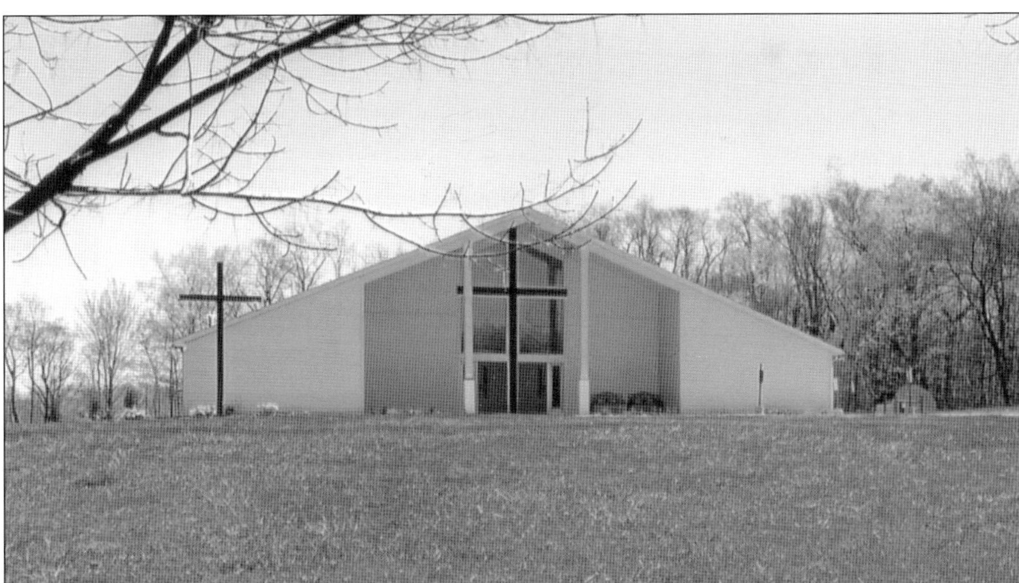

The first Sunday morning worship service for Covenant Community Church was held on January 10, 1993, with Pastor Mark Hill officiating. This ministry started out with six families who wanted to form a vibrant church in Holland. For the first six years, services were held at the former Boys and Girls Club on South Main Street. Construction for a permanent church began in 1999 at 10039 Savage Road. The name of the church was changed to Hope on the Hill in 2014.

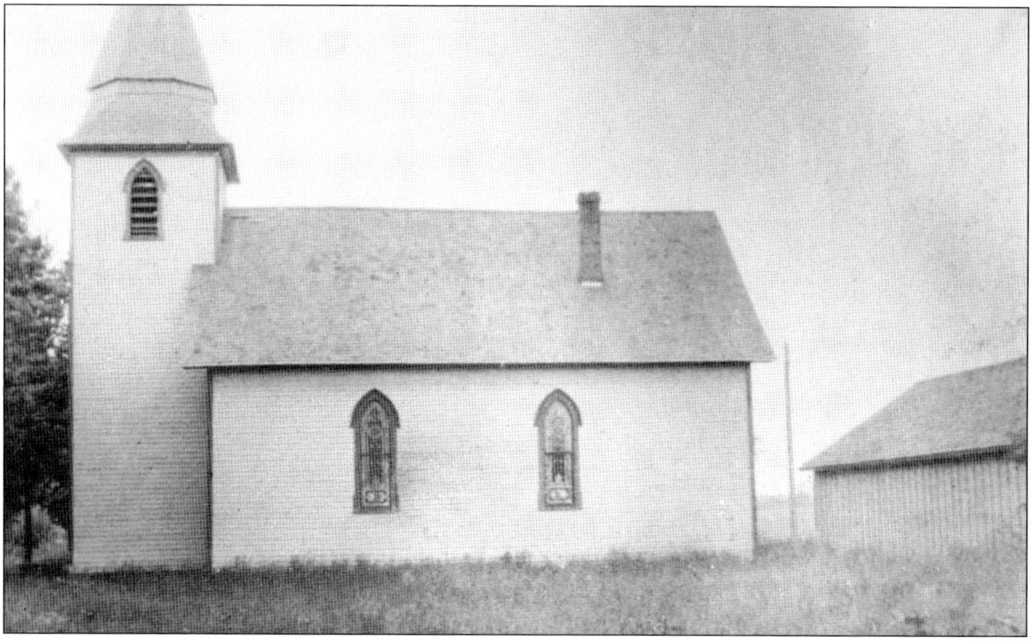

In 1884, St. Joseph's Roman Catholic Church, a mission church, was constructed on the corner of Park and Garfield Streets (73 Park Street). The church was destroyed by fire on October 24, 1918. For the next six years, the parish held services in the Putnam Hotel (the current site of Holland Hotel).

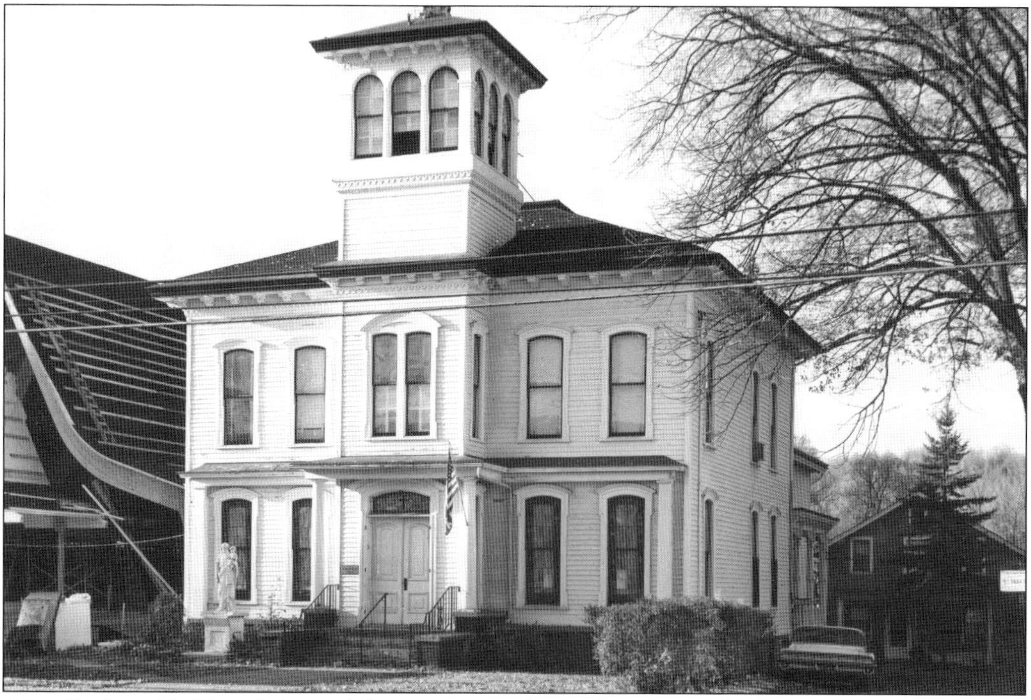

After St. Joseph's Church burned down in 1918, the Dickerman-Zaph residence (46 North Main Street) was purchased and converted into a church. No longer a mission church, Masses were now celebrated weekly, with the first being held on October 5, 1924, by Rev. John W. Klimek.

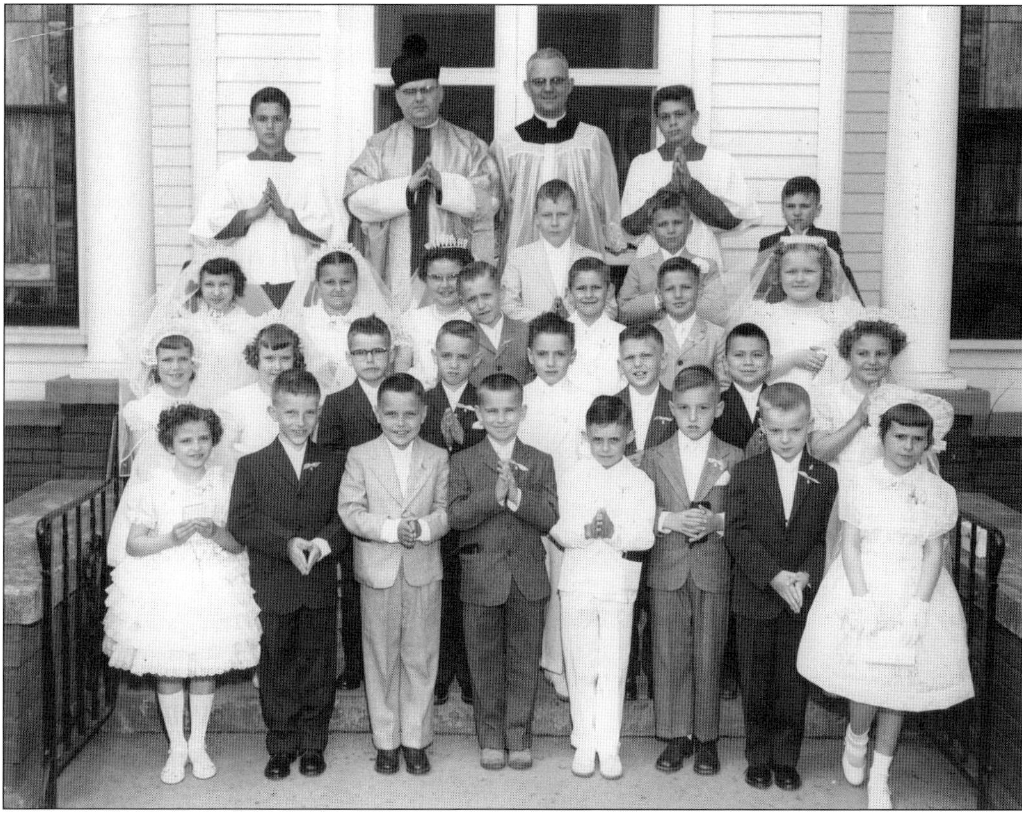

Pictured on the front steps of the old church is a First Communion class from the early 1960s. Rev. William E. Wendzikowski officiated and served as parish priest from 1954 to 1964. His nephew, Rev. Monsignor Mecislaus S. Wendzikowski, was also appointed St. Joseph's parish priest from 1979 to 1999. (Courtesy of Eileen Rickettson.)

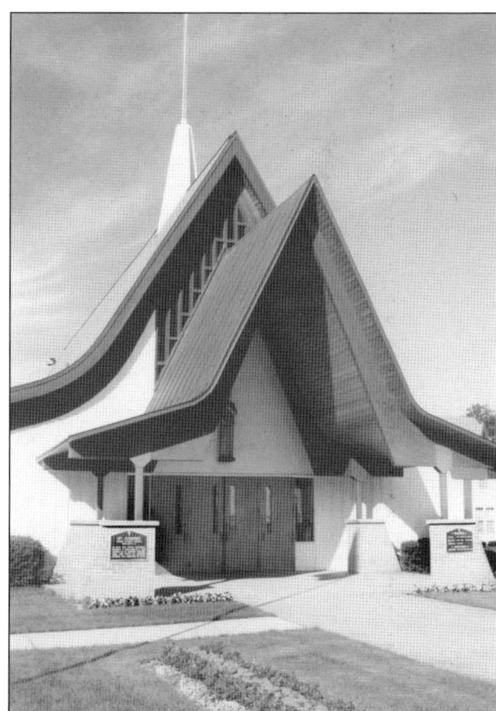

In the 1960s, a building fund was established for a new church to address the needs of St. Joseph's growing parish. Excavation began in May 1966 for the new church, an arm's length from the existing church. The first Mass was celebrated in the new church on May 1, 1967. In 1968, the new rectory was completed and the old church demolished. (Courtesy of St. Joseph's Roman Catholic Church.)

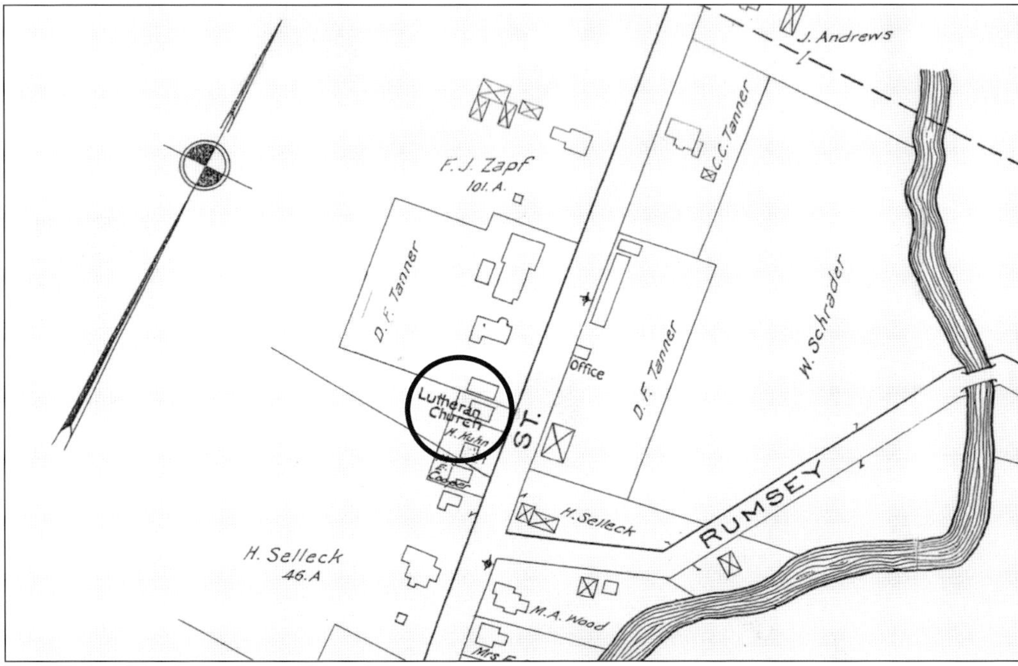

The German Lutheran church was organized in Holland in 1874, and services were conducted in German. The first trustees of the society were Joseph Wolff, George Leonhardt, and John Brodbeck. A house of worship was built the same year. It was on the west side of North Main Street, next to D.F. Tanner's property. The first minister was Rev. E. Reissig, who came from the Kingdom of Saxony. The original church was closed and either torn down or moved to another town in the 1920s or 1930s.

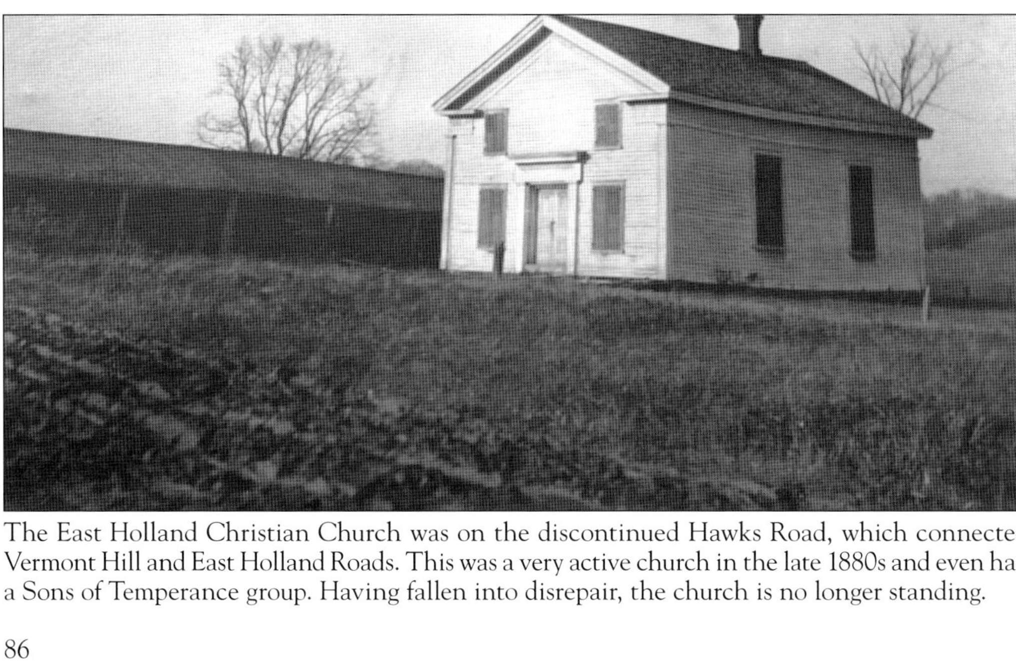

The East Holland Christian Church was on the discontinued Hawks Road, which connected Vermont Hill and East Holland Roads. This was a very active church in the late 1880s and even had a Sons of Temperance group. Having fallen into disrepair, the church is no longer standing.

Eight

Sports and Recreation

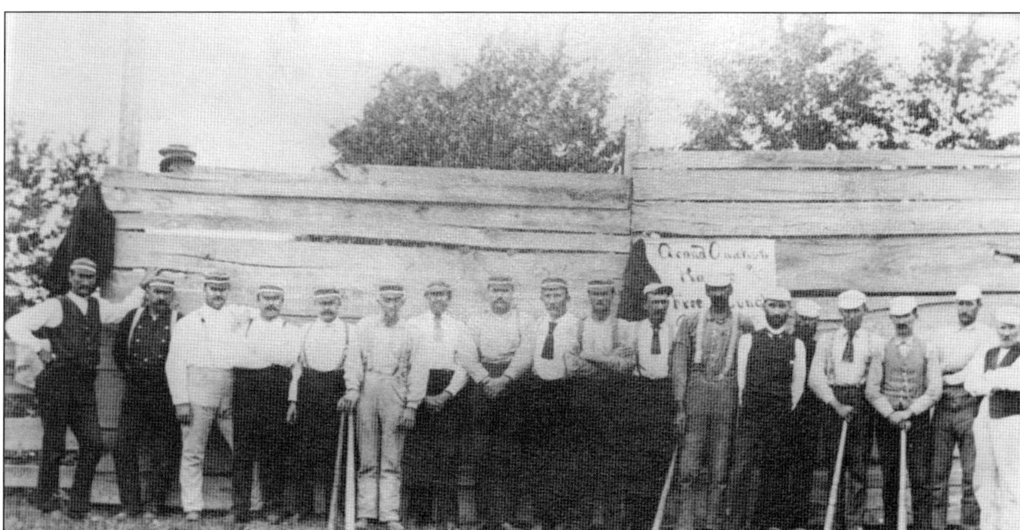

Baseball was always a popular sport in rural townships like Holland. This is the oldest baseball picture found in the town's archives. It is a photograph of the Fats and Leans from the 1888 season. From left to right are Herbert Bucknam, Vonley Orr, Hiram Savage, Albert Challis, John Bolender, Ichabod Griggs, Nathan Allen, David Goodell, John Wagner, Henry Spaulding, A. Forbes (Pennsylvania Railroad station agent), Barrett Hunt, William Jackson, Clark Hill, Joseph Wolfe, Wesley Bucknam, Howard Rosier, and Homer Mowrey Morey.

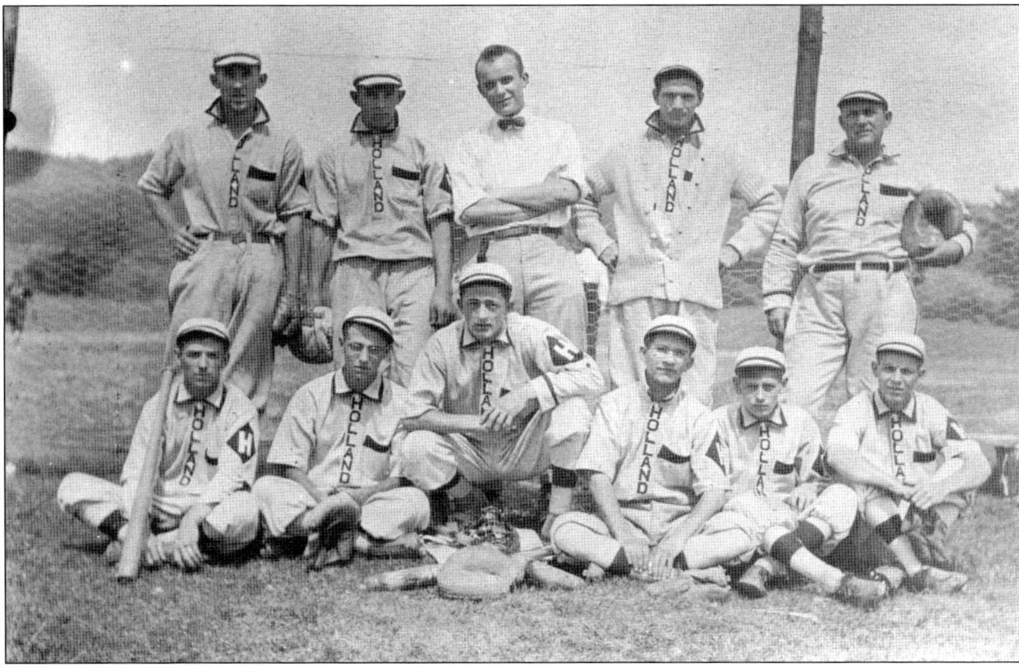

The 1910 Holland baseball team included, in unknown order, Nelson Whitney, Lloyd Whitney, Lavines Cornwall, Gene Dillon, Leslie Cross, Earl Manchester, Fritz Greenwall, Earl Bangert, Perry Eickner, Louis Knowles, and Don Thornton. During a May 1913 ball game, catcher Fritz Greenwall was tragically killed by a ball thrown home from second base.

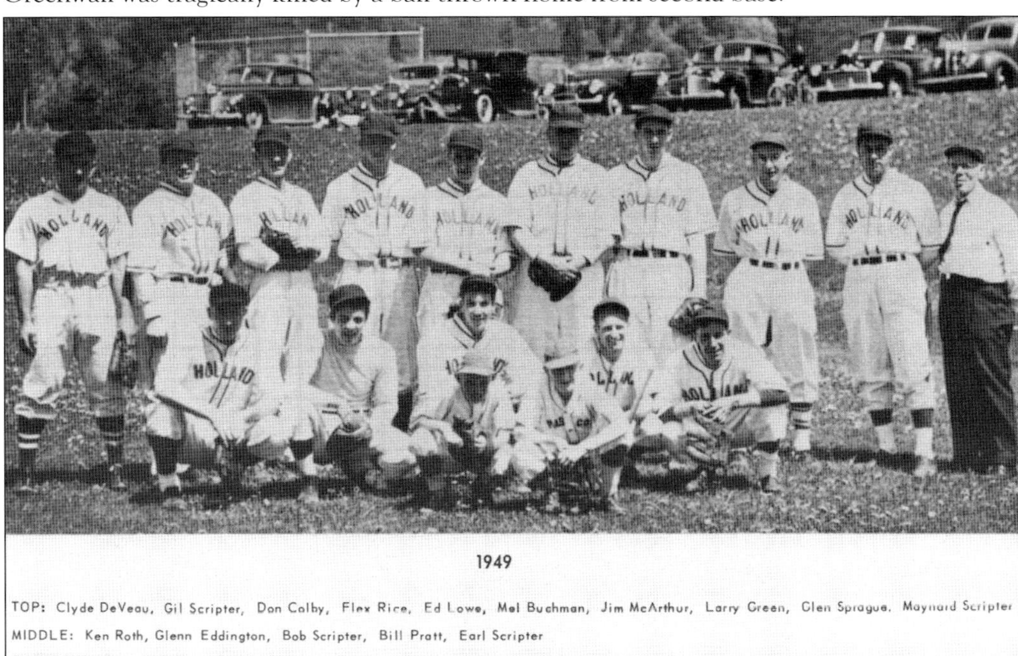

Holland's 1949 town team is pictured here. At this time, games were played on the high school's baseball field. Fans parked their cars in an area above the field and watched the games from the small hillside that surrounded the diamond.

In the 1960s, Holland's town team was a major force, earning the title of Central League champions for the years 1964 to 1968 and again in 1970. Holland was just one of the many teams that participated in the Buffalo News Suburban Baseball League. From left to right are (first row) Glenn Kline (bat boy), Ted Goller, Ross Charles, Donald Wangelin, Gary Haas, Philip Roth, James Joyce, Harry Armond Kline (manager), and Charles Breeser (bat boy); (second row) William Pratt (commissioner), Norman Wangelin, James Higley, Gordon Hessel, Kenneth Major, Daniel Berry, Byron Roth, and Fred Reimers. (Courtesy of Charles Thum.)

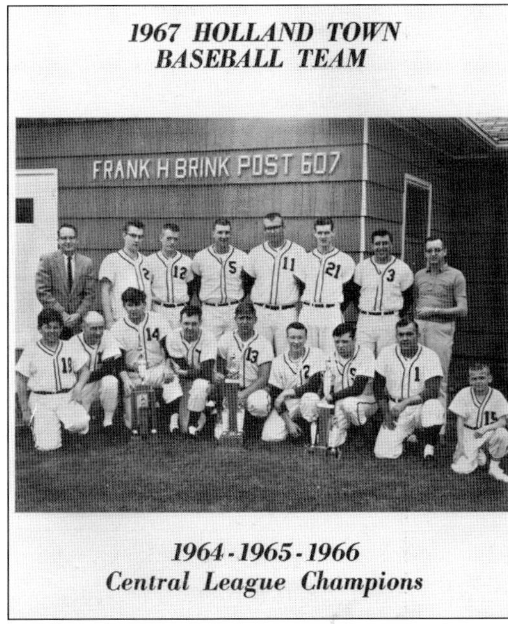

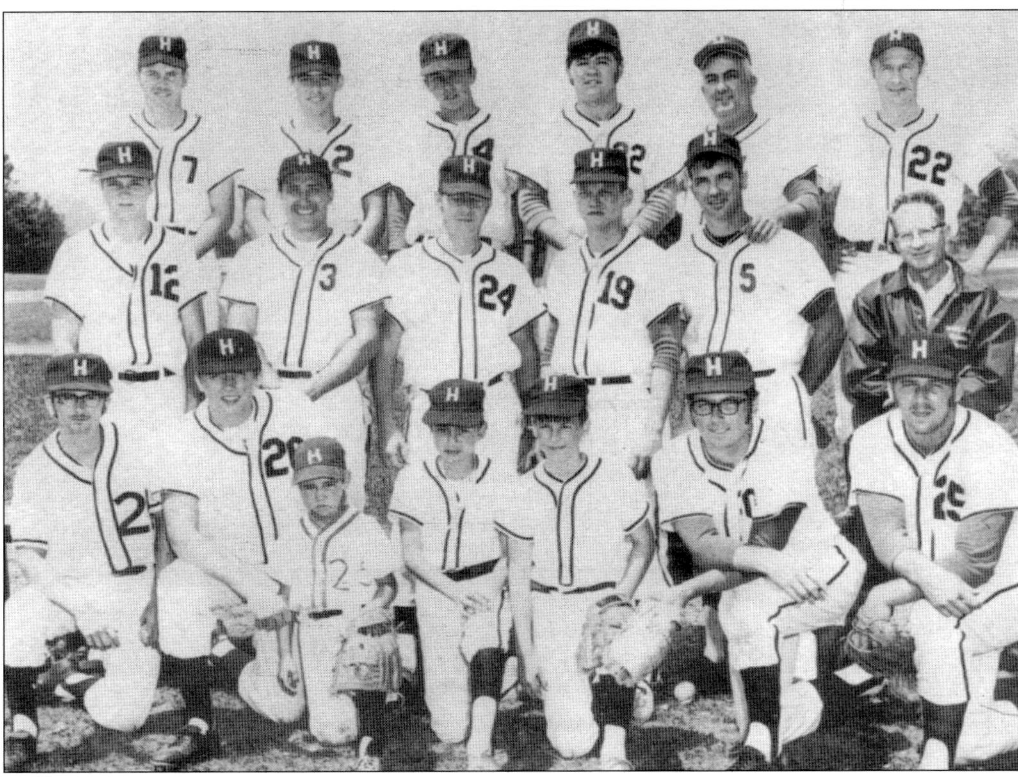

Holland's 1970 championship team is, from left to right, (first row) Merritt Eddy, Daniel Peckham, bat boys Armond Kline, Jerry Helper, David Langendorfer, Charles Thum, and Daniel Copeland; (second row) Glen Ramsey, Byron Roth, Norman Wangelin, James Kramer, Gordon Hessel, and William Pratt (commissioner); (third row) Donald Wangelin, Thomas Polanski, Glenn Kline, Ross Charles, Armond Kline (manager), and Ted Goller. (Courtesy of Charles Thum.)

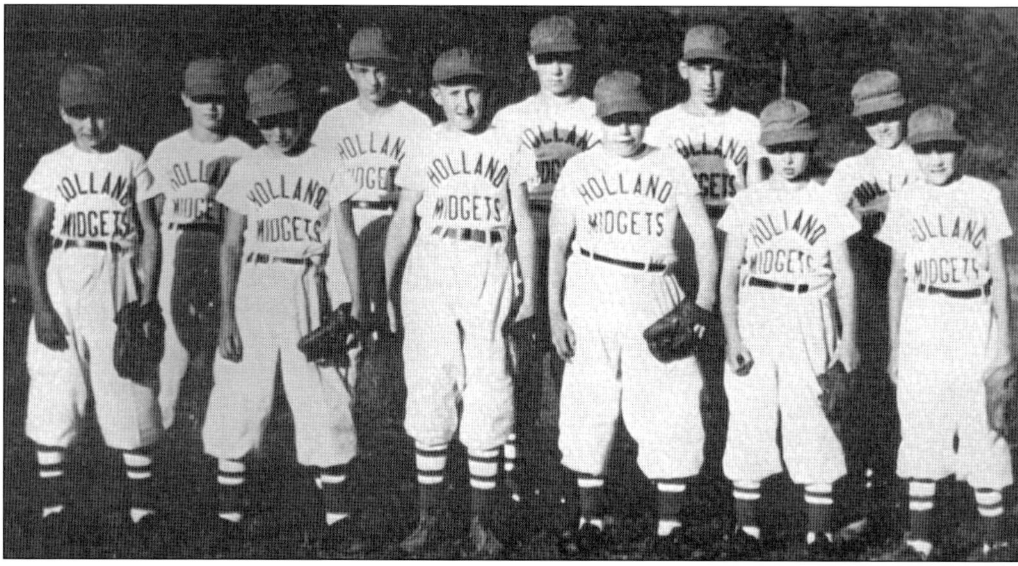

One of Holland's little league teams, the Holland Midgets, is pictured in this team photograph from 1950. (Courtesy of Charles Thum.)

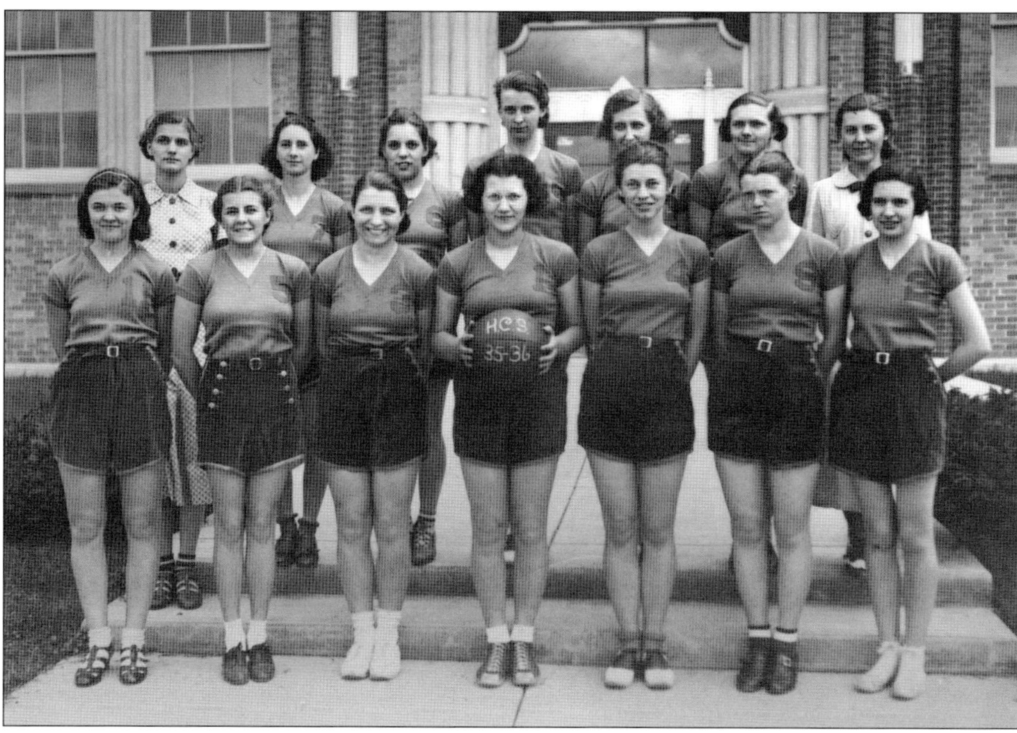

The 1935–1936 Holland High School girls' basketball team is, from left to right, (first row) Dorothy Edington, Hildred Thau, Monnie Roth, Alma Neischel, Eileen Niehus, Esther Becker, and Mary Tanner; (second row) Hazel Sweetapple, June Wheeler, Joan Bancroft, Eleanor Morrell, Kathryn Preston, Kathleen Smith, and Miss Minsker.

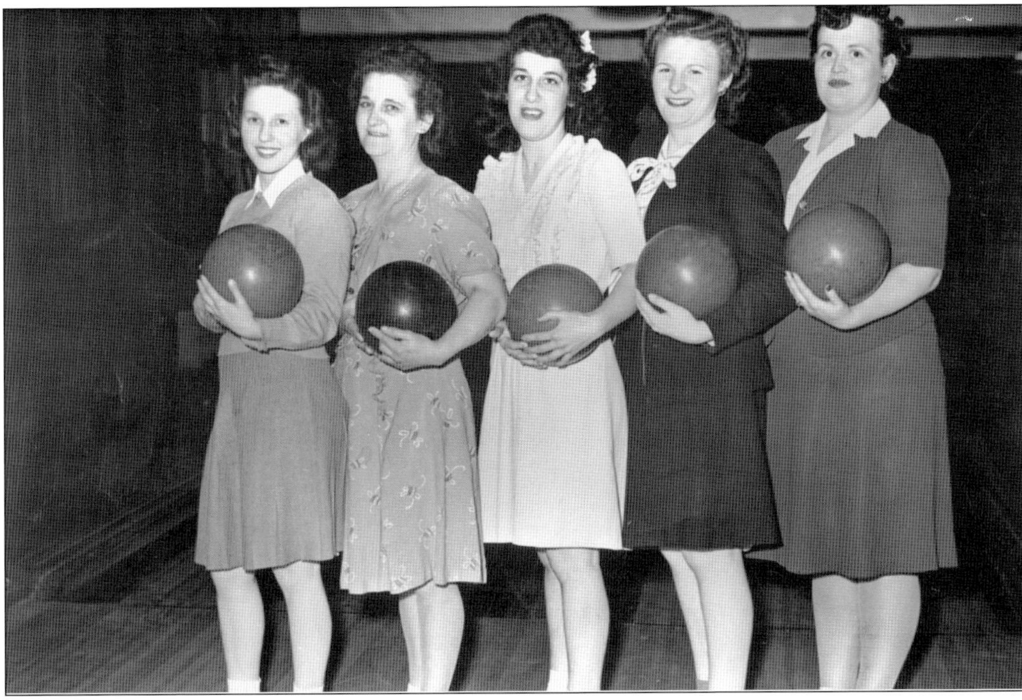

Local bowling alleys provided leagues for this popular pastime. This ladies' team above includes, from left to right, Esther White, Emma Colby, Betty Colby Rehrauer, Doris Welsted Thompson, and Dorothy Koerner Kimball. Members of the men's team below are, from left to right, (crouching) Leland Joyce; (second row) Claude Renfro, LaVern Osgood, Ray Miller, and Gerald Hiller.

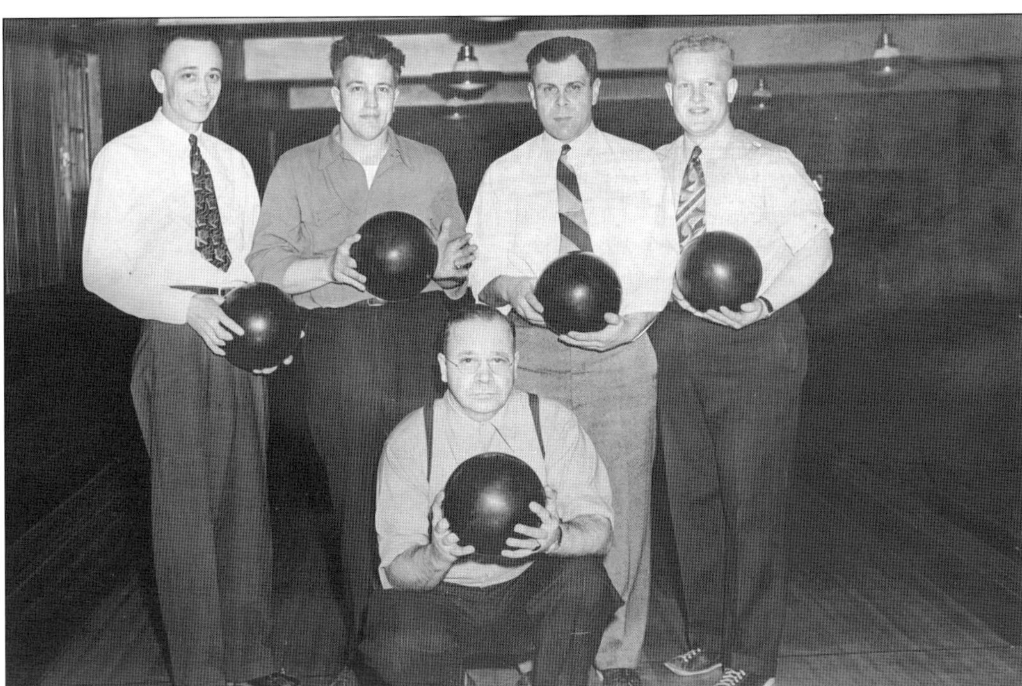

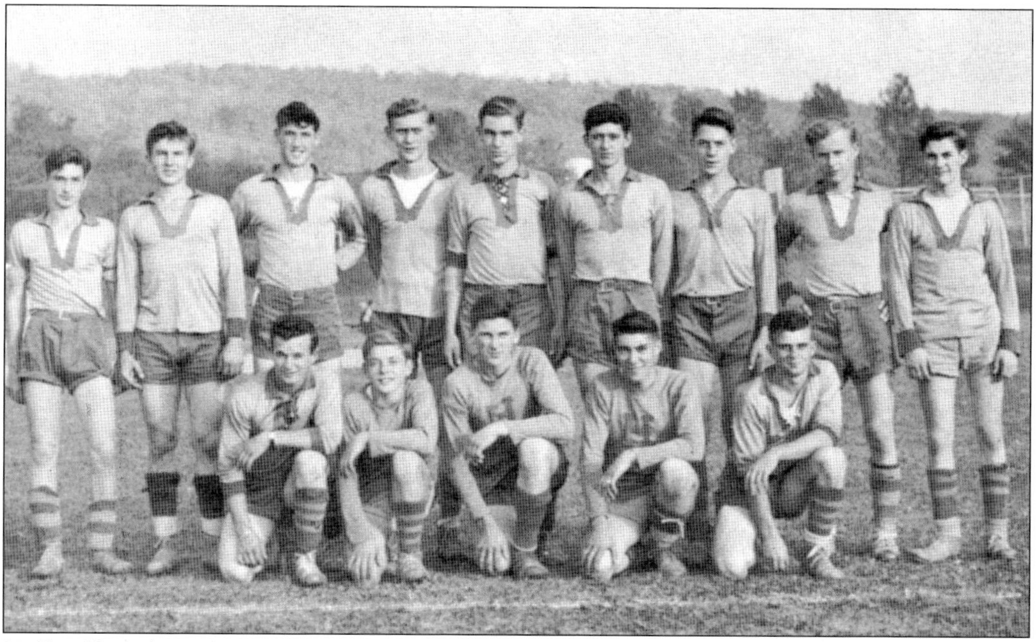

Holland has always been known for its outstanding soccer programs, which was quite a distinction for a small, rural school. Some of the competition included high school teams from North Collins, Woodlawn, Machias, and Deveau Military Academy of Niagara Falls. The 1948 boys' varsity team is, from left to right, (first row) Kenneth Lingenfelter, Donald Heim, Donald Morrell, Colin Gould, and Bud Bohadlo; (second row) Paul Allshouse, Norbert Bakowski, Clifford Rice, Norbert Borowski, Richard Wilkins, William Jones, Donald Austin, Joseph Szulewski, and Raymond Edington.

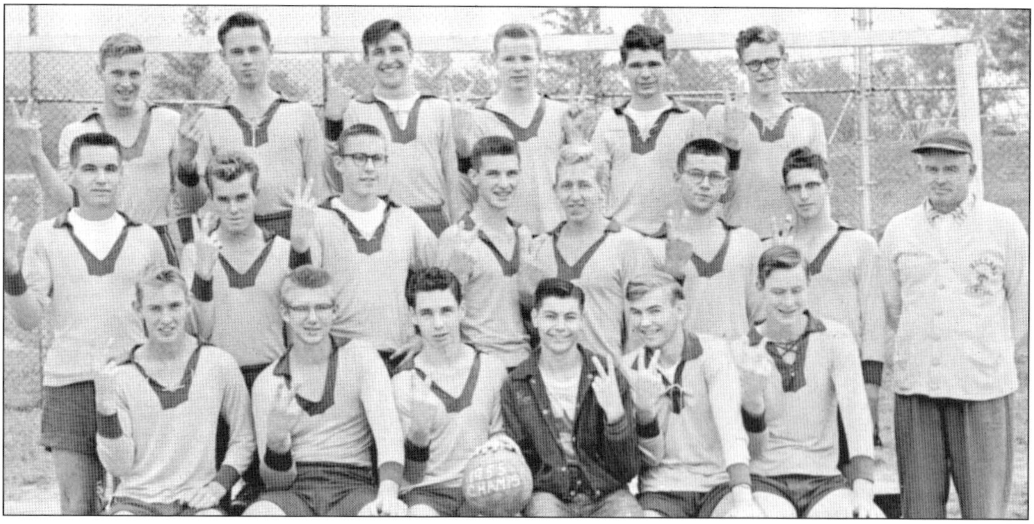

The 1955 high school soccer team captured the Section VI championship for the second consecutive year and finished with an undefeated season. It beat high school teams from Amherst, Frontier, Williamsville, North Collins, and Gow. From left to right are (first row) David MacArthur, Kenneth Major, Edward Lewis, Ronald Rhodes, Kenneth Higley, and David Faries; (second row) Melvin Szarleta, Nelson Merlau, Richard Farrar, Gordon Hessel, Russell Major, Burt Farrant, William Guilmain, and Coach Floyd Peckham; (third row) Ronald Heppner, John Spalis, Byron Roth, William Weaver, Bert Smith, and Robert Reisdorf.

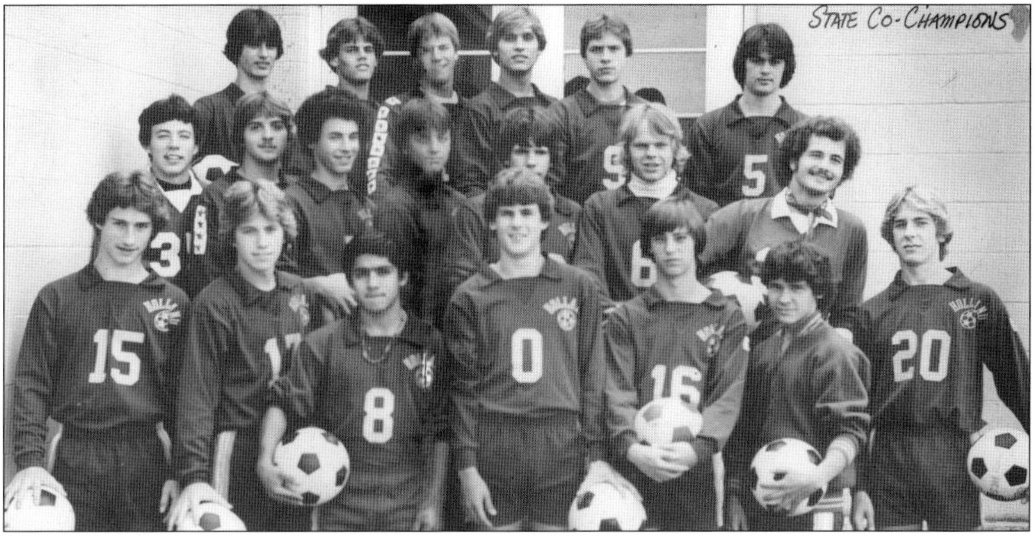

In 1982, Holland Central earned more than a regional win for the boys' soccer team; this was the year it battled for the title of New York State Class C champion. After a hard-fought game, Holland and Mattituck-Cutchogue Union Free School were named co-champions, as neither team could break the 1-1 tie. The team was coached by Russell Wiseman, and Jobie Ramsey scored the only goal for Holland. At the time, this was Holland's lone state title in any sport. Team members are, in alphabetical order, James Buckley, Russ DeLuca, Jeffrey Dix, Joel Fallon, Joseph Fridman, Mark Jauquet, Todd Jones, Matthew Kramer, Brian Leach, Jeffrey Lewis, Robb Lewis, Eric Lynch, Daniel Meacham, Kip Palmateer, Scott Pla, Daniel Rahn, Jobie Ramsey, Michael Raymer, Ismael Renteria, Gregory Schurr, Timothy Schurr, Thomas Schweizer, and Todd Young. (Courtesy of Russell Wiseman.)

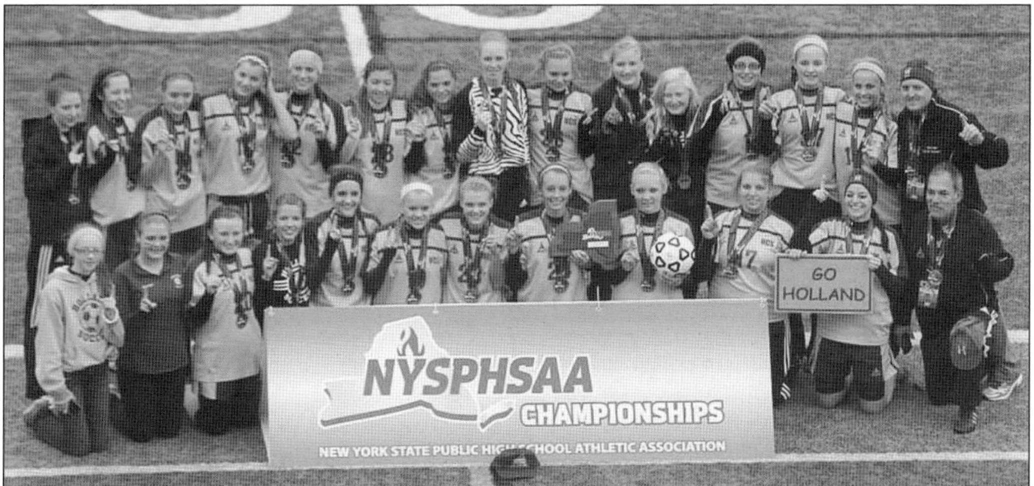

The first New York State championship for Holland Central School's girls' soccer program was in 2013. With a score of 2-1 over Haldane Central School, Holland won the Class C championship. From left to right are (first row) ball girls Caitlyn Caltagirone and Kara Schmidt, Jana Pagano, Laura Schiltz, Julia Grupp, Molly Zientek, Olivia Schmidt, Samantha Maloy, Chelsea Grupp, Shania Hacker, Angela Pagano, and coach Craig Fredette; (second row) Micheala Jones, Alicia Massara, Megan Caltagirone, Jenna Lewis, Kristin Heitzhaus, Cameron Wangelin, Gillian Wangelin, Haley Hymers, Melissa Trawinski, Elizabeth George, Melissa Nuedeck, Junna Jewell, Cassidy Slocum, MacKenzie Maier, and coach George Schmidt. (Courtesy of George Schmidt.)

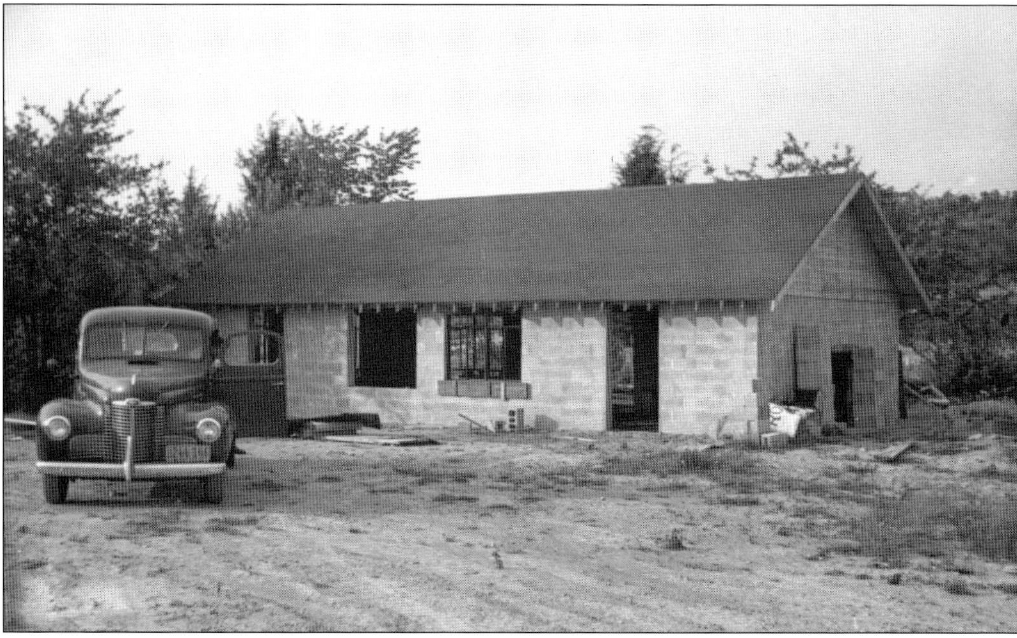

Holland's Rod and Gun Club was founded in 1937 as a multiple-use facility for area sportsmen. The clubhouse is pictured above under construction in the late 1930s and completed, below. The club sits on over 29 acres. The complex has a stocked two-acre pond, picnic area, and shooting ranges. It is home to many shooting leagues, as well as the high school's air rifle team.

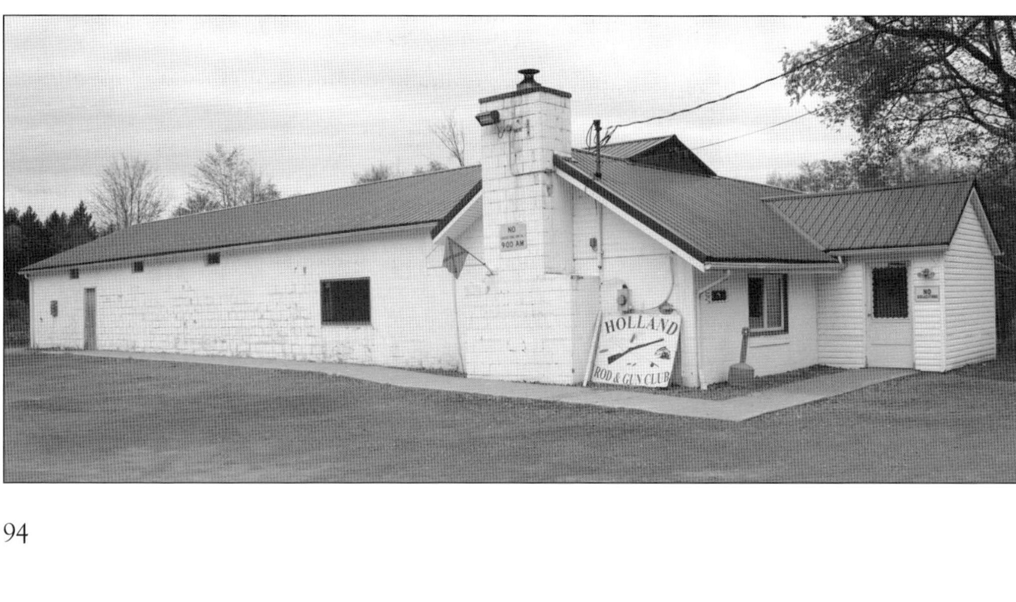

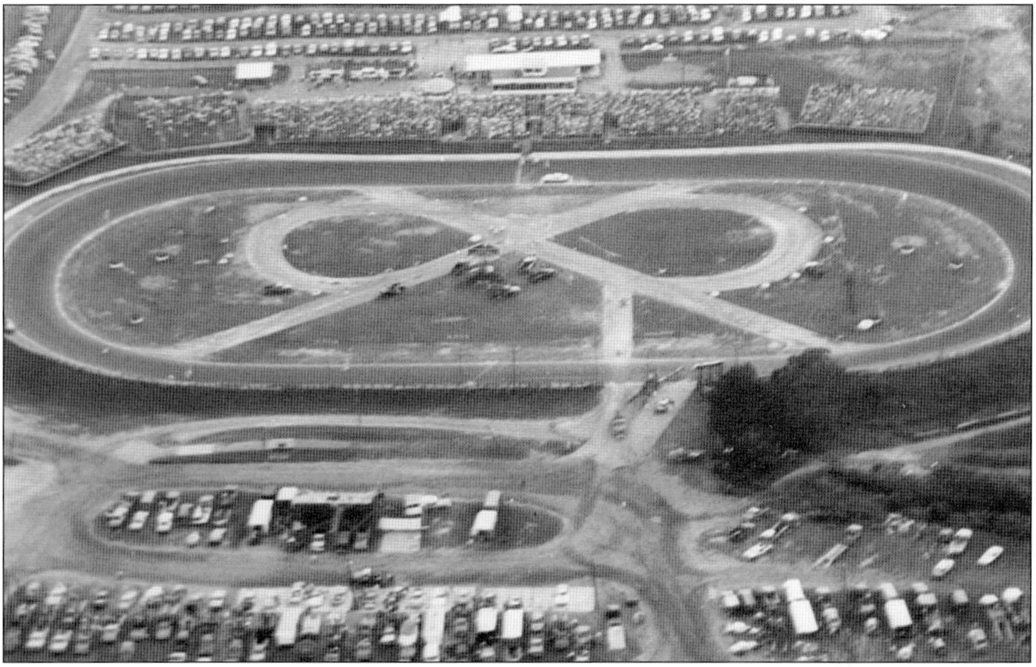

Started in 1960 by three young men, Ronald Bennett, Richard Knox, and Gordon Becker, Holland International Speedway was carved out of a farm field on Holland Glenwood Road in the small rural township of Holland. This aerial photograph was taken in 1993.

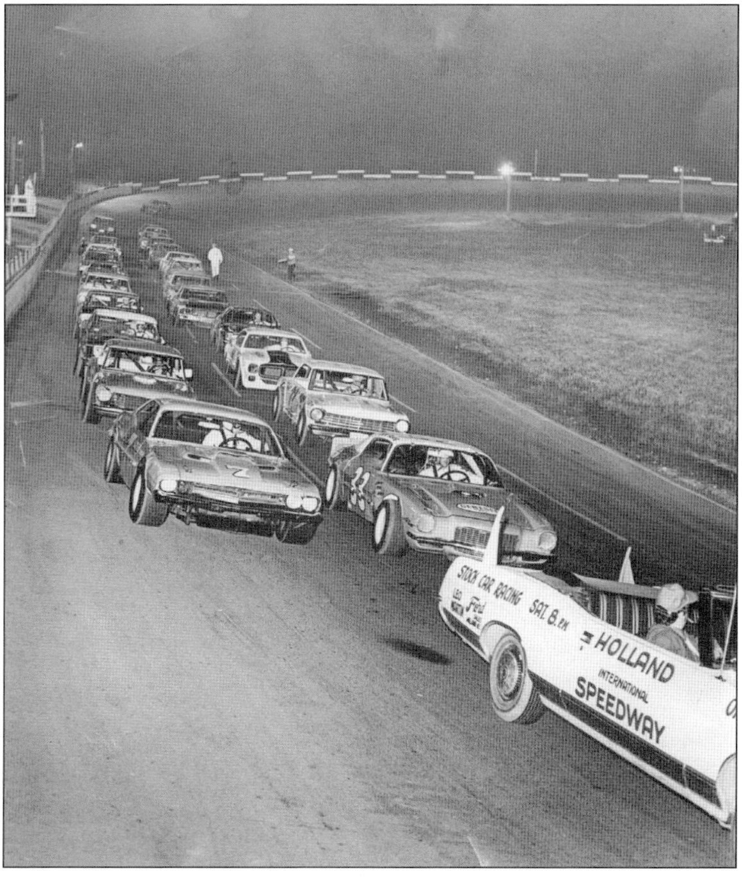

The Holland International Speedway Leo Martin Ford pace car is shown leading the late model field toward the green flag in the 1970 Kendall 100 race. Pole-sitter Dick Flaig (No. 33) and Art Clark (No. 7) are in the first row. (Courtesy of Holland International Speedway.)

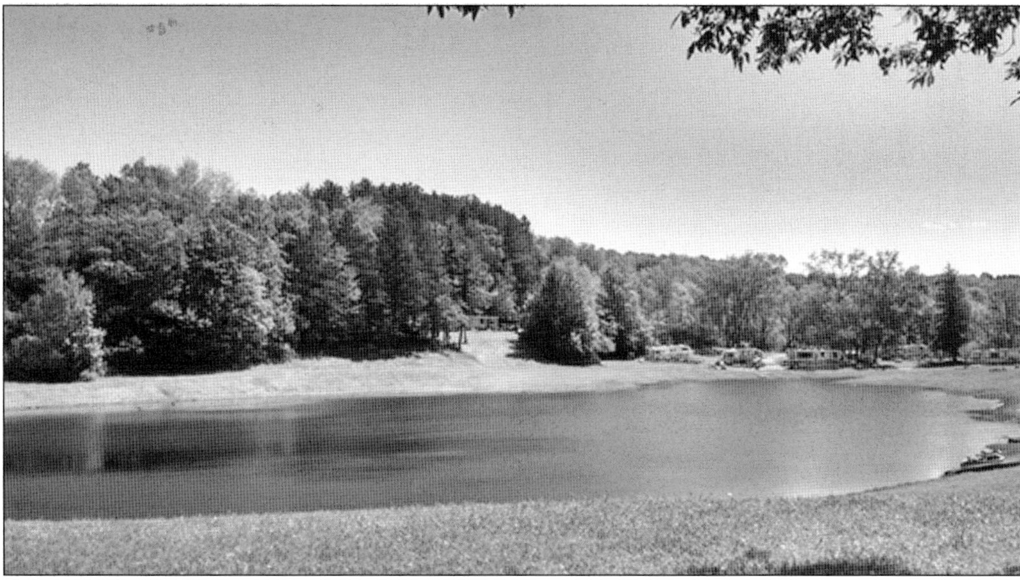

Three Valley Campground occupies over 500 acres in Holland. What started as Boy Scout Camp Ti-Wa-Ya-Ee in 1928 was converted into a family-oriented campground by the Helmich family in 1980. The Long House, the camp's kitchen, dining, and recreation house, is still there today. Campers enjoy miles of hiking and biking trails, as well as fishing, swimming, and fabulous views of the hillside.

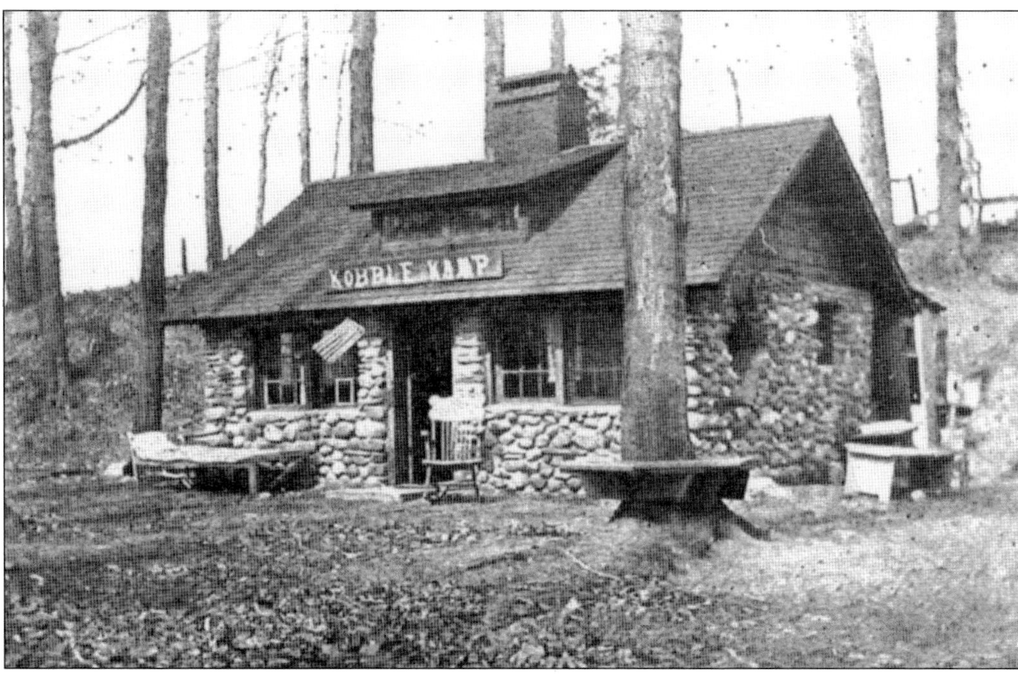

Kobble Kamp was on the west side of Route 16 south of the hamlet of Holland on an old road branching toward Burlingham Road. From 1912 to 1950, it was used for camping and group picnics. Built in 1912 by C.H. House, a dentist in town, the building was constructed of cobblestones gathered from a dry branch of Cazenovia Creek.

Nine

COMMUNITY

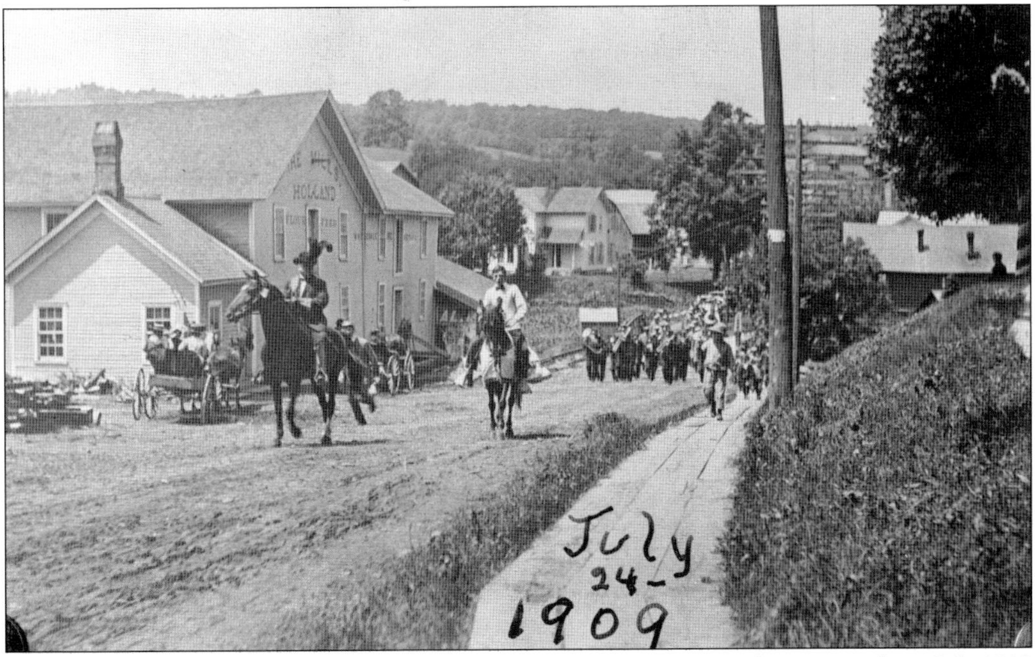

Holidays and special celebrations were almost always reasons for parades. Pictured is a July 1909 Old Home Day parade heading south on Main Street; Griggs Mill can be seen on the left. Named the Calithumpian Parade on an old advertising poster, the day was dedicated to raising money for the Baptist Church Repair Fund. In addition to the parade, an inspection of the fire department was held at 10:00 a.m., followed by lunch and speeches by former residents. A baseball game that featured Old Timers versus Young Stars started at 3:00 p.m., and the evening's entertainment of musical and literary numbers began at 8:15 p.m.

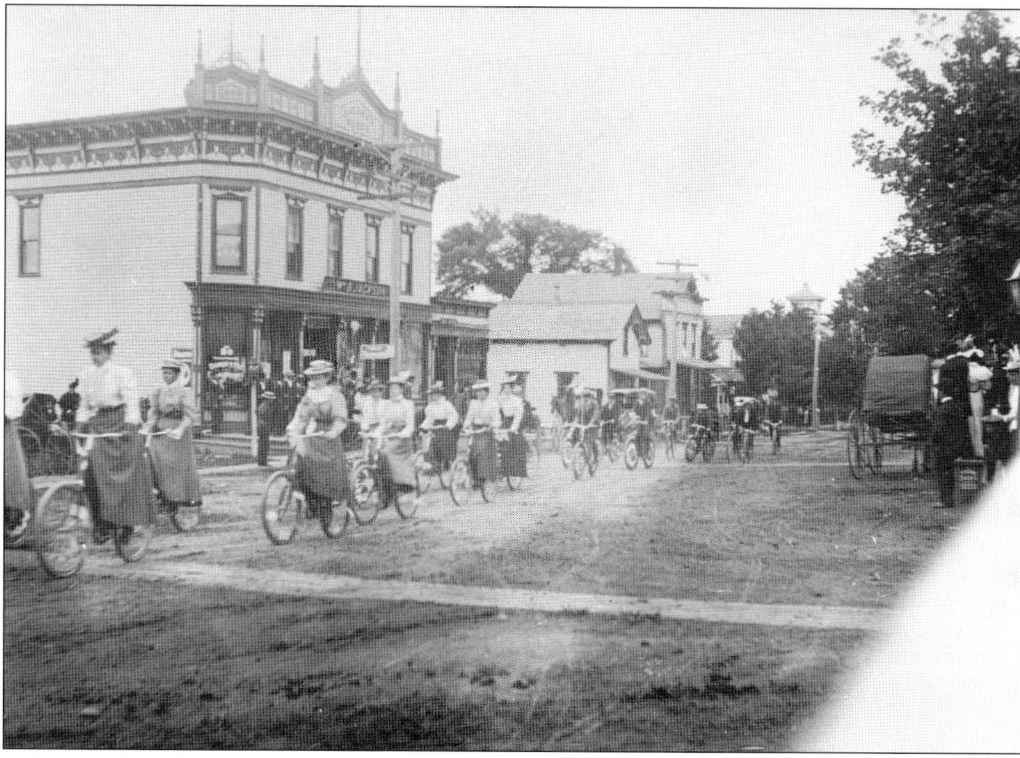

Ladies on bicycles are shown in this parade photograph on Main Street near today's traffic signal. Buggies pulled over to watch from the roadside, and a plank crosswalk can be seen in the foreground.

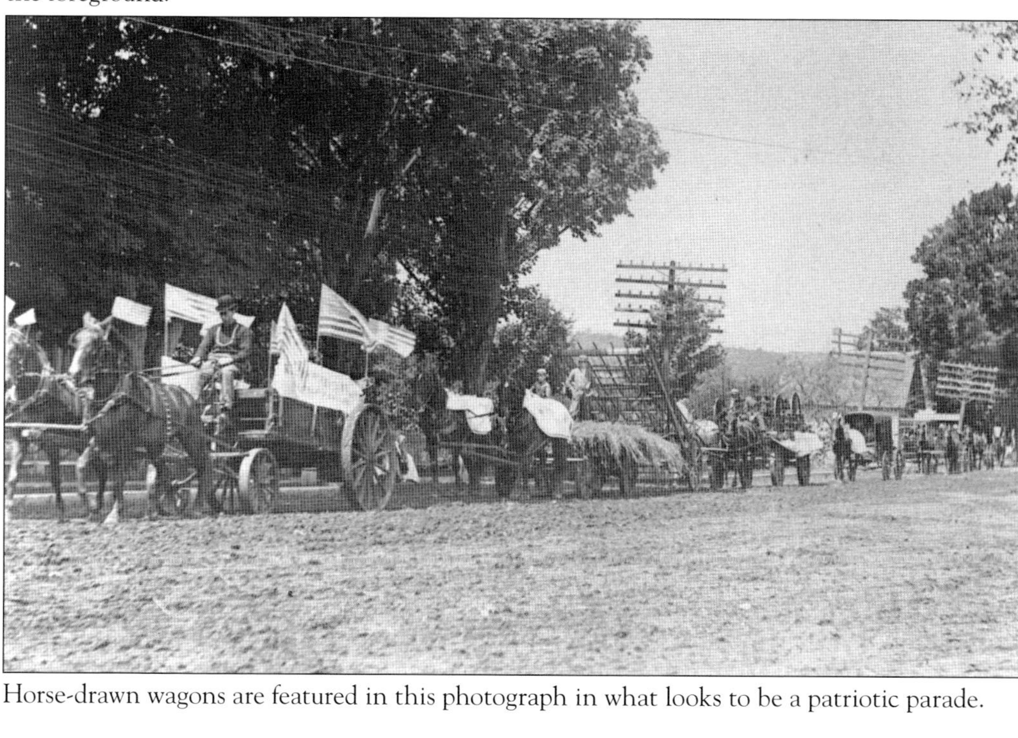

Horse-drawn wagons are featured in this photograph in what looks to be a patriotic parade.

In the late 1800s, Holland had several societies or social organizations that community members (mostly men at that time) could belong to. One of these was the Independent Order of Odd Fellows. Members were guided by three values: friendship, love, and truth. Pictured is the invitation cover to the dedication ceremony of Holland's Lodge No. 631, which took place December 16, 1892.

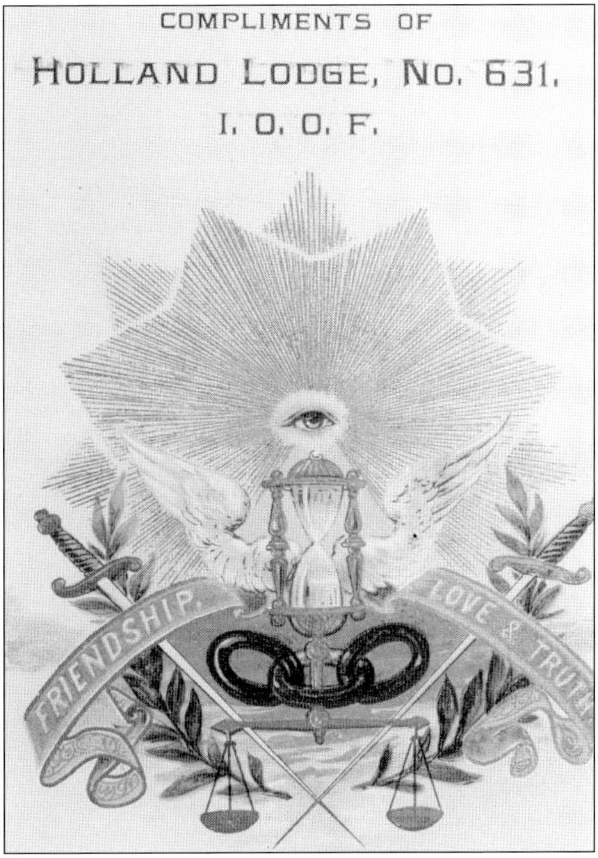

The Knights of the Maccabees were a fraternal organization whose members contributed money to provide minimal insurance to widows and orphans of members. This eventually became a life insurance company. Pictured are members of Holland's Lodge No. 39 in 1890.

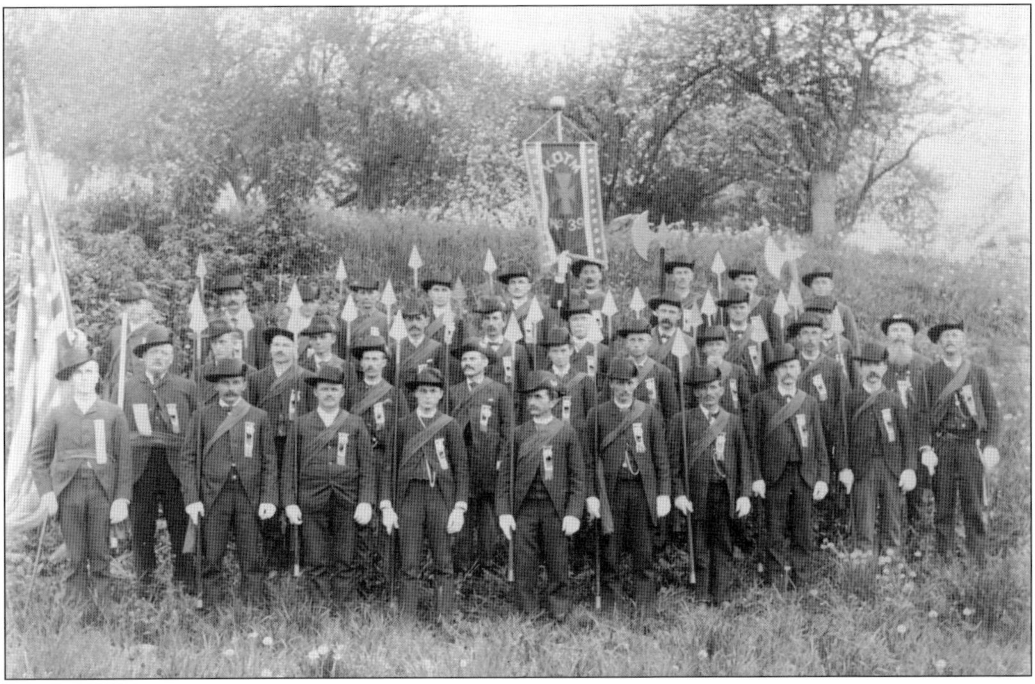

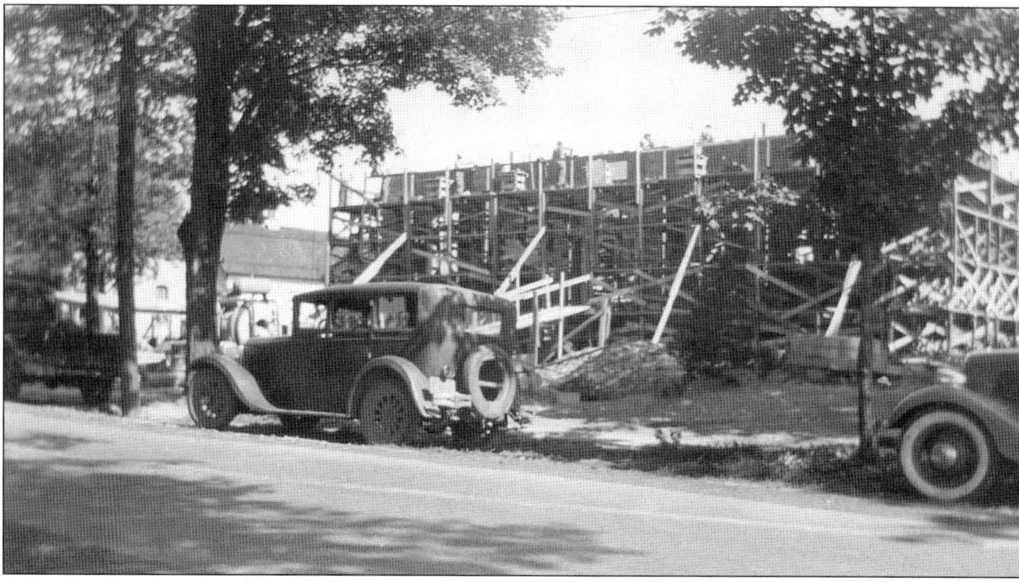

After Holland's schools centralized in 1931, local government moved into the former village school on Pearl Street and used it as the town hall. A fire caused by painters using gasoline torches to burn off old paint gutted the building. A new, brick town hall was built on this site by the Works Progress Administration and completed in 1935. This photograph shows the new structure in progress.

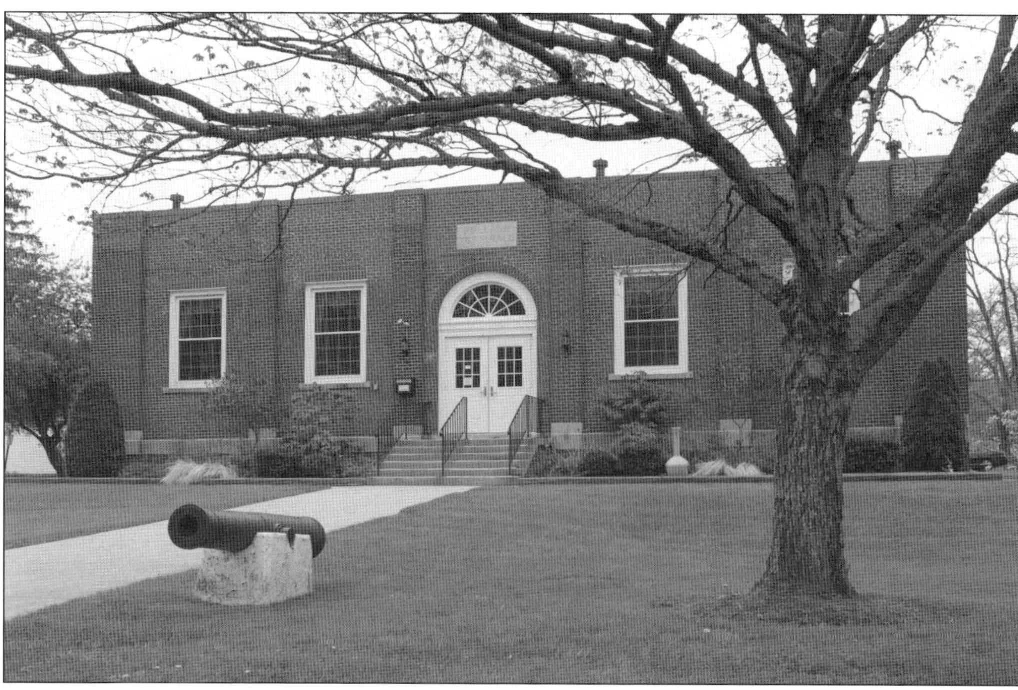

This photograph shows the town hall in its current state. It houses offices for local officials, a courtroom, and a town board meeting hall. Of note is the gun on the front lawn, a Civil War 12-pound naval gun.

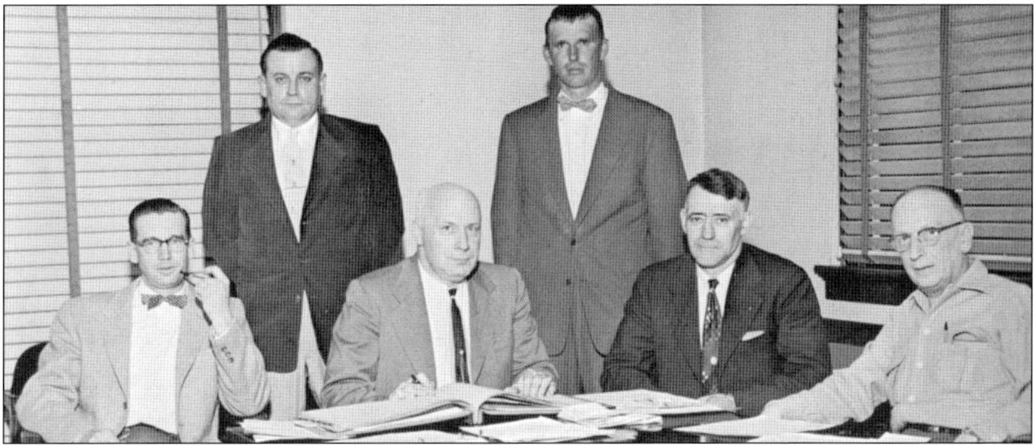

Local government office holders for 1956 are, from left to right, (seated) Sheridan Geer, justice of the peace; Harold Haws, supervisor; Robert Schreiber, councilman; and Donald Moore, justice of the peace; (standing) Theodore Bucknam, town clerk; and Kenneth Major, councilman.

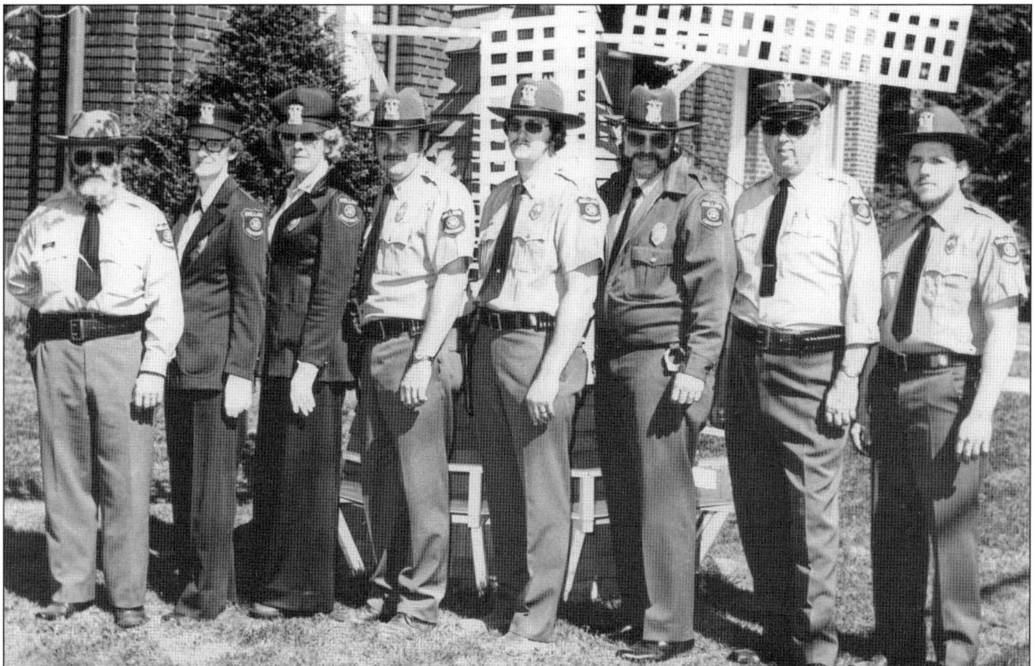

This 1970 photograph of Holland's constabulary includes, from left to right, Richard Wolfe, Faith Wheaton, Marilyn Linde, William Place, Richard Quant, Paul Appleby, Melvin Bucknam, and Michael Hamm.

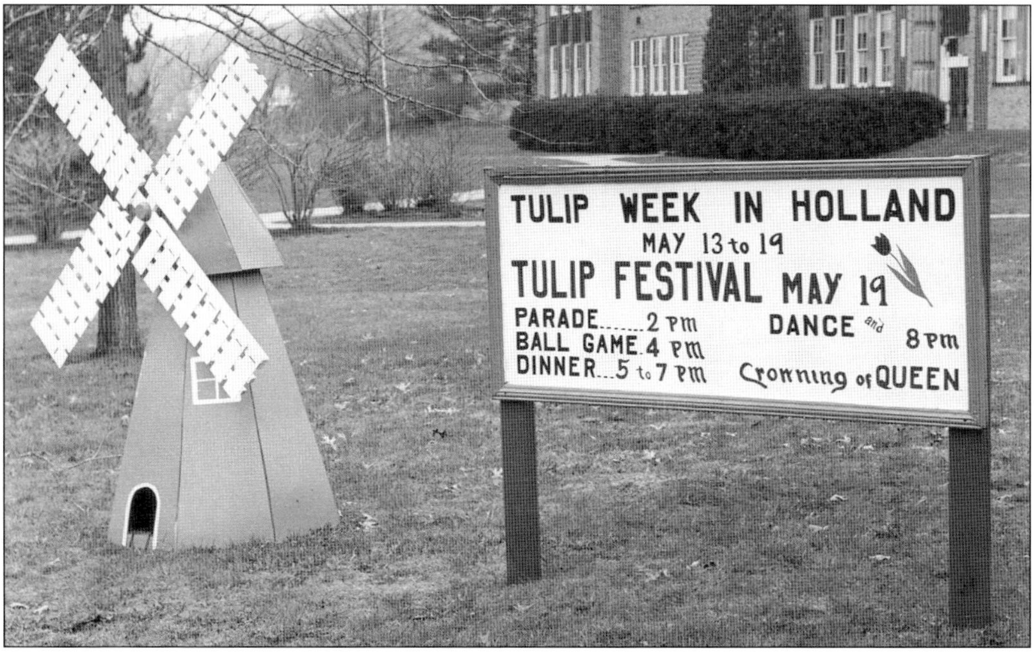

Sponsored by Holland's Kiwanis Club, the Tulip Festival is the largest of Holland's annual community events. The first Tulip Festival was held in 1956, when the Kiwanis Club of Holland was relatively new. Members were searching for a community activity that would develop into an annual affair. Every May, the community looks forward to the festivities that bring together current and former families. Pictured is early signage in preparation for the big event.

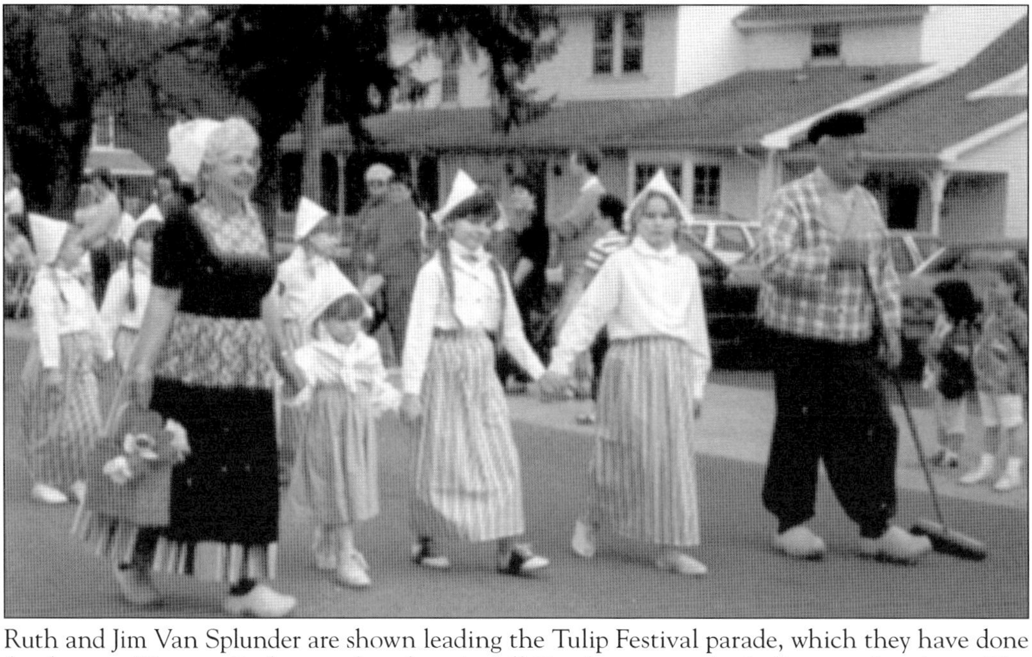

Ruth and Jim Van Splunder are shown leading the Tulip Festival parade, which they have done for the past 30 years. Each year, they dress in full Dutch costume, including wooden shoes. The Van Splunders have given their time and many talents to school and community organizations, especially to Holland's Kiwanis Club. (Courtesy of Larry Johnson.)

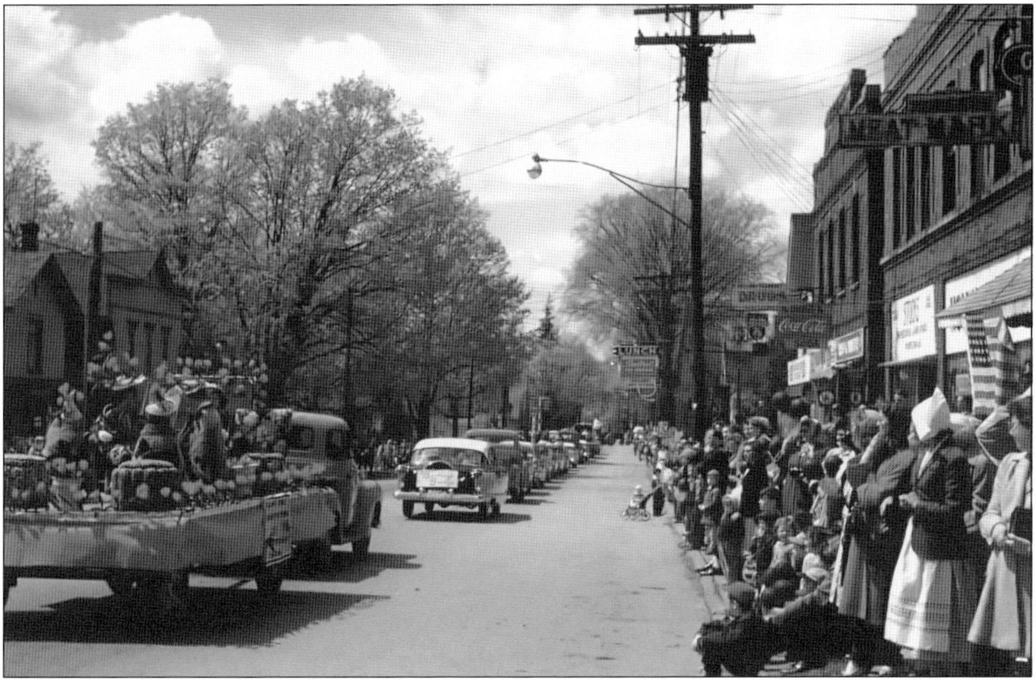

Pictured is the 1957 Tulip Festival parade. Residents and out-of-towners gather on Main Street to watch, some dressed in Dutch costumes.

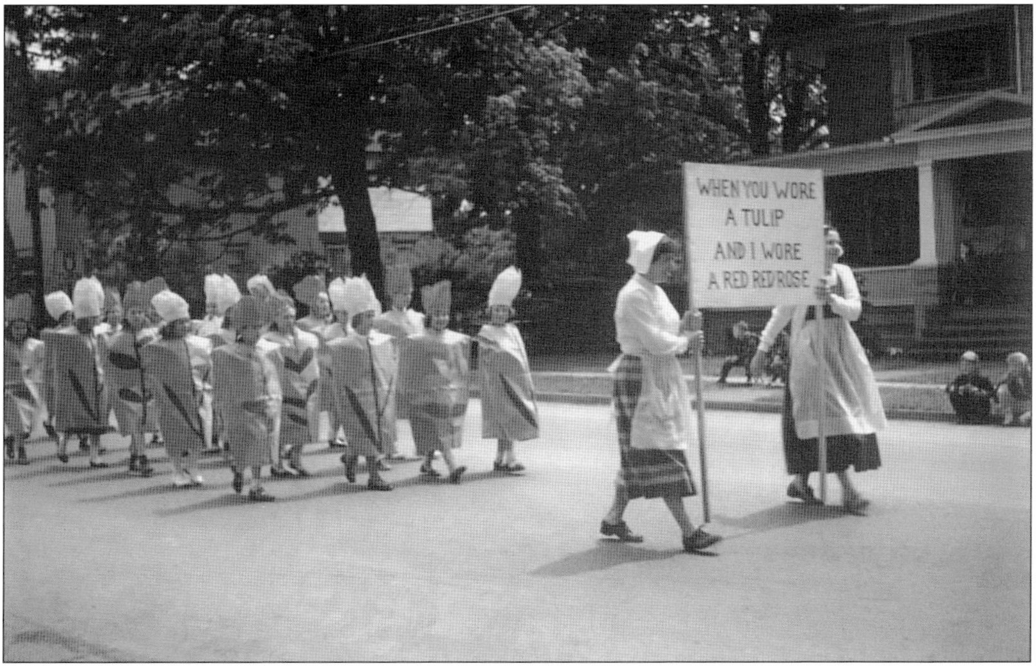

This Brownie troop, dressed as tulips, marches with their leaders in the 1957 Tulip Festival parade.

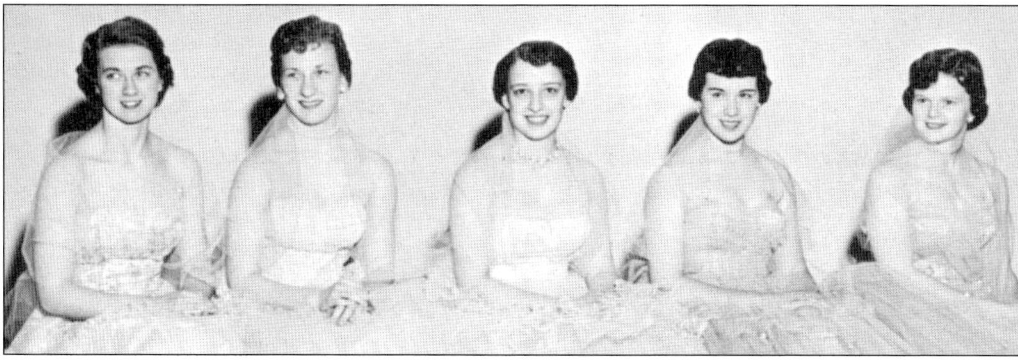

The crowning of the Tulip Festival queen has been a tradition from the very beginning and continues today. The very first queen candidates in 1956 are, from left to right, Virginia Copeland, Gail Laser Lewis, Betty Heitman, Barbara Hossenlopp, and Marcia Kirkby Hazlett. Betty Heitman was honored with the crown.

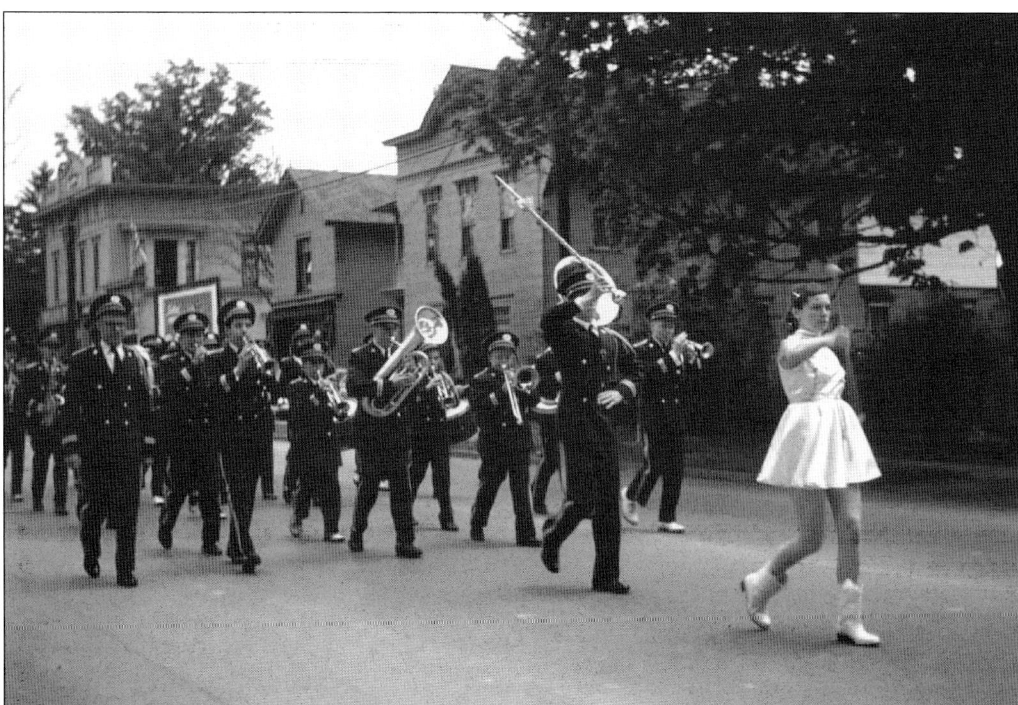

Holland's high school band, with its majorette, marches in the 1957 Tulip Festival parade.

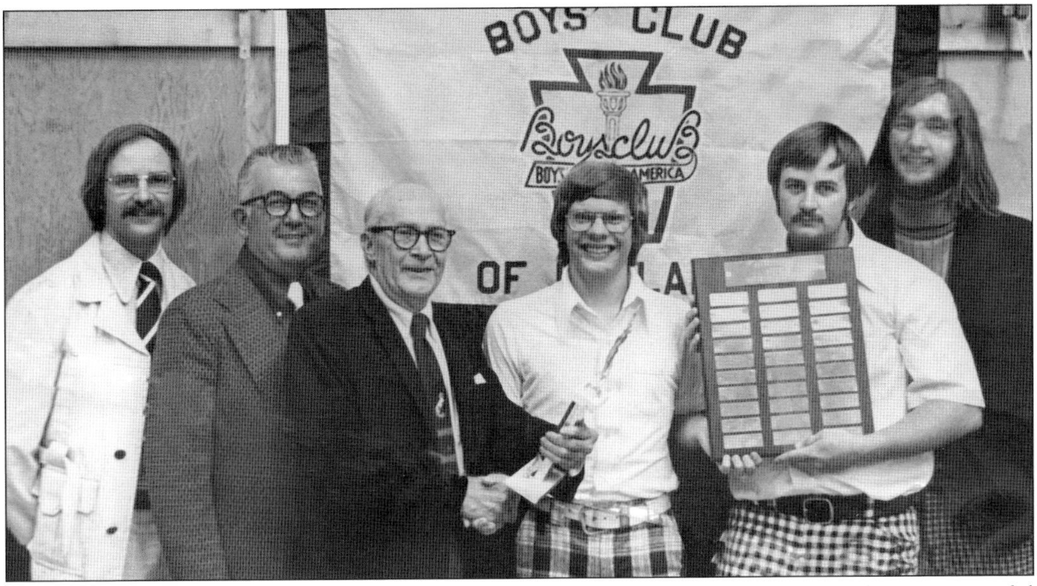

The idea for a Boys' Club in Holland is attributed to local Jay Baxtresser. After a successful community-wide capital campaign, the Boys' Club of Holland received its national charter on September 14, 1971. The former Methodist church on Main Street was purchased in 1972 and was the home for the club until 2013. This picture, from the club's early days in 1975, shows Timothy Baker receiving the Boy of the Year award. From left to right are Robert Seibold (staff); Harry Armond Kline (staff); Jay Baxtresser (founder); Timothy Baker (Boy of the Year); James Coatsworth (program director); and Timothy Roberts (staff). (Courtesy of Holland Boys and Girls Club.)

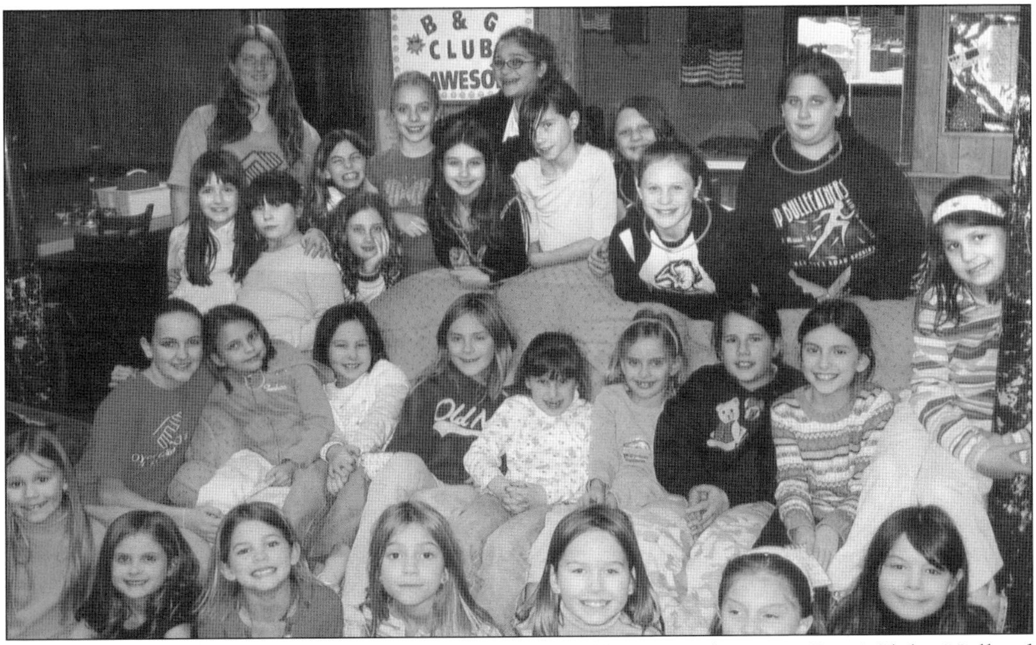

When the national headquarters changed its charter allowing girls to join Boys' Clubs, Holland promptly followed suit and changed its name to the Boys and Girls Club of Holland. Pictured is a group of girls enjoying their time at the club. (Courtesy of Holland Boys and Girls Club.)

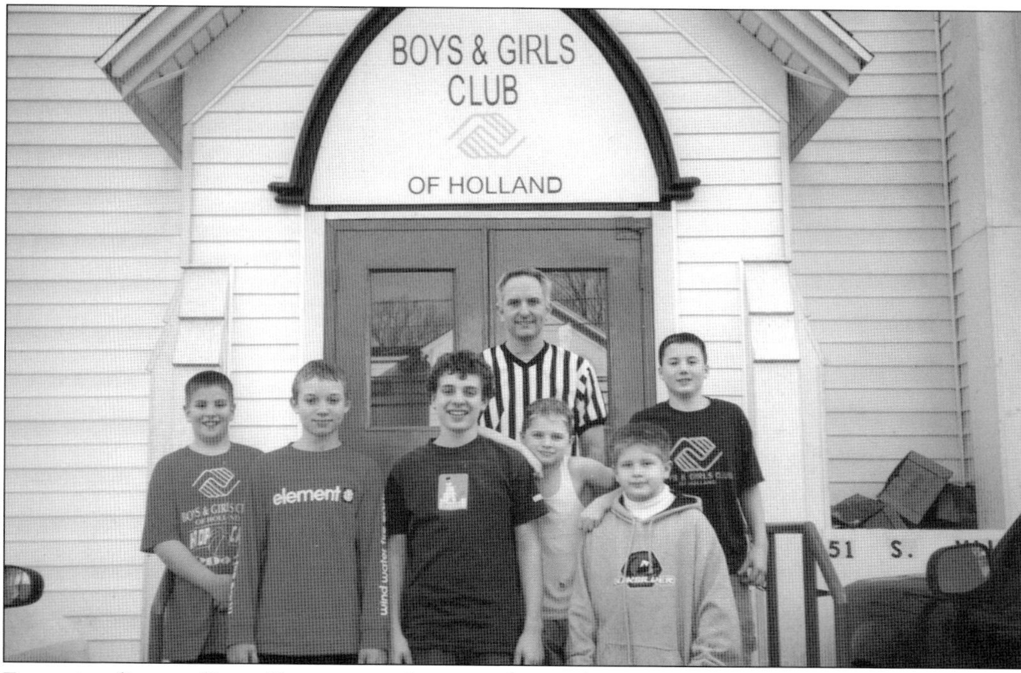

Executive director Brian Tavernier is shown with members outside the old Main Street Boys and Girls Club. Tavernier started as program director in 1997. He was a driving force behind the club's successful campaign to relocate. (Courtesy of Holland Boys and Girls Club.)

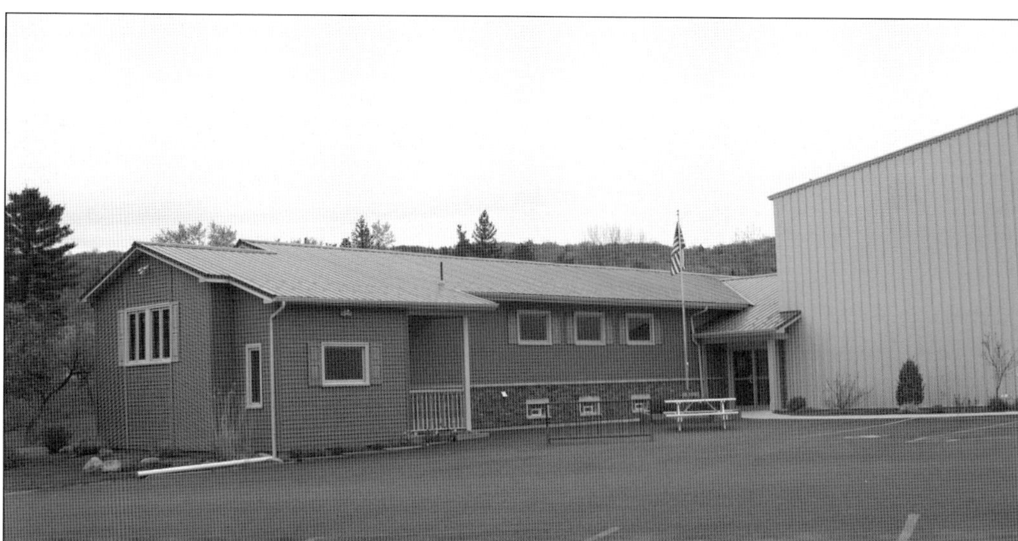

In April 2009, Holland's Boys and Girls Club purchased a former Jehovah's Witness hall and started renovations to the building. A 9,500-square-foot gymnasium was added to the existing building, and on November 4, 2013, the doors were opened to members for the first time.

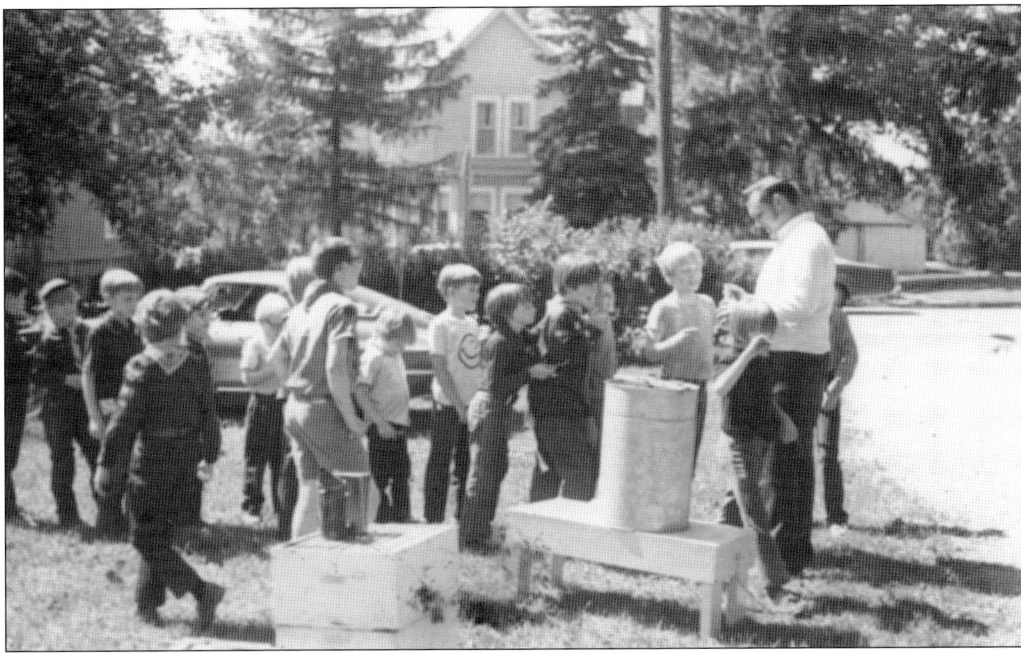

In this June 1972 photograph, a group of Holland Cub Scouts tastes honey from Bruce Goodman's bees. Holland is a tight-knit community, and residents are happy to share talents and hobbies with the younger generation. (Courtesy of Janet Palmateer.)

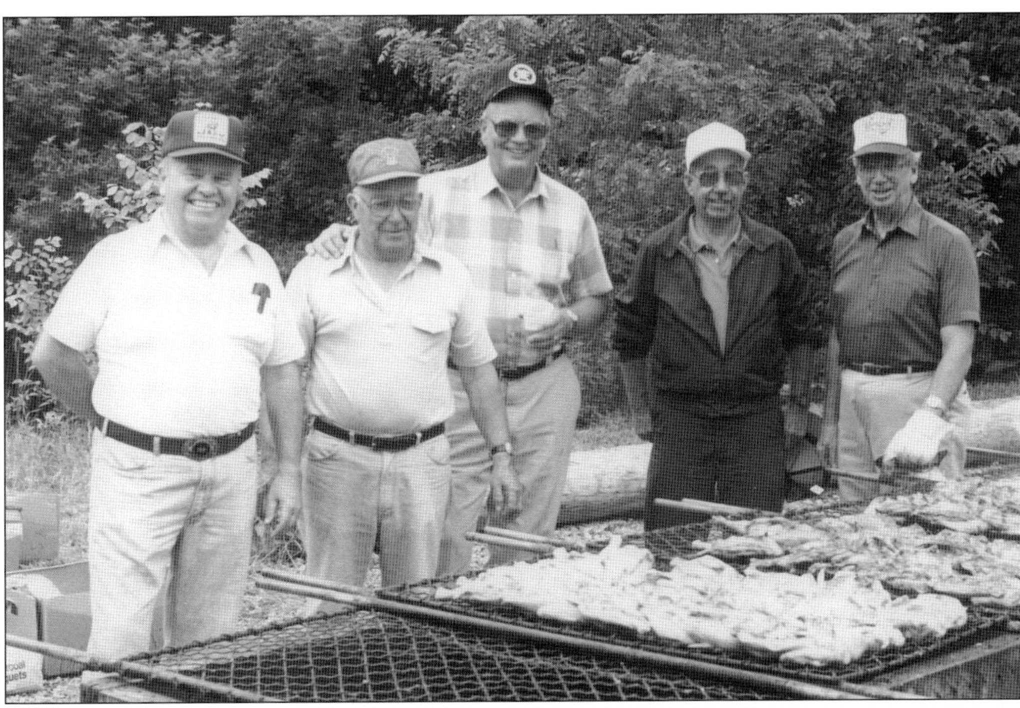

These five well-known men from Holland were always helping out in the community, whether through Kiwanis or local government. They are, from left to right, Rodger Joyce, James Van Splunder, Robert Logel, Robert Blackman, and Sheridan Geer.

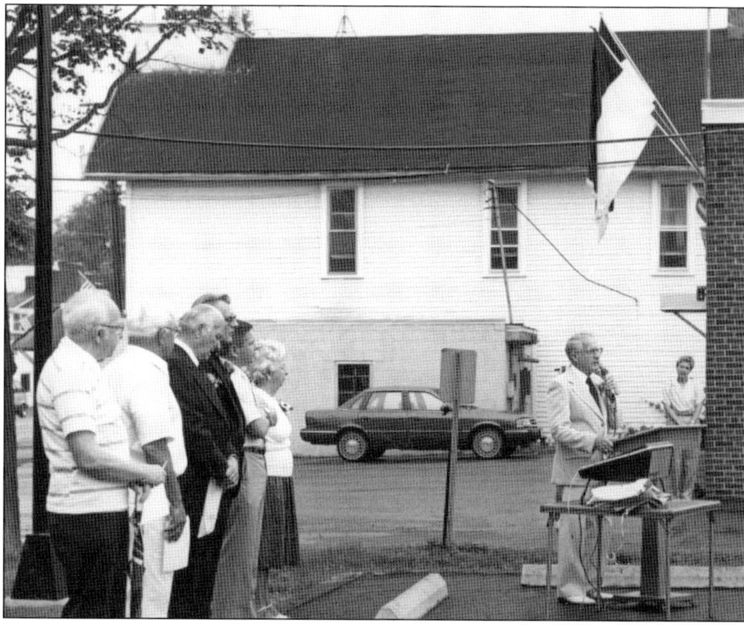

The community came together to create a living memorial to four Pratt sisters who grew up in Holland and a sister-in-law, all tragically killed in a car accident on September 1, 1988. Named the Five Sisters Memorial, trees and flowers in clusters of five were planted next to the town's fire hall on Main Street. Pictured is William Pratt, husband of the late Mary Pratt, addressing the crowd.

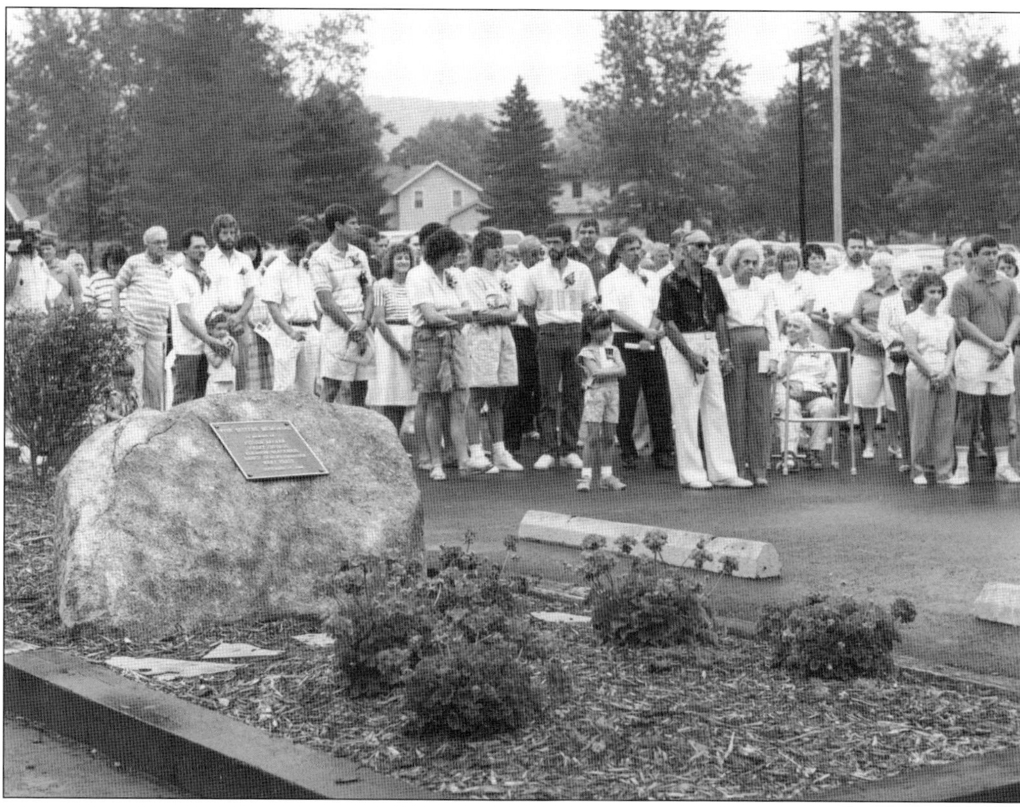

This is a picture of the Five Sisters Memorial at the dedication on July 4, 1989. The boulder and plaque, hauled from the Becker farm in Holland, are in memory of sisters Esther Pratt Becker, Eleanor Pratt Blackman, Juliet Pratt George, Nancy Pratt Schuppenhauer, and sister-in-law Mary Pratt.

Ten

Business District

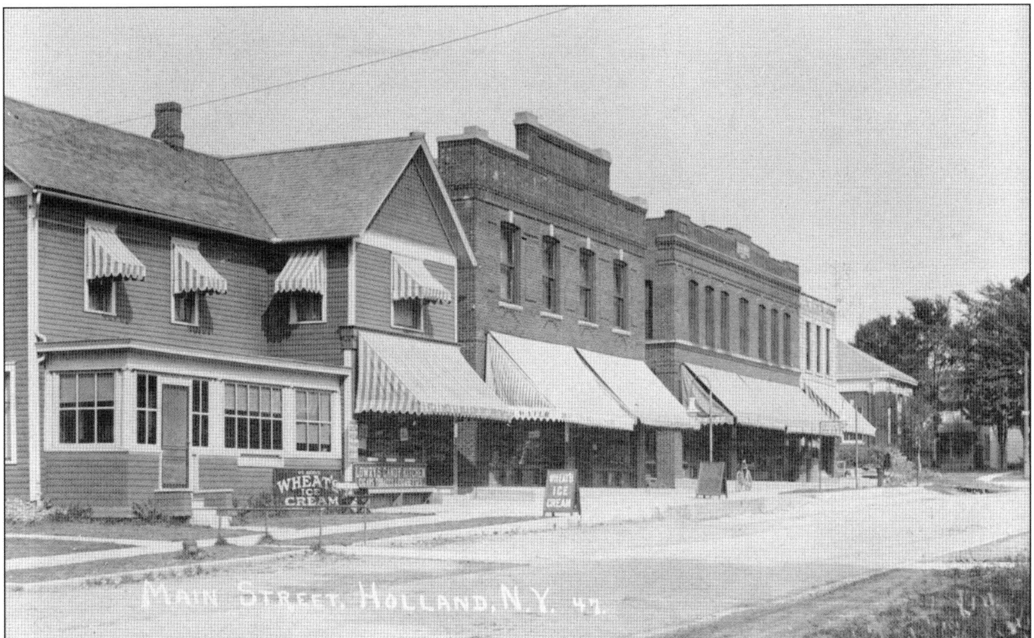

Leander Cook opened the first store in Holland in 1817 near the Orr mill site; it closed after less than two years. The next store was established by William Hoyt and Mr. Flinn on the east side of Main Street. This remained in business until 1832. Joseph Howard and Philip Riley established a mercantile business, and Riley later became sole proprietor. This photograph shows the east side of Holland's business district around 1920. From left to right are Lowry's Candy Kitchen and ice cream parlor, a dry goods grocery, a hardware store, and a meat market. The Bank of Holland can be seen on the far right.

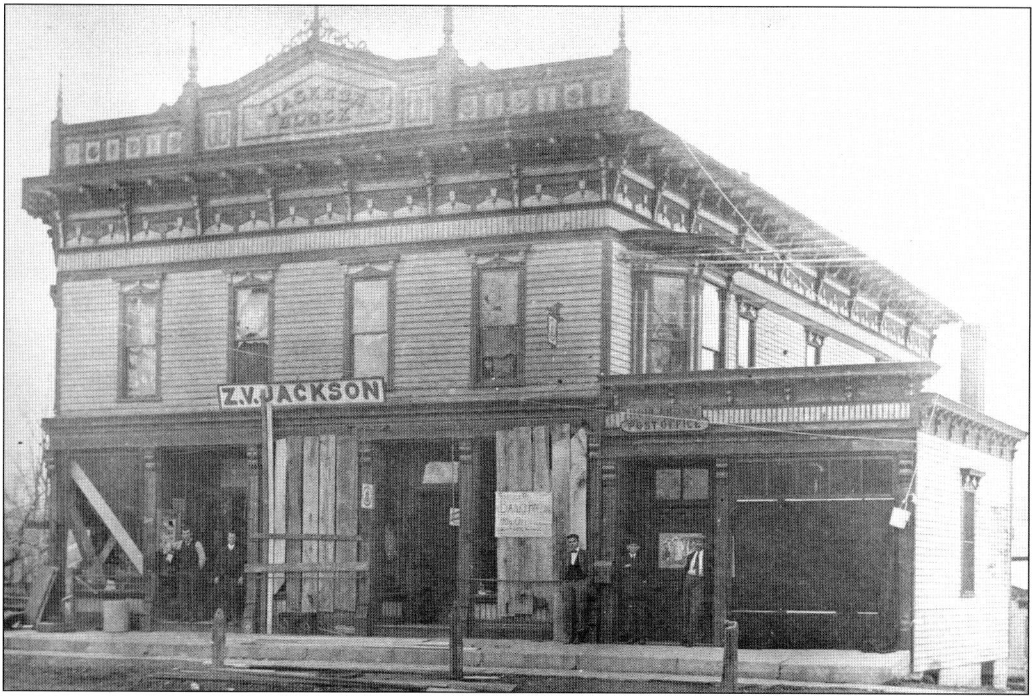

The Jackson Block was established in 1888 by Z.V. Jackson at 2 North Main Street. It housed a large general store and sold dry goods, clothing, boots, shoes, and the like. The post office was in the attached building on the right. The block was later owned by William Jackson, a relative of Z.V. and a notable businessman in Holland. This building still stands today and is home to a law firm and speedway office.

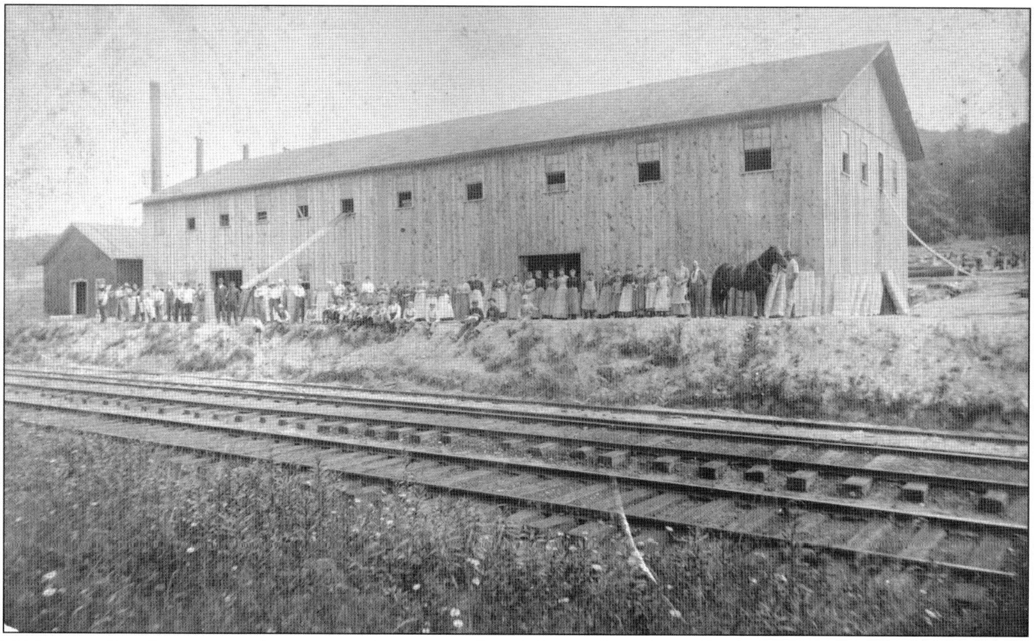

This was the shirtwaist factory on the east side of the railroad tracks on today's Edgewood Drive. This photograph was taken in 1893; the factory burned down on August 21, 1914.

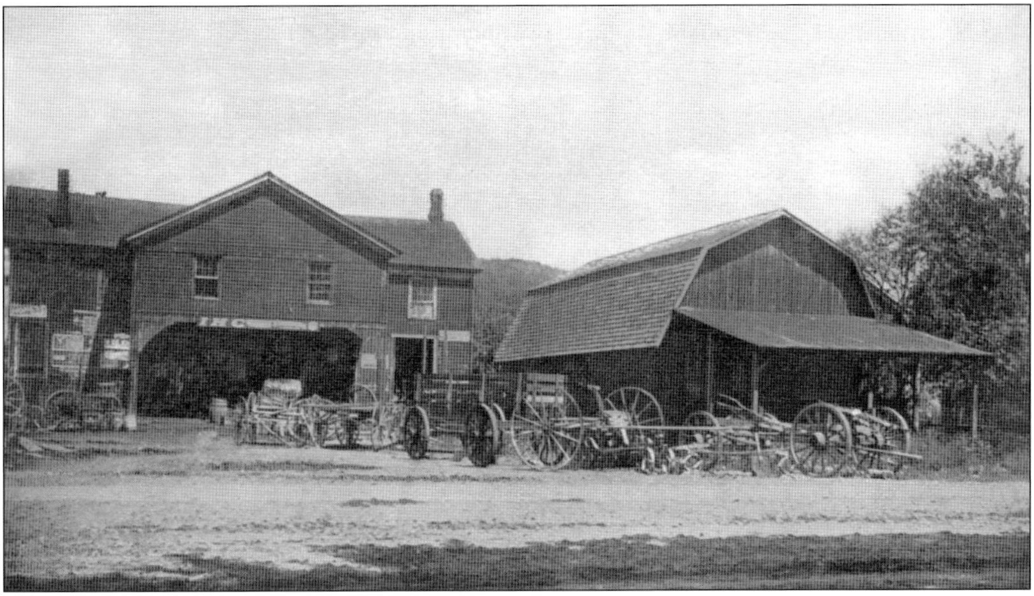

Pictured are the wagon shop owned by Henry Bangert and the blacksmith shop owned by Frank Dillon. Bangert was a woodworker who made sleighs, spokes for wagons, and the like. Dillon was a blacksmith for many years who later sold his business to Roland Davies. Davies continued until there was no longer a need for a blacksmith. These shops were located on Main Street on the site of the current Holland Fire Hall.

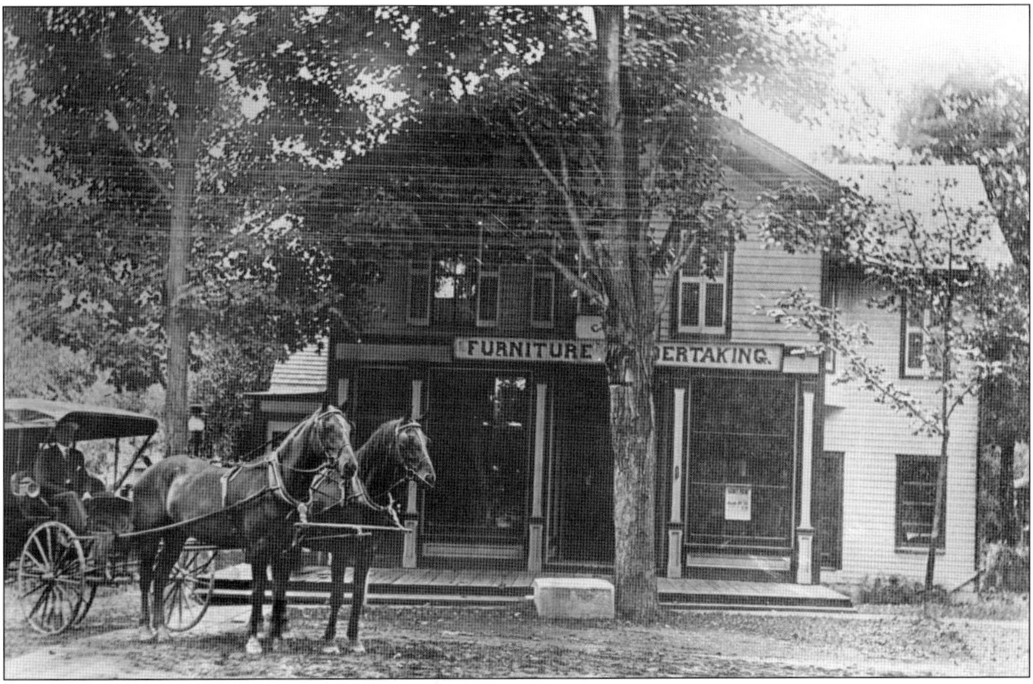

Built in the 1850s by the Orr family (mill owners) this building was first known as a furniture store operated by Ashford Cutler. In the late 1800s, the Main Street business developed into a funeral parlor operated by Cutler and Charles Sill. Wellman Bucknam purchased the building in the 1940s and took over. In later years, the building burned and had to be demolished.

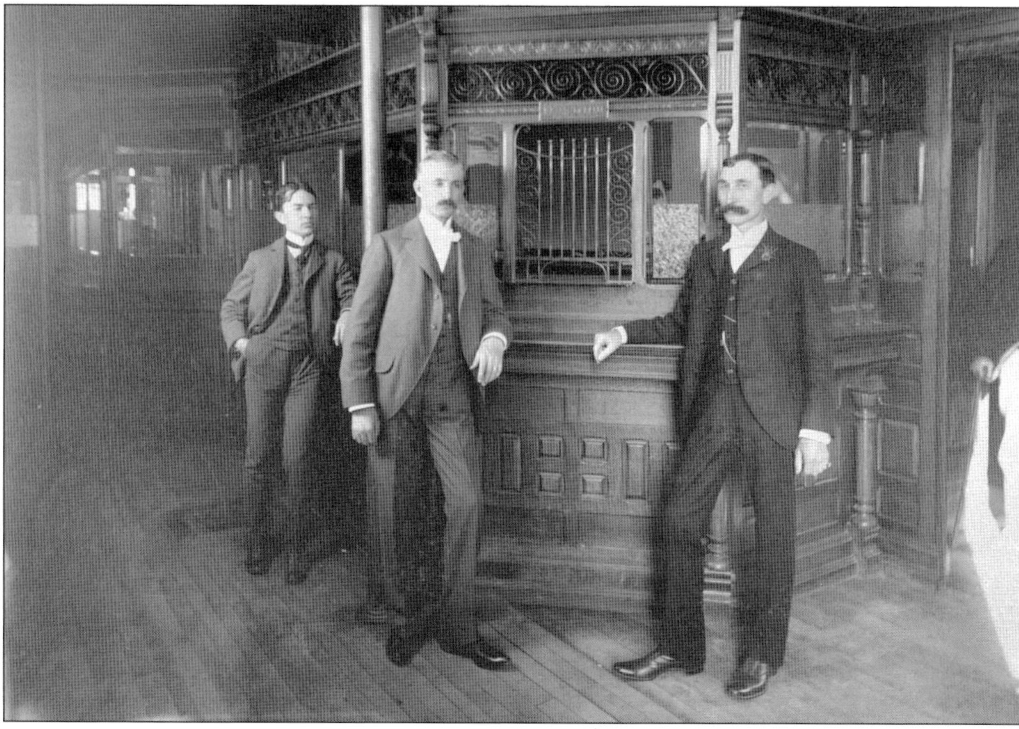

In 1893, a group of local businessmen decided it would be a great advantage to the community to establish a bank in Holland. With $25,000 in stock, the bank received its charter from the New York State Banking Department on October 21, 1893. Pictured are the first employees of the Bank of Holland. From left to right are Albert Earle, George Merrill (cashier), and William Jackson (president).

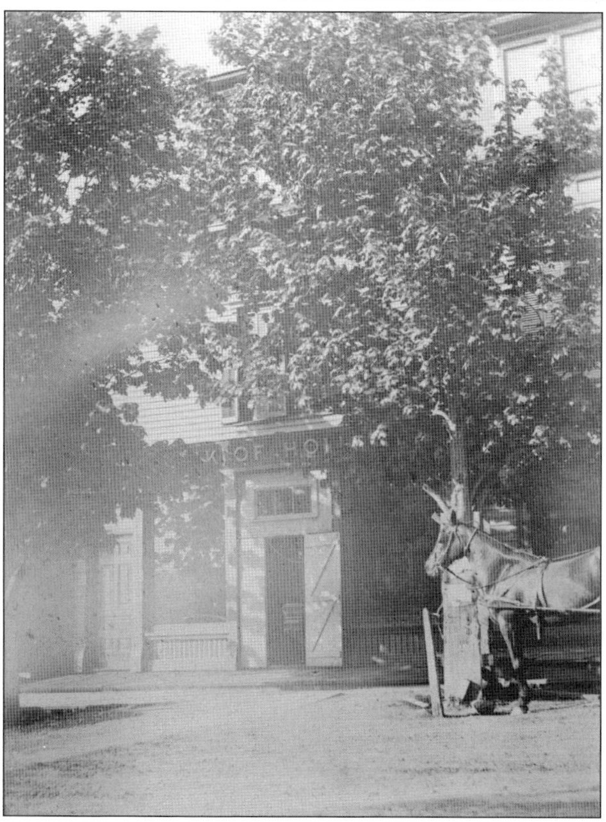

The Bank of Holland was first located in an area inside the Whitney Block on Main Street. Bank deposits at the end of the first year were $44,877; the first dividend of six percent was paid in 1895. At the beginning of the 20th century, deposits had reached $100,000.

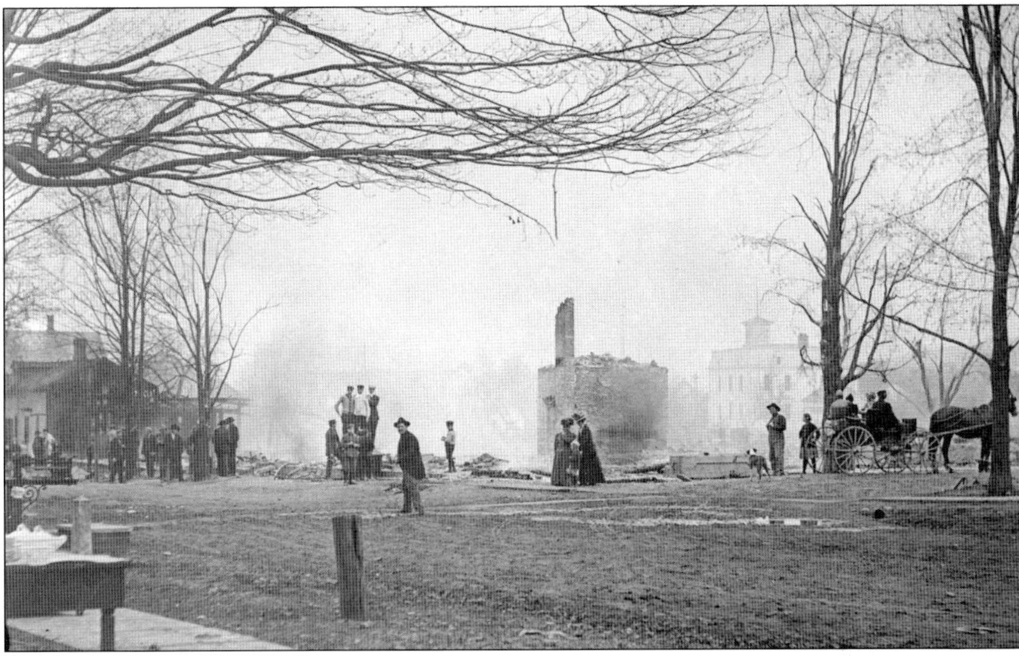

On April 5, 1910, the worst fire in the history of Holland wiped out the business district on the east side of Main Street. The fire was discovered at 1:00 a.m. in the rear of Parkinson's Drug Store. Besides the drugstore, other buildings destroyed were the Bank of Holland, Odd Fellows hall, Ralph Whitney's general store, Paul Wurst's hardware store, Philip Riley's jewelry and dry goods store, Sergel's millinery store, the medical office of Dr. Troupe, the dental office and apartment of Dr. Sidney Moore, the L. Bailey photography studio, residences of Homer Morey and Irving Blakeley, and the barn of Lafayette Colby. On the west side of Main Street, Schreder's Meat Market and the Jackson Block were badly scorched, and windows in the post office were broken by the heat. The center brick structure is the vault of the Bank of Holland, which was intact.

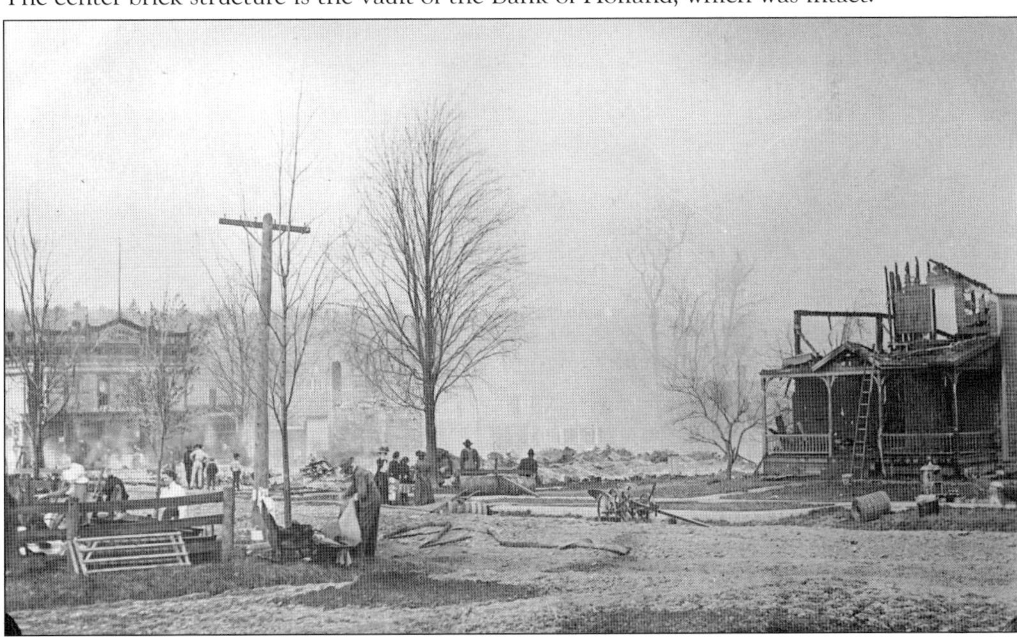

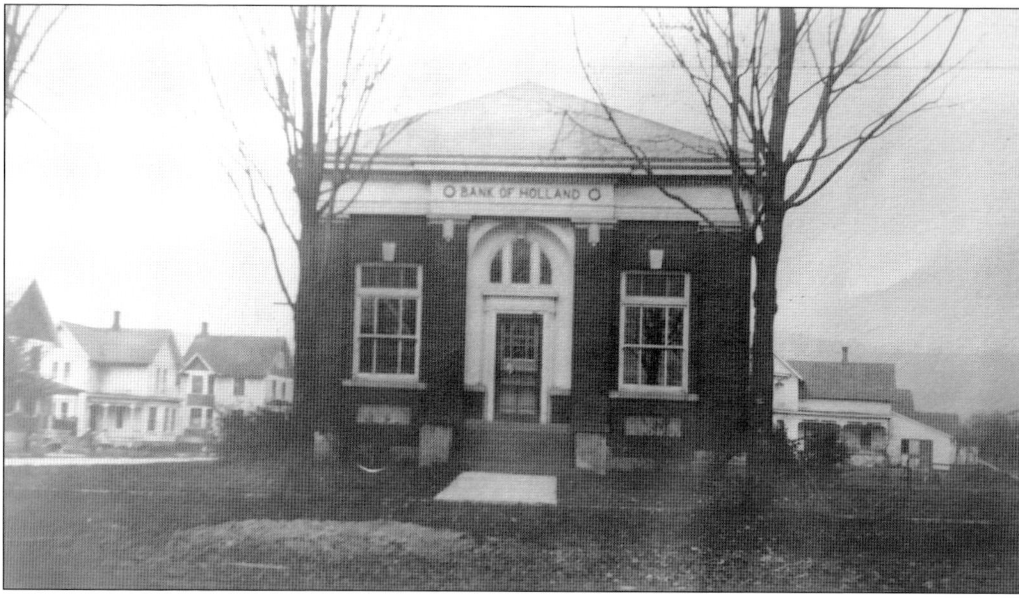

Immediately after the fire, bank directors planned a new bank building. They purchased property at the corner of Main and Vermont Streets, and the new building was completed and occupied in 1911. In addition to William Jackson, subsequent bank presidents include George Merrill, Robert Watson, Paul Wurst, R. Stanley Wood, Harold Haws, Mark Luderman, and Timothy Dickey.

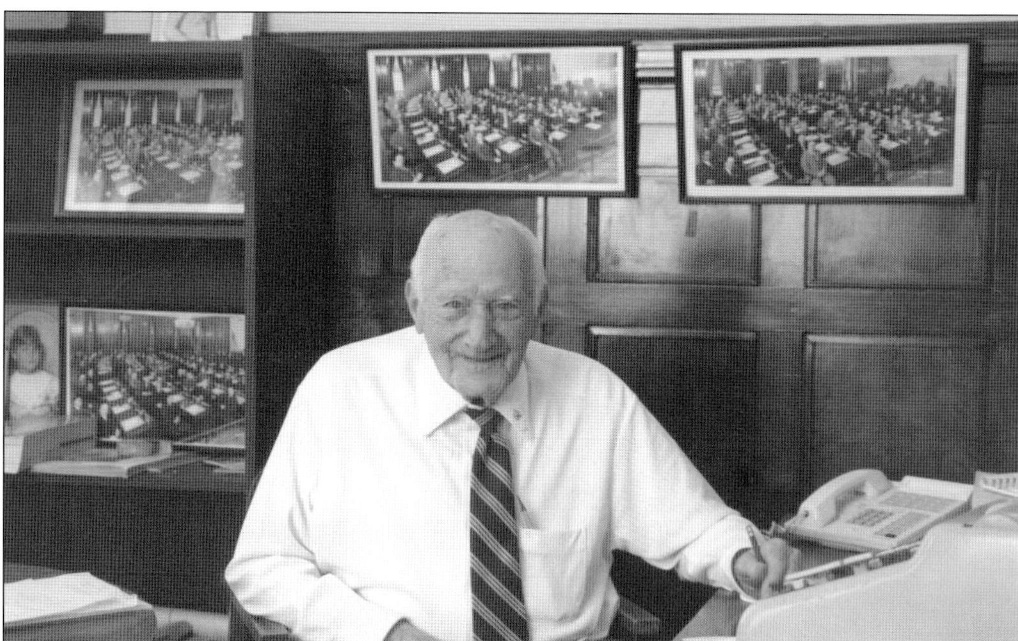

Harold C. Haws holds the honor of being the longest active bank president in the United States, having retired in 1995 at the age of 94. Starting in 1923, Haws worked a remarkable 72 years at the Bank of Holland, holding the title of president since 1958. He was also involved in town government, serving as town supervisor for 14 years and councilman for another four years. Harold Haws passed away in 1998 at the age of 96.

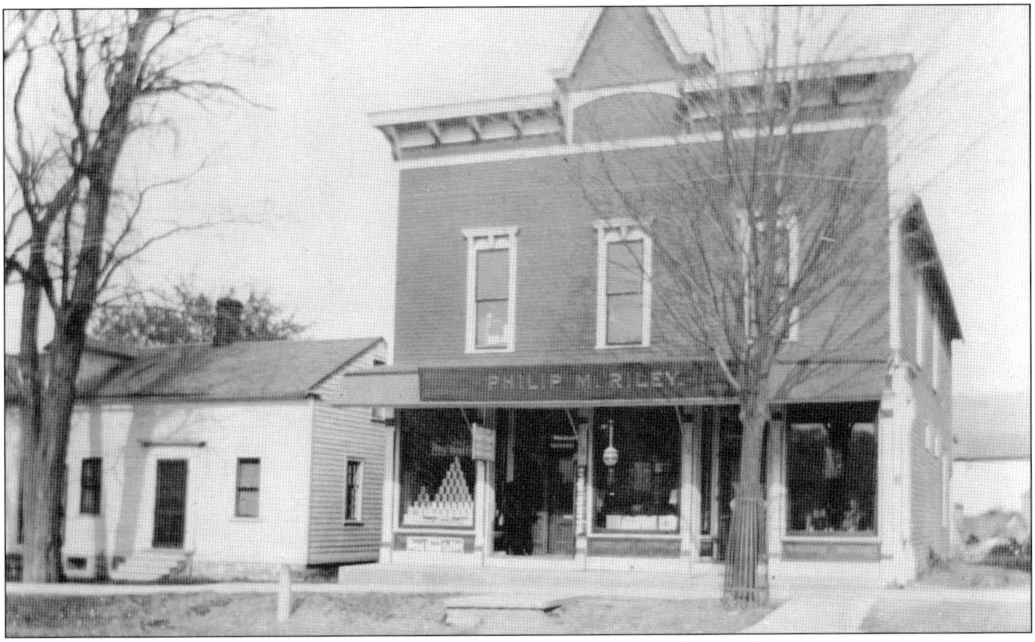

One of Philip M. Riley's businesses was the Riley Jewelry Store, located in the business district on Main Street. The second floor of this building was a concert hall. The store specialized in diamonds, watches, clocks, and jewelry. It also carried chinaware and sterling and plated silverware. Eye glasses were furnished and fitted here, too. This was one of the buildings destroyed in the 1910 fire.

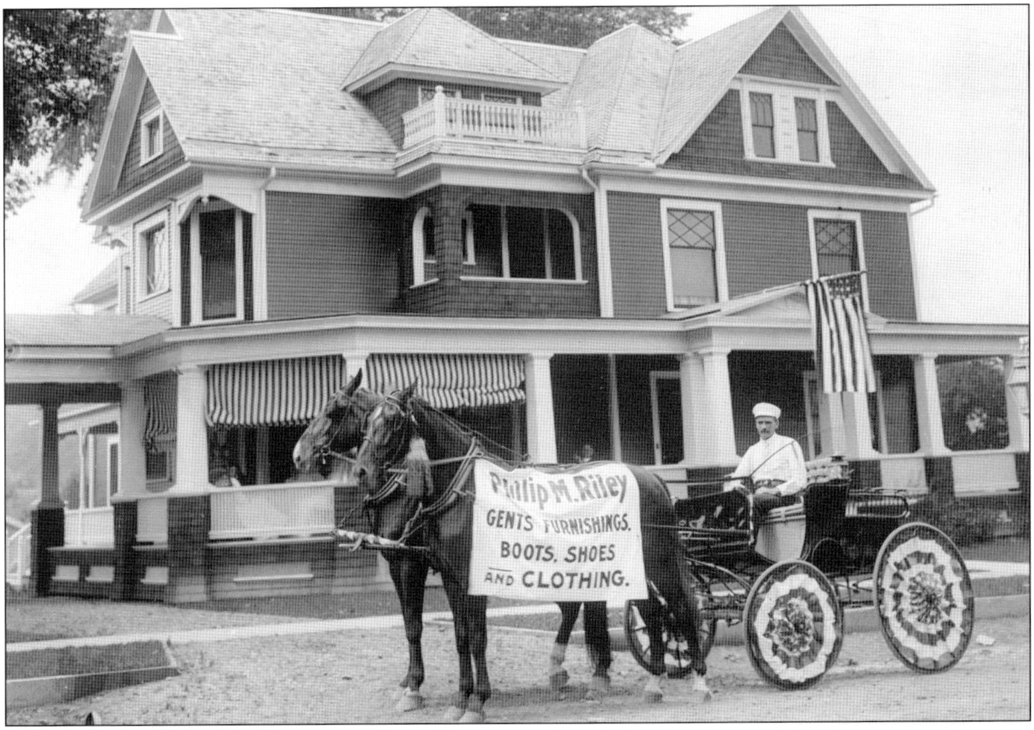

This photograph shows Philip M. Riley in front of the Riley home on Main Street. He is most likely participating in a parade while advertising his business.

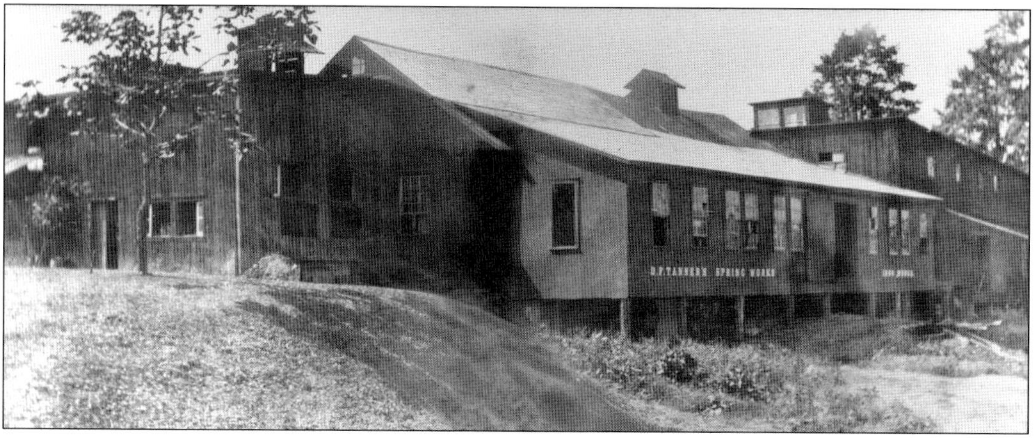

In 1899, Holland became the home of the D.F. Tanner Spring Works, a manufacturer of wagon springs, wheelbarrows, neck yokes, and whippletrees. It sold these products all over the eastern United States, including through Sears, Roebuck & Company. The business expanded into lumber, paint, hardware, and feed. It also produced commercial truck bodies.

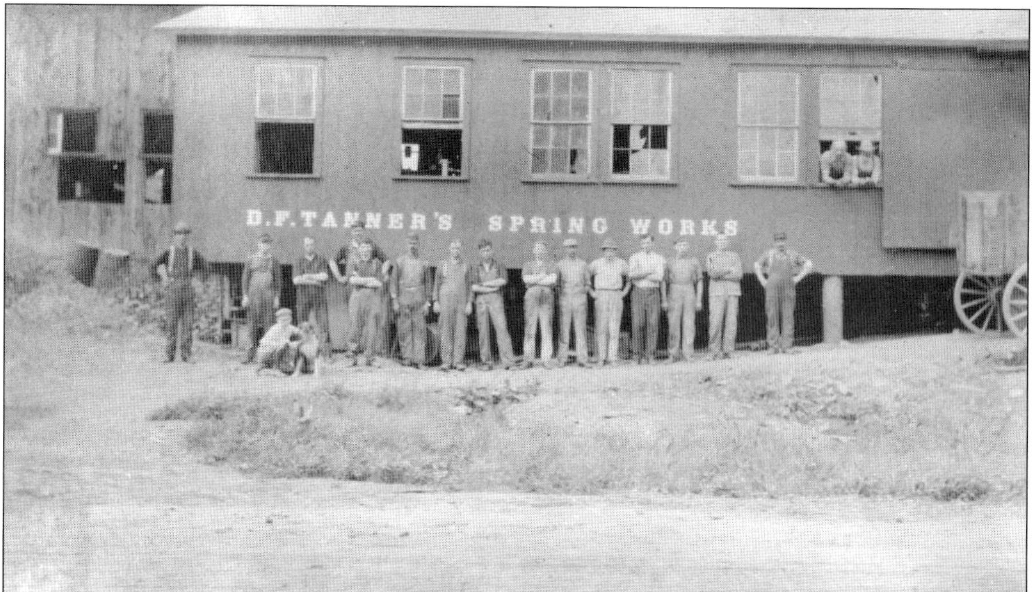

Here is a turn-of-the-20th century picture of shop workers outside the D.F. Tanner Spring Works.

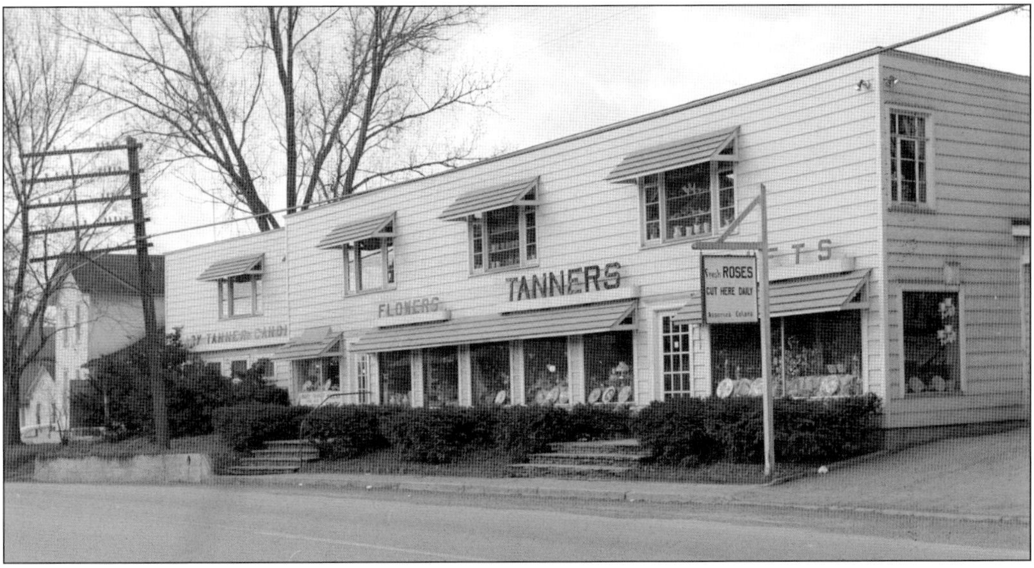

Tanner's Gift Shop was a destination for shoppers near and far. The Tanners were known for their fresh-cut flowers; at one time, there were 17 greenhouses with 30,000 rose bushes. The first greenhouse was built in 1923. A gift shop was added in 1941 where Mary Tanner made and sold her delicious candies. Exquisite gifts were displayed and sold in the gift shop. The business was discontinued in the early 1970s.

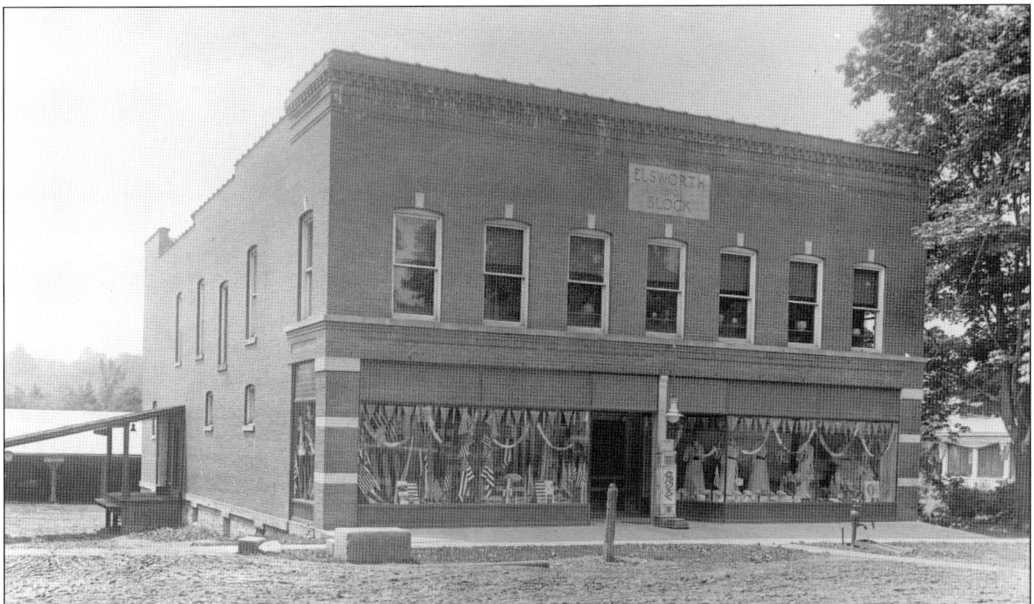

In 1910, Isaac Elsworth and his son, Frank, built the Elsworth Block on Main Street and relocated their Mill Street store (seen on the cover) to this location. Opened in 1911, it was the largest department store of its type in the surrounding area. In 1937, Elsworth's store closed. Just before World War II, it reopened as a woodcraft manufacturing business, and later, it became the Star Molding Company and Holland Crafts, making toys, candles, syrup products, and other novelties and employing about 60 people. In the 1960s, the store was remodeled and became a Red and White grocery store, owned and operated by the Jack Moore family.

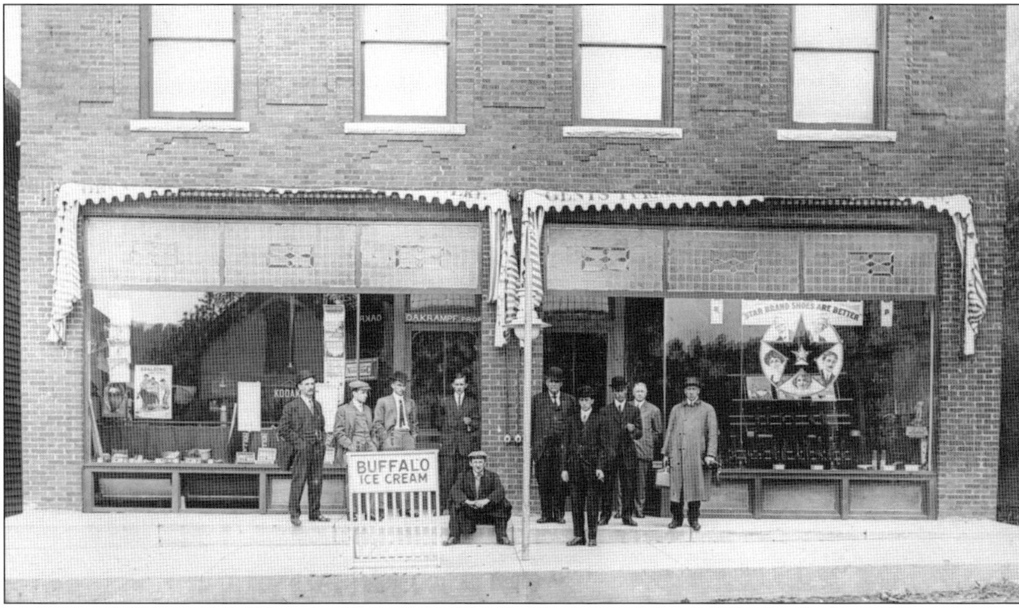

After the 1910 fire, this Main Street building became home to a drugstore (left) and jewelry store (right). Later, Fred Guenther operated a grocery store in the right side, while the drugstore remained. In the early 1960s, Joseph Buckley became partners with Pete Lowe, who was pharmacist at that time. Buckley purchased the building and became sole owner around 1966. The drugstore area was expanded to occupy both sides of the building. Buckley's daughter, pharmacist Claire Buckley Mackiewicz, took over the family business in 1995.

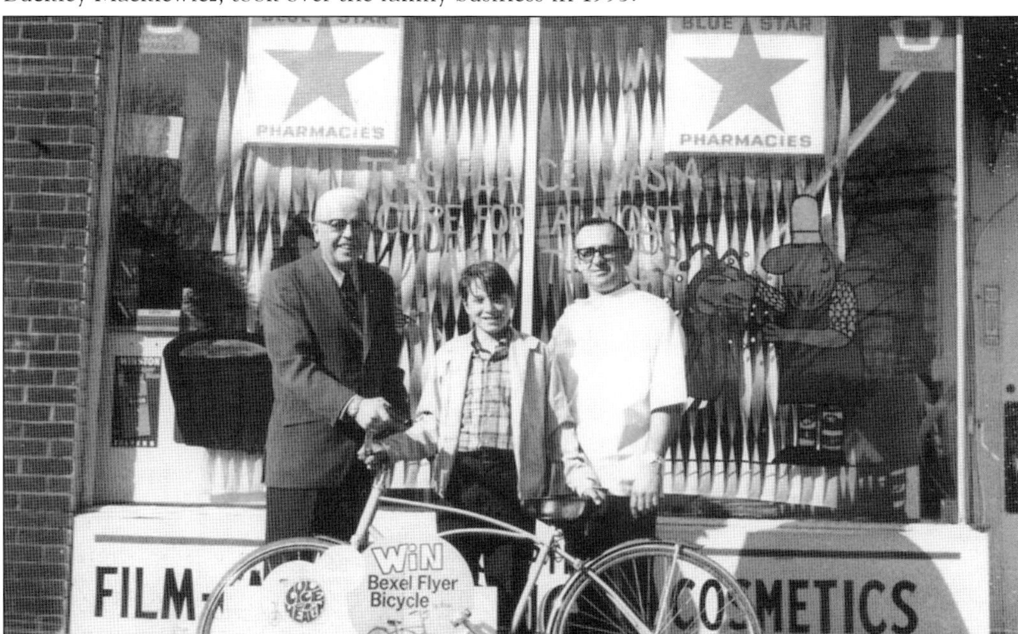

Pictured are, from left to right, Harold Brumsted (school superintendent) and Joseph Buckley (owner, Holland Pharmacy) awarding a Bexel Flyer bicycle to a student contest winner in front of the pharmacy. (Courtesy of Claire Buckley Mackiewicz.)

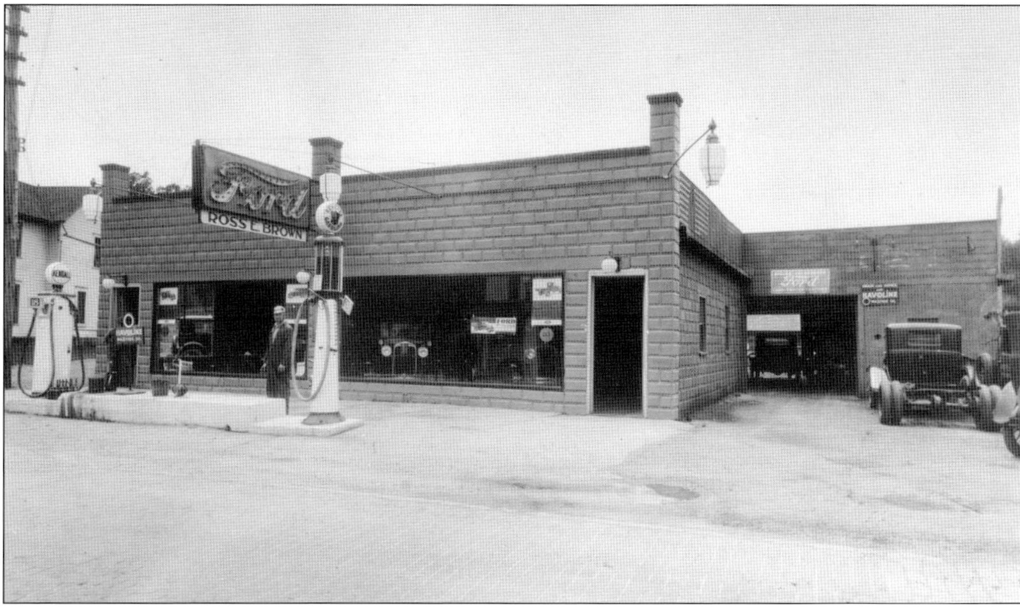

In 1923, Ross E. Brown opened a Ford garage and service station on the site presently occupied by Upstate Automotive Group. Later owners of the Ford garage were Layton Charles, Glenn Sprague, Ralph Phillips, and Leo Martin.

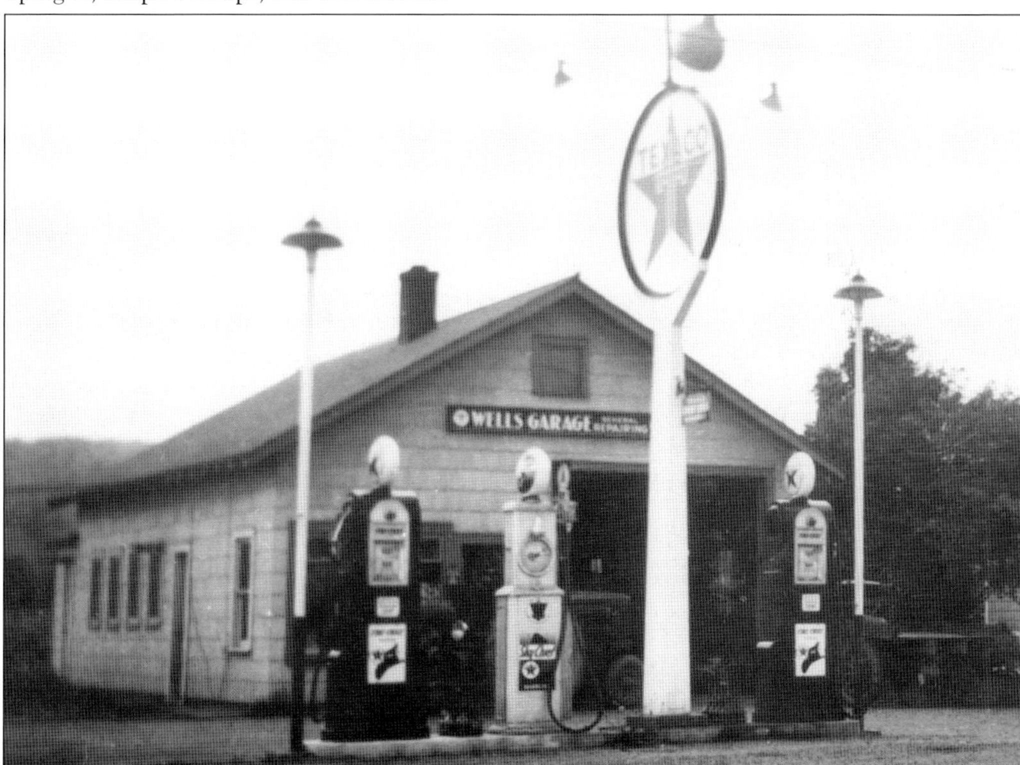

Wells' Texaco Station is shown in 1943. It was on Olean Road (at the present location of Crosby convenience store) and was owned by Robert Wells.

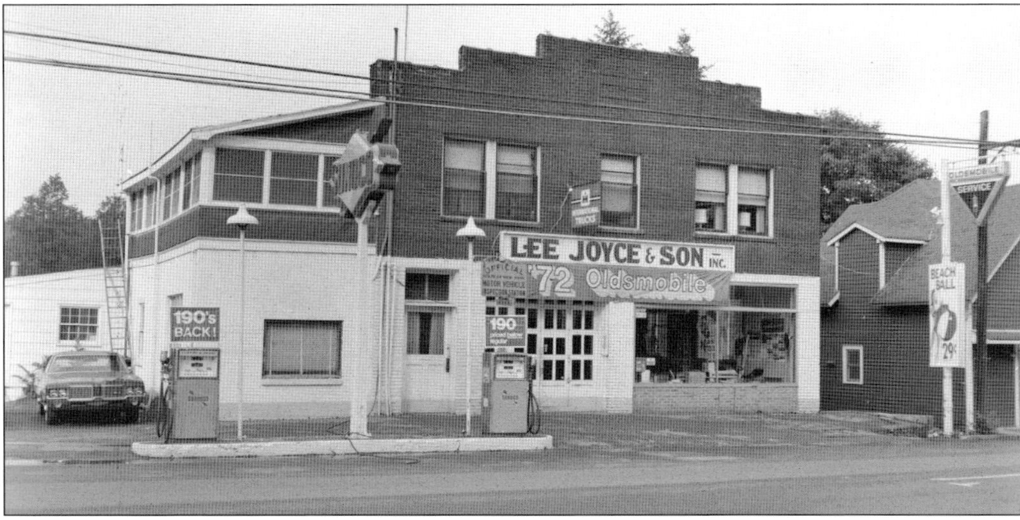

Leland Joyce opened a garage in Holland in the fall of 1934 and became an Oldsmobile and International dealer in 1936. During World War II, Joyce turned his garage into a machine and tool shop. His son Rodger entered the family business in 1951. Always active in the community, Joyce was elected town supervisor and served from 1958 to 1967. He was also a member of the Holland Fire Department for 32 years, 14 of which he was fire chief. Joyce was also a member of Holland Central School Board of Education for 14 years.

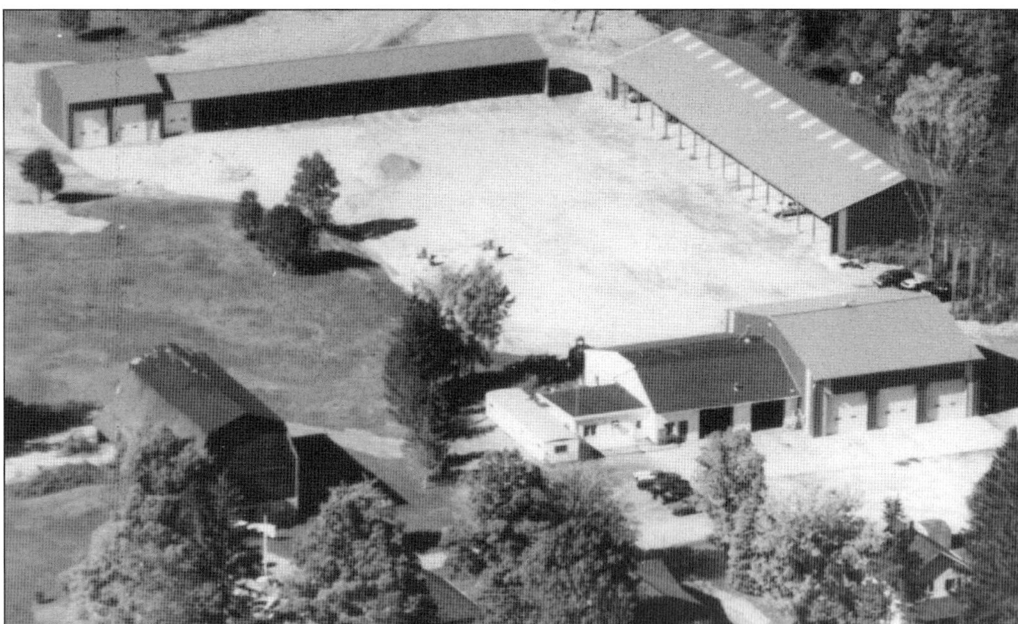

Formed in the mid-1950s, H.L. Draper Trucking was a family-run business started by Howard Draper. In the late 1960s, the name changed to HowGen Transport Company, a combination of the owners' names—Howard and his wife, Genevieve ("Ginger"). During this time, the company's fleet grew to 34 vehicles, a mix of straight trucks and tractor-trailer combinations. Through the years, there have been very few major highway projects in Western New York that this firm did not have a hand in. In 1984, when Richard Draper purchased the business, the name changed to Draper Trucking. This aerial view is from the early 1970s. (Courtesy of Draper Trucking.)

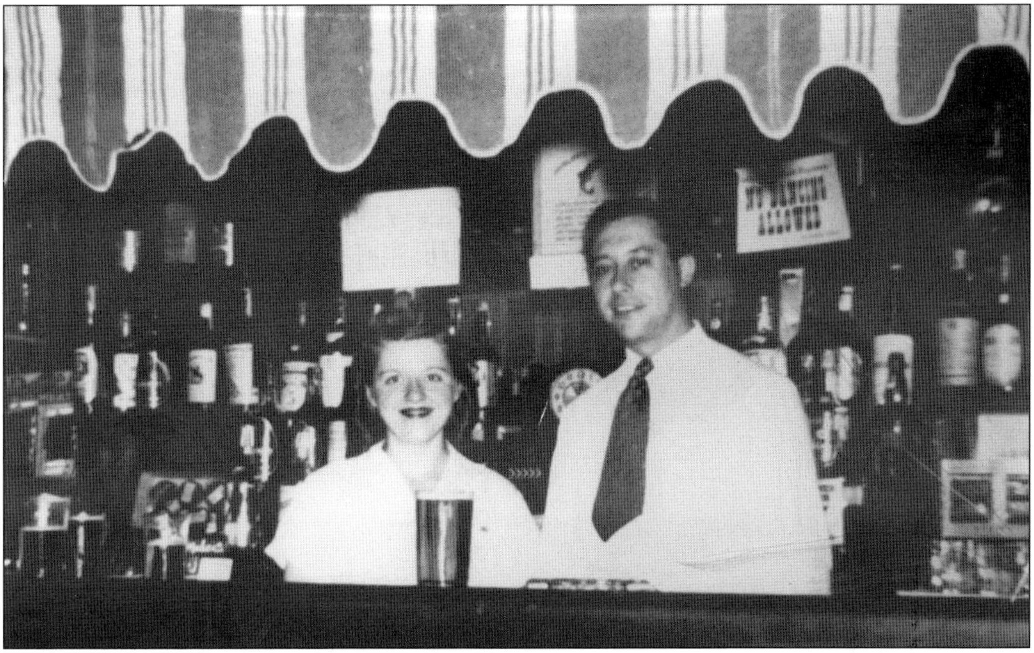

The Holland Willows was built in 1936 by Roy Knox. Named for the huge willow trees that surrounded the property on Savage Road, it continues to be a favorite spot in the community. Glenn and Ella Sprague bought the restaurant and bar combo before World War II and ran it until it burned in 1953. After the fire, Howard and Alva Ebert took ownership. Other owners in the 1950s and 1960s included Tom and Tony Galante and Ronald and Bernice Smith. Ronald Pilkington and his family have owned the business since the early 1970s. Pictured are Glenn and Ella Sprague behind the bar during their tenure.

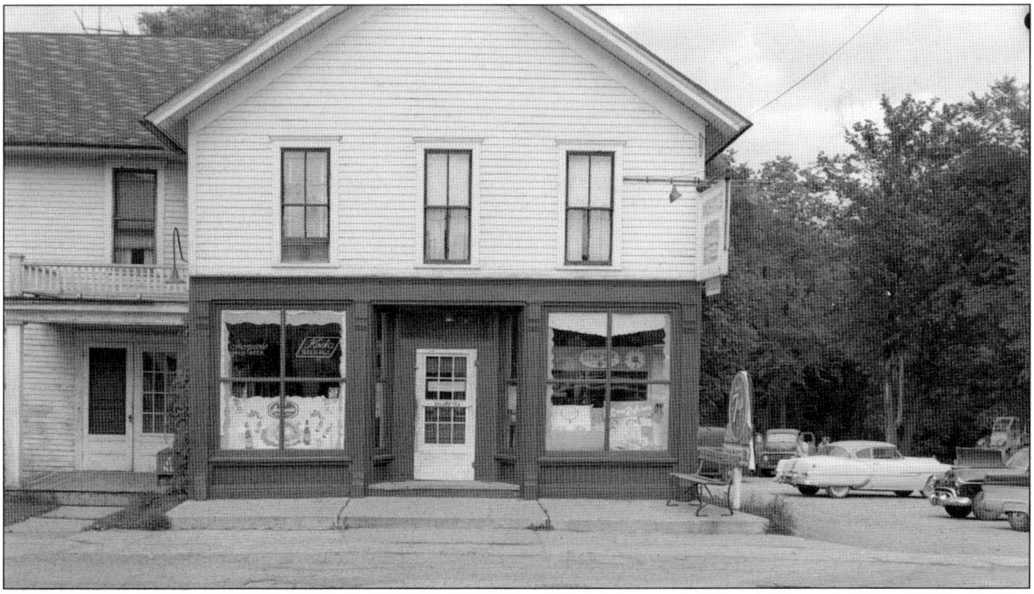

This is a photograph of Wilson's Store on North Main Street, near the Cazenovia Creek bridge. It was owned by Mick and Margaret Wilson and was later sold to Leslie Schiltz, who made it Schiltz's Deli. The building was torn down in 1988 to make way for a new bridge over the creek.

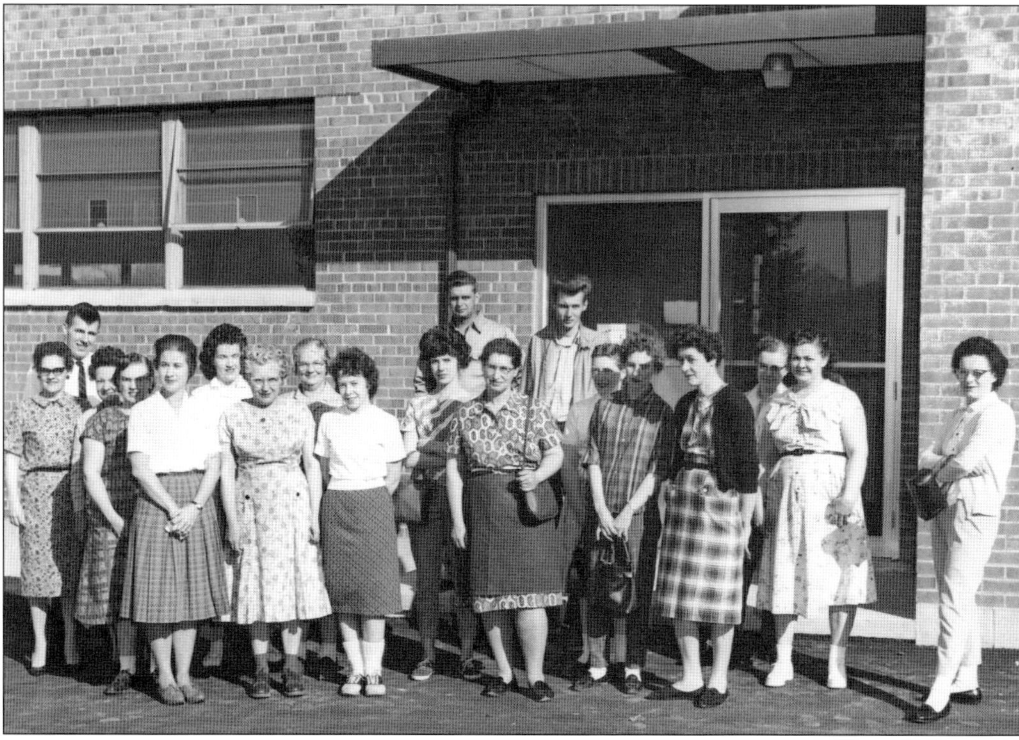

In the early 1960s, the Fisher-Price toy company added a facility in Holland to help with its production needs. This is a 1962 photograph of the first group of employees at the Holland facility. Known names are, in alphabetical order, Janet Banks, Norman Bapst, Dorothy Berg, Esther Bristol, Ellen Close, Ealda Grizer, Kathy Hall, Ruth Hopkins, Evelyn Kaiser, Jane McArthur, Gloria McVay, Stacy Mosser, David Musty, Mavis Pixley, David Schurr, Ruth Weisner, Alice Wickett, and Lolita Woodruff.

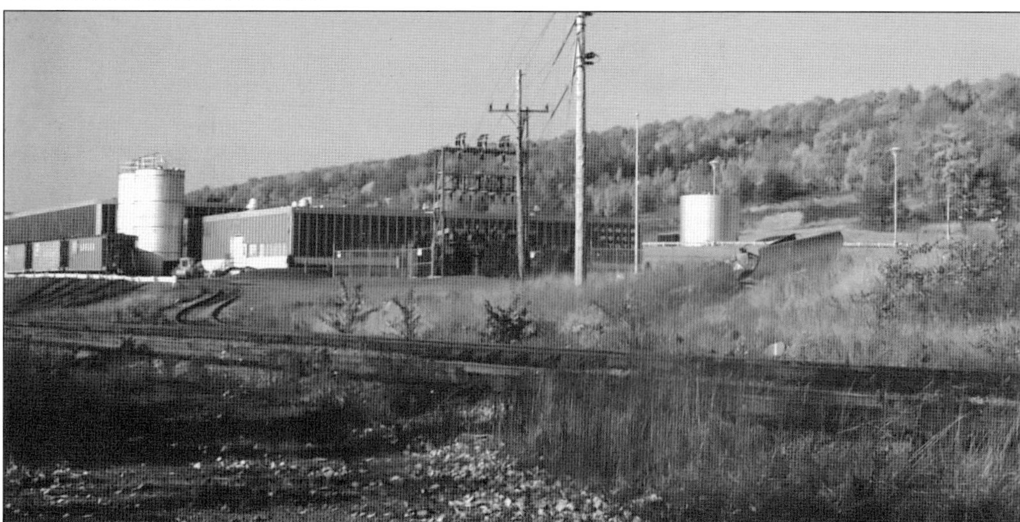

This photograph shows the Fisher-Price Holland plant around 1970. Its specialty was molding plastic parts for toys. The plant was closed by headquarters in 1990. Staroba Plastics now occupies the building at 42 Edgewood Drive.

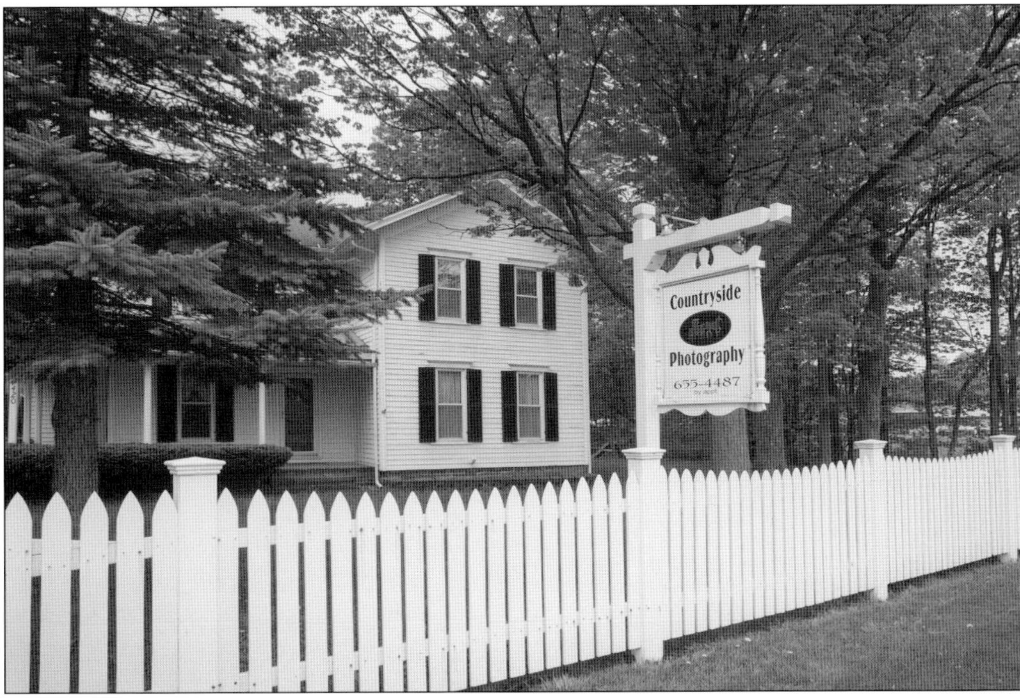

Built in the late 1870s, this was once the home of the Sellecks—Randall J., wife Grace, and daughter Bertha. It has been the residence of the Saviano family since 1980. They also operate their family business, Countryside Photography, at this location on Olean Road.

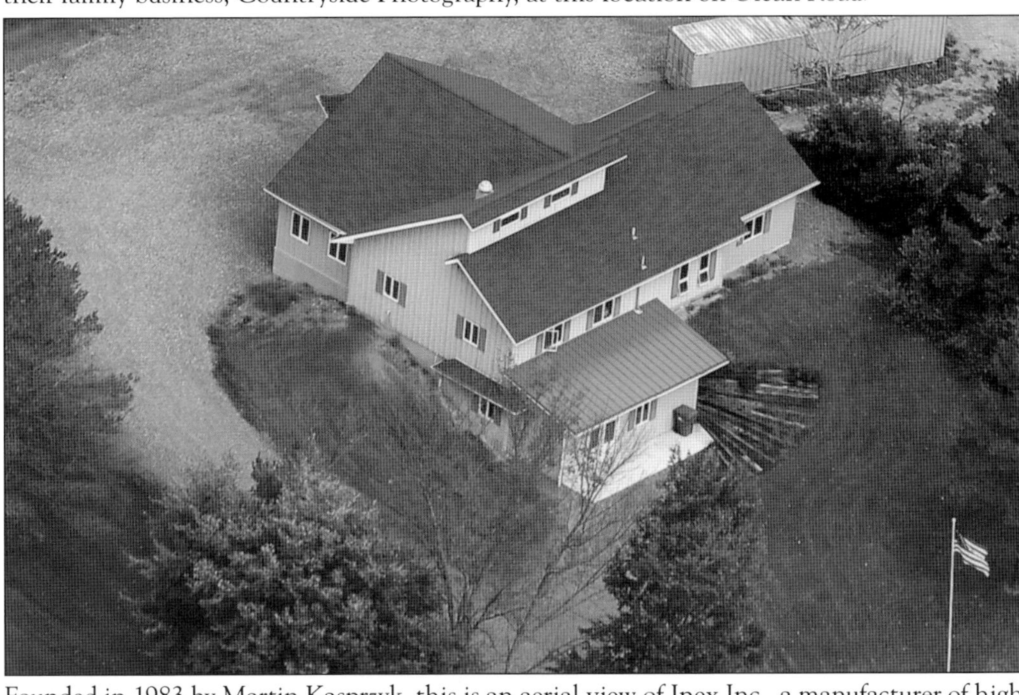

Founded in 1983 by Martin Kasprzyk, this is an aerial view of Inex Inc., a manufacturer of high-temperature ceramic materials used in industrial furnaces and chemical processes. Later, partner Michael Kasprzyk became sole owner and president. This facility was built in Holland in 1993.

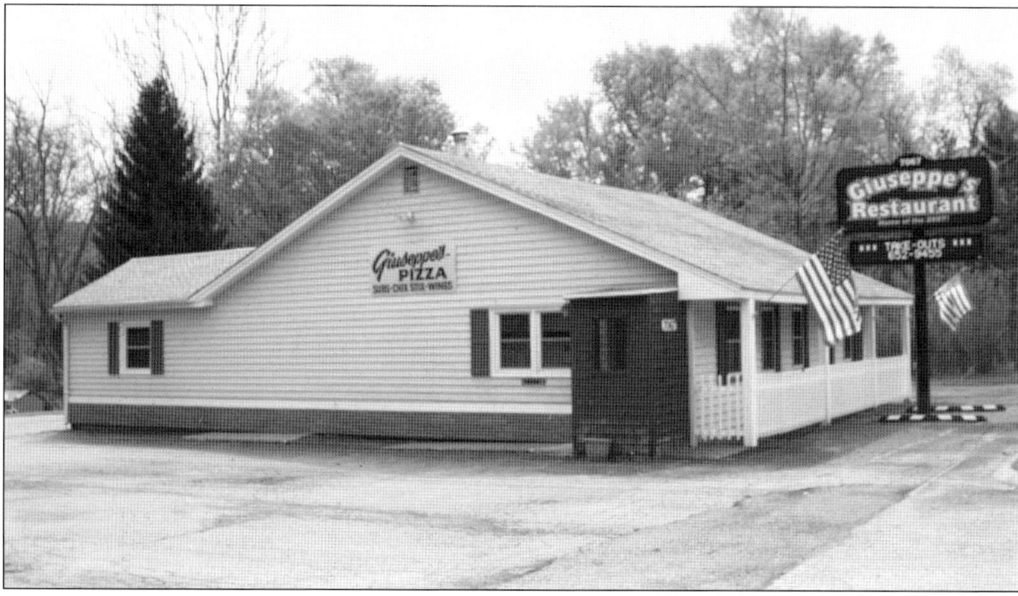

The Blue Bird Inn was once located on this Olean Road property. The inn was a popular restaurant, bar, and dance hall that was destroyed by fire. In the 1950s, Ray Gerstung purchased the land, constructed the current building, and operated it as a diner. Later owners included Elizabeth and Roy Gee. In 1971, Allen Kerlin became owner, and it was called Giuseppe's Restaurant, specializing in Italian cooking. His wife, Patricia, and their daughters all worked at the family business. Tina Fronckowiak, a waitress under Kerlin's ownership, and her son Jeffrey purchased the business in 2011. It is still known for serving homemade meals, including Italian specialties and desserts.

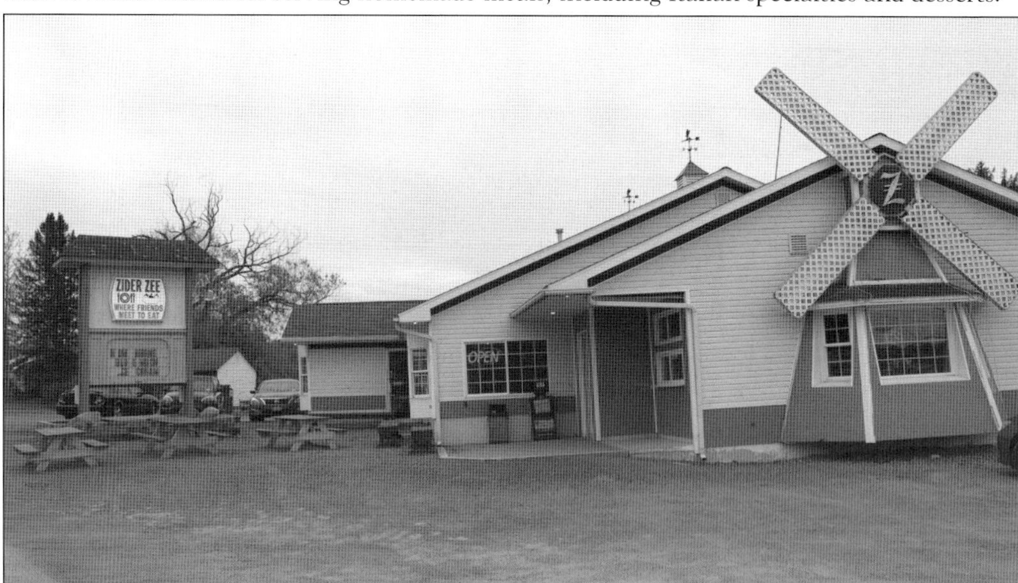

The Zider Zee restaurant was started by Joseph Inglis in April 1958. It originally operated as a seasonal hot dog and ice cream stand. Joseph's wife, Mildred, gave the restaurant its name, keeping it Dutch-themed to coincide with Holland. The restaurant has had several owners over the years, including Lloyd Mest, Tom and Dianna Galante, LaVonne Smith, and current owner Nelson Rauch. It is especially known for its homemade pies.

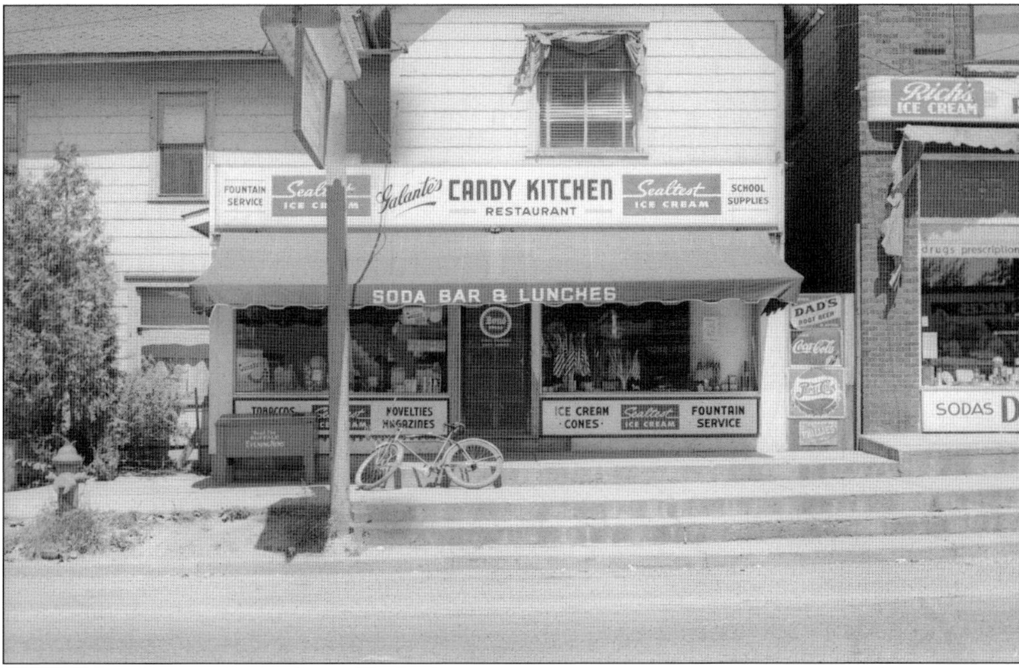

The Candy Kitchen was in the business district on Main Street. It was especially popular with teens; they could order from the soda fountain, listen to music, play pool, and socialize. This photograph is from 1950, when it was owned by the Galante family.

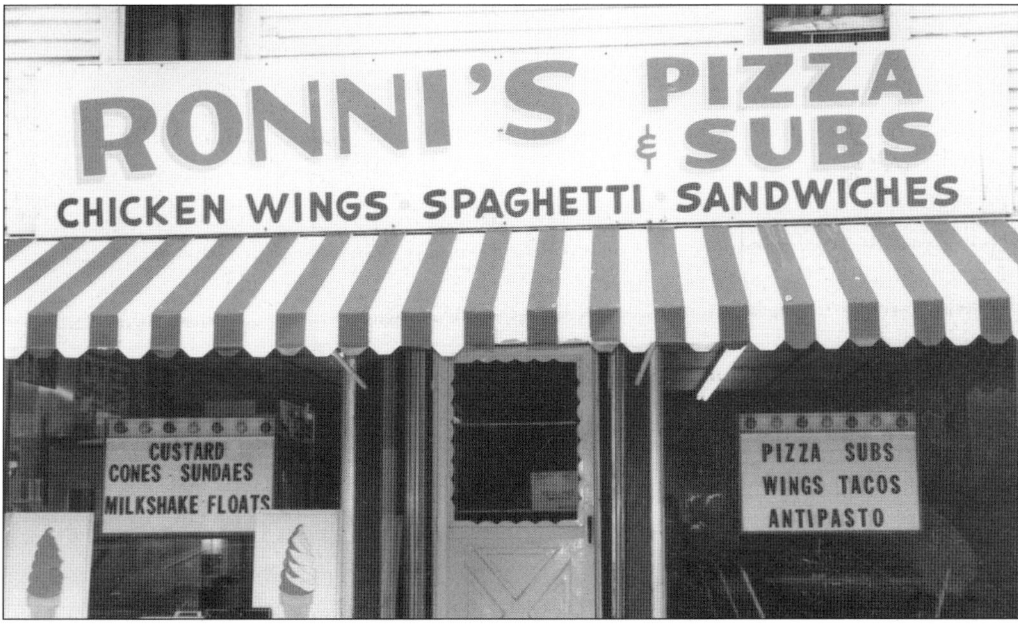

In 1981, John Vitali and his son Greg opened a pizzeria at 25 North Main Street. After John retired in the late 1980s, Greg took over the business, and he successfully runs it to this day. This photograph was taken in 1982.

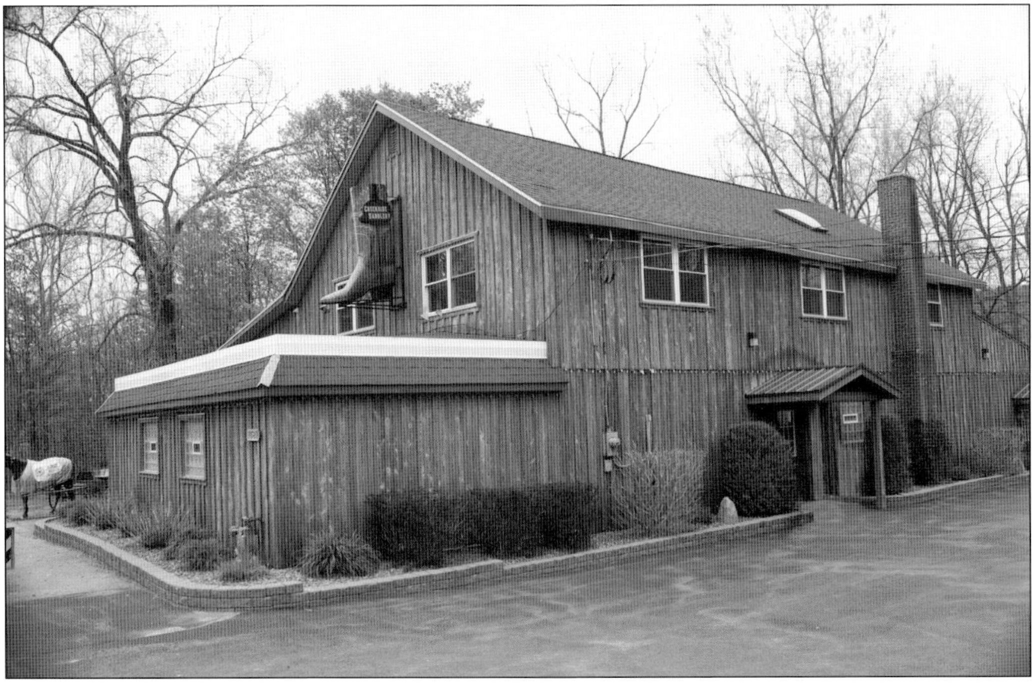

Pat's Tack Shop was started in the mid-1980s by Patricia Mary. The store specializes in Western and English riding apparel, including hats, boots, and jewelry, and everything horse-related, such as halters, blankets, and tack. In 2006, she decided to sell the business, and David Blendinger became the new owner, changing the name to Creekside Saddlery.

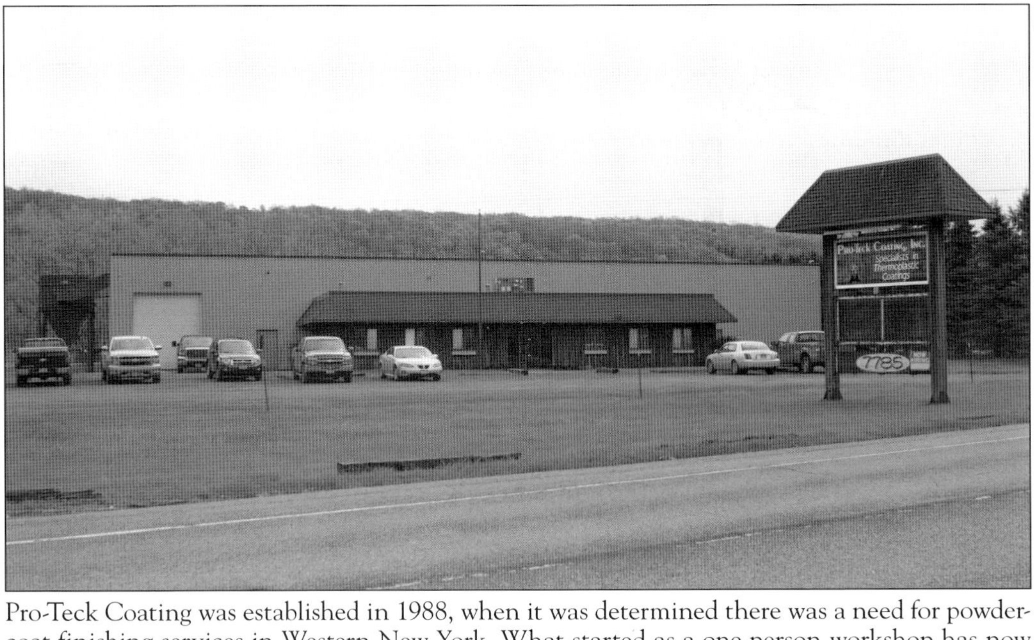

Pro-Teck Coating was established in 1988, when it was determined there was a need for powder-coat finishing services in Western New York. What started as a one-person workshop has now grown to 22 fulltime employees. The business operates out of its 25,000-square-foot production facility on Olean Road in Holland.

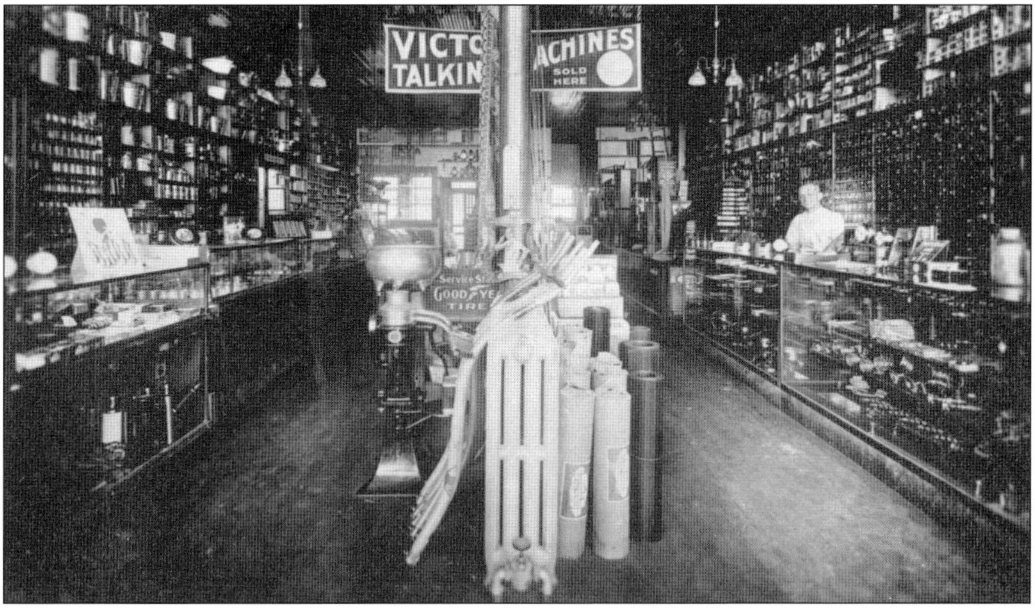

Holland's hardware store, operated by Paul J. Wurst, was destroyed in the great 1910 fire. Wurst rebuilt a brick structure at the same site and named it the Paul J. Wurst Block, which housed the hardware and other businesses. Jacques Kirkby and his wife, Cora, operated the new hardware store. They sold the business to Robert James around 1948. Later it was purchased by Robert Gates. From 1960 to 1977, it was owned by Robert Duthie. The Lowe family took ownership in 1977. This is a picture of the interior of Kirkby Hardware with Jacques Kirkby behind the counter in the early 1920s.

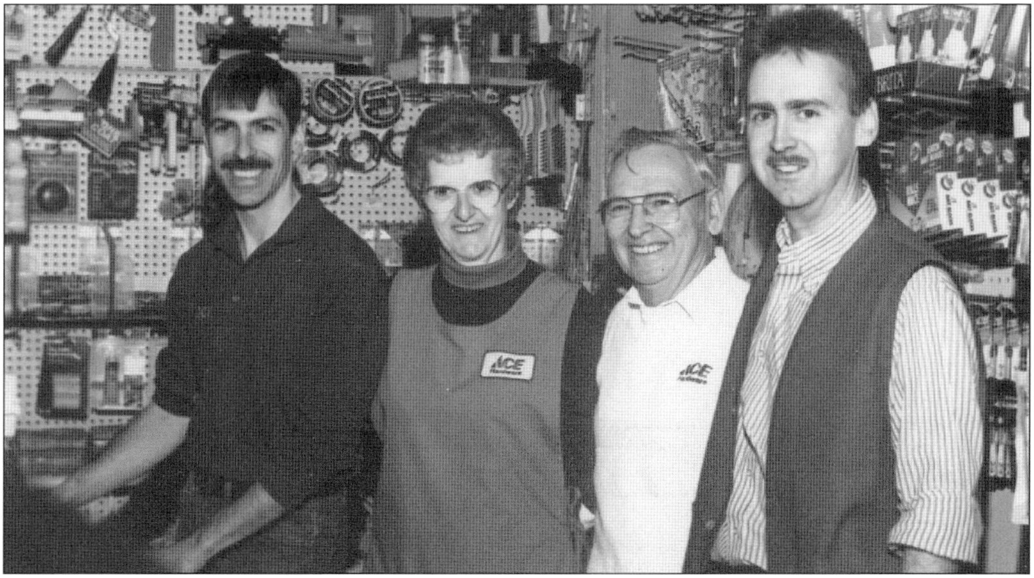

In 1977, Ralph and Donna Lowe purchased Holland Hardware and ran it as a family business with their two sons. This photograph was taken at their 20-year anniversary in 1997. Pictured from left to right are Donald, Donna, Ralph Sr., and Ralph Jr. Donald and Ralph Jr. operate the store to this day. Their father, Ralph Sr., was an active member of the Holland Historical Society and took pride in gathering information on the town's history and sharing it with others.

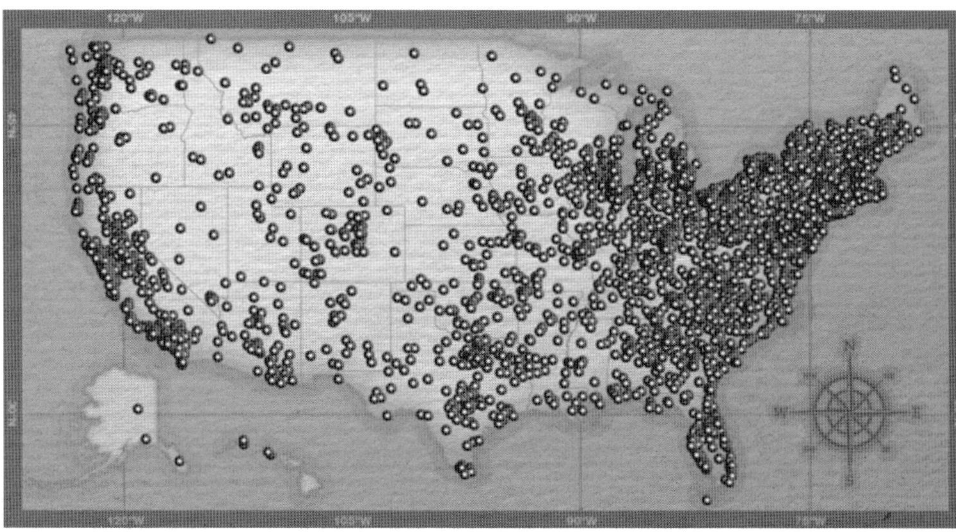